**CLAIM FREE GIFT**

# 2 Free Gifts

FREE EBOOK

FOREX TRADING GUIDE

# BOOK 1

## "OPTIONS UNLOCKED: YOUR JOURNEY TO TRADING SUCCESS BEGINS"

# OPTION TRADING:
# A Beginners Crash Course

CARTER HERROLD

*First Published by Herrold Publishing 2023*

*Copyright © 2023 Carter Herrold*

*All rights reserved. No part of this book may be reproduced
or used in any manner without the prior written permission of the copyright owner,
except for the use of brief quotations in a book review.*

*Due to the high level of risk, options trading may not be ideal for all investors. Trading options can lead to significant financial losses, it should be noted that past performance is not indicative of future results. To begin with options trading activities, fully understanding the dangers associated with this field is vital as well as considering your current financial situation along with risk tolerance and targets for investment. In this book, strategies and techniques are based on the author's experiences and research. However, there is no guarantee of success for these approaches in all market environments. When trading options, they are subject to market volatility and other factors that can influence trade outcomes. As a result, the authors hold no responsibility for financial losses or failed transactions.*

*First Paperback edition September 2023*

*Published by Herrold Publishing Inc.*

# TABLE OF CONTENTS

- INTRODUCTION .................................................................................................................. 4
- CHAPTER 1 ........................................................................................................................ 5
- DECODING OPTIONS: A BEGINNER'S GUIDE TO FINANCIAL OPPORTUNITIES ...................... 5
  - UNDERSTANDING THE BASICS: WHAT ARE OPTIONS? ................................................... 5
  - UNDERSTANDING THE CONCEPT OF OPTIONS AND HOW THEY DIFFER FROM STOCKS ...... 6
  - EXPLORING THE ADVANTAGES OF TRADING OPTIONS .................................................... 8
  - INTRODUCING THE TWO TYPES OF OPTIONS: CALL OPTIONS VS. PUT OPTIONS ............... 9
- CHAPTER 2 ...................................................................................................................... 11
- NAVIGATING THE OPTIONS MARKET: YOUR FIRST STEPS TO TRADING ............................ 11
  - OPENING A BROKERAGE ACCOUNT AND GAINING ACCESS TO OPTIONS TRADING ......... 12
  - LEARNING ABOUT OPTIONS CHAINS AND INTERPRETING OPTIONS SYMBOLS ............... 14
  - UNDERSTANDING EXPIRATION DATES AND STRIKE PRICES .......................................... 16
- CHAPTER 3 ...................................................................................................................... 19
- CALL AND PUT OPTIONS REVEALED: THE POWER OF CHOICE .......................................... 19
  - DIVING DEEPER INTO CALL OPTIONS, THEIR FEATURES, AND PROFIT POTENTIAL .......... 19
  - UNDERSTANDING PUT OPTIONS AND THEIR ROLE IN PORTFOLIO PROTECTION ............. 21
  - REAL-LIFE EXAMPLES ILLUSTRATING HOW CALL AND PUT OPTIONS ARE USED IN THE MARKET ........ 22
- CHAPTER 4 ...................................................................................................................... 24
- MAKING YOUR FIRST OPTIONS TRADE: A STEP-BY-STEP ADVENTURE .............................. 24
  - GUIDE WALKTHROUGH OF PLACING A SIMPLE OPTIONS TRADE ON A BROKERAGE PLATFORM ........ 24
  - GRASPING
  - TIPS FOR MANAGING THE TADE AND MONITORING ITS PERFORMANCE ........................ 26
- GLOSSARY ....................................................................................................................... 27
- TRADERENCES ................................................................................................................. 28

# INTRODUCTION

This book is a beginner's crash course in options trading. It will teach you the basics of options, including what they are, how they work, and how to use them to achieve your investment goals.

If you've picked up this book, you're likely intrigued by the potential of options, perhaps having heard stories of traders leveraging these instruments to amplify their returns or hedge their portfolios. But, like many, you might also find the concept of options a tad overwhelming. Fear not; this crash course is designed precisely for individuals like you—eager learners standing at the threshold of a vast and dynamic financial landscape.

Options trading is a skill, an art, and a science, not just another type of investment. At their heart, options offer flexibility by providing various methods that may be customized to meet your financial objectives, level of risk tolerance, and market forecast. Whether you want to protect your investments, generate additional income, or speculate on market movements, options can be your powerful ally.

However, with great power comes great responsibility. The characteristics that make options attractive—such as leverage—can also magnify losses. Hence, a solid understanding is crucial before diving in.

In this book, "Option Trading: A Beginner's Crash Course," we will embark on a journey, starting with the foundational concepts and gradually delving into strategies, risk management, and practical applications. By the end of this guide, you'll have a robust understanding of options, armed with the knowledge to make informed decisions in the market.

Options trading is a potent tool that investors can use. Before you begin trading, it's crucial to understand the dangers involved. You will learn the basic principles of options trading from this book to decide if they are the proper investment for you.

I hope you enjoy this book and find what you need to get started with options.

Good luck!

# CHAPTER 1
## DECODING OPTIONS: A BEGINNER'S GUIDE TO FINANCIAL OPPORTUNITIES

The world of finance is rich with opportunities, and one avenue that often captivates the imagination of investors is options trading. Options are versatile financial instruments that offer a unique way to profit from market movements, manage risk, and create strategic positions. If you're new to options trading, fear not – this beginner's guide will decode the complexities and open doors to exciting financial possibilities.

### UNDERSTANDING THE BASICS: WHAT ARE OPTIONS?

A contractual agreement known as an option provides the holder with the right, but not the authority, to buy or sell a particular asset at a predetermined price at any time throughout the option's term. This agreement grants the holder the privilege of doing so but not the deficit. In options trading, we encounter two primary categories: call options and put options.

- **Call Options:** Call options enable the holder to buy an asset at a designated price (exercise price) before a specific date (expiration date). Call options are often used by traders who anticipate the cost of the underlying asset to rise.

- **Put Options:** Put options provide the holder the right to sell a particular asset at a specific price within a certain amount of time, but only if they meet certain conditions. Put options are commonly used by traders anticipating the underlying asset's price to decline.

Decoding options unlock a world of financial opportunities. From generating income to hedging risk and speculating on market moves, options provide a versatile toolkit for traders. As a beginner, approach options trading with caution, respect for risk, and a commitment to ongoing education. With time and experience, you can harness the power of options to enhance your financial journey and achieve your trading goals.

## UNDERSTANDING THE CONCEPT OF OPTIONS AND HOW THEY DIFFER FROM STOCKS.

Options trading is often perceived as a high-risk investment strategy that seasoned professionals typically pursue. There is no doubt that options trading is risky and requires adequate experience and knowledge to be successful. However, options also offer an excellent opportunity for individual investors who wish to expand their investment portfolios.

Options are exquisite agreements that grant you the extraordinary opportunity to engage in the thrilling world of future market value trading. They bestow upon you the divine right, yet not the burdensome obligation, to partake in the said market at a predetermined price on or before a designated date. Options contracts on assets are standardized financial instruments that, by paying an option premium, grant their holder (buyer or taker) the right, but not the obligation, to buy or sell at a previously established price and during a predetermined term, a certain quantity of the individualized asset in the contract.

Options can be actively traded on regulated exchanges and in the decentralized over-the-counter market. There exist two fundamental categories of options in the realm of trading. A call option grants the holder the privilege to initiate the purchase of the principal asset at a prearranged price within a specified timeframe. A put option gives the holder the freedom to exercise their right to sell the underlying asset at a prearranged price on or before a selected date. The exercise price is the price assigned in the contract, while the expiration date or maturity is the date defined in the contract. It is imperative to highlight that an option grants the holder the privilege to take action. The option holder is not constrained to exercise their right. This is the key differentiating factor between options and forwards/futures, as options provide the holder with the choice, rather than the obligation, to buy or sell the underlying asset. Please be aware that while there is no upfront cost associated with entering into a forward or futures contract, acquiring an option involves a premium cost.

**Differences between options and stocks**

Options and stocks are two essential concepts in finance and investment.
- When you trade stocks, you exchange ownership of a company. By comparison, when you buy or sell option contracts, you are trading in the potential, or obligation, to buy or sell the principal stock. Owning an option alone does not grant ownership of the underlying security nor entitle the holder to receive dividend payments.
- Options, conversely, are derivative instruments that grant the purchaser the privilege (yet not the compulsion) to purchase or sell a principal asset at a predetermined price on a predetermined date. In other words, unlike stocks, options do not represent a share in a company but a kind of agreement or contract between two parties.
- Both stocks and options can be bought and sold in the financial markets. Stocks are traded on stock exchanges, while options are purchased and sold on the options market.
- Stocks are a kind of ownership credential in large companies, while options are bets on a particular stock's rise and fall.
- In the trading realm, stocks offer greater convenience than options, as options tend to carry higher inherent risks over extended periods.
- Stocks, being untethered to a specific time frame, exhibit a fluidity that spans numerous years. Conversely, options, the embodiment of time-bound contracts, have expiration dates that span a spectrum ranging from a few weeks to a few months.
- Anyone can trade shares, but the options are limited to the owners of the company and the fund management authorities in particular.

In summary, options and stocks are financial instruments useful to investors in different times and situations. It is essential to know these options well and use them responsibly and appropriately to maximize the benefits of our investments and reduce financial risks.

**EXPLORING THE ADVANTAGES OF TRADING OPTIONS**

**1. Flexibility**
Flexibility is a significant advantage of trading options, providing investors various strategies and approaches to adapt to various market conditions. Options offer versatile trading opportunities, making them a valuable tool for speculative traders and risk-averse investors. Options are very flexible instruments. As well as allowing you to take very risky positions, they also serve to reduce and control risk. You can invest in purchase (call) or sale (put) options, which allows you to obtain benefits in bullish, bearish, and lateral markets.
Flexibility is a crucial advantage of trading options, allowing investors to employ diverse strategies based on their market outlook, risk appetite, and investment objectives. Whether seeking speculative opportunities, income generation, or risk management, options provide a versatile toolkit for traders to navigate dynamic market environments. As with any financial instrument, understanding options thoroughly and having a well-thought-out trading plan are essential for maximizing the benefits of flexibility in options trading.

**2. Leverage**
Leverage is a crucial advantage of trading options, allowing investors to control a larger position in the asset with a relatively small investment. This feature makes options attractive for traders seeking amplified returns and enhanced trading opportunities. One of the primary benefits of leverage in options trading is the potential for amplified returns. "Options enable investors to control a significant amount of the underlying asset with only a fraction of the asset's actual value," states Hull.
Leverage also grants options traders flexibility in position sizing, allowing them to adjust their exposure to the market based on their investment objectives. According to CBOE (2021), options contracts come in various sizes, allowing traders to "fine-tune their risk exposure and tailor their positions." This adaptability enables traders to participate in different market scenarios while managing risk effectively.

**3. Hedging**
Options contracts are frequently used as hedging instruments. Trading with options allows us to cover an entire portfolio of shares or any other instrument or position. We understand by covering a portfolio, eliminating, or reducing the risks of losses if prices move unfavorably to our investment, maintaining as much as possible the profit potential when they move in favor.
A simple example of a hedging strategy with options would be to buy put options on stocks already held in the portfolio so that if the prices of those stocks decline, exercising the put option can help mitigate losses. So, for example, let's say we buy 100 shares of a stock at $50, expecting the market

price of those shares to rise. To protect against lower stock prices, we purchase put options with an exercise price of $48, thus paying a premium of $2 per share. Let's imagine that the share price drops to $30, in which case we can exercise our option contract, selling each share for $48 instead of $30. However, if the share prices were to go above $50, we would not need to exercise the contract and would only lose the premium paid for each share.

It is essential to consider purchasing put or call options to effectively hedge your investment portfolio using options depending on your market outlook and directional bias. You should buy put options if you think the market will go down. If you think the market will increase, you should buy call options. When buying options, you must ensure that the option's expiration date is far enough away and that the strike price is appropriate.

**4. Risk Management**

The risk is limited in operations, with options designed for this purpose. When buying an option contract, the buyer only pays the initial premium, which will depend on certain factors. Once the exercise or strike price and the number of contracts that you want to buy and, therefore, the capital that you want to risk (which depends on the premium and the number of contracts) have been set, you will not have to worry about the Sudden market movements if we wait for the expiration, since we will have invested a certain amount of money. We cannot lose more than this.

**INTRODUCING THE TWO TYPES OF OPTIONS: CALL OPTIONS VS. PUT OPTIONS**

**Call option**

A call option gives the owner/contract holder (the call option buyer) the right to buy the principal shares at a specified price before expiration. Call options are generally purchased when the price of the asset stock is expected to rise. When an investor buys a call option, he expects the underlying value to rise in the markets; that is, it has bullish expectations. Suppose your bet is correct when the expiration date arrives, and the underlying price is higher than the exercise price set in the contract. In that case, you will be interested in exercising the option since you can buy the cheaper underlying asset. Conversely, if the price does not rise as expected and the exercise price is higher than that of the underlying, he will not exercise the option and will lose the investment made, that is, the premium.

**Put Options**

In a put or put option, the buyer has the right, but not the obligation, to sell the underlying at a fixed price on the expiration date. The put seller assumes that obligation. The purchase of a put option is justified when the investor has bearish expectations. If the price of the underlying decreases, you will want to exercise the option and sell at the strike price, which is higher. Otherwise, he will not exercise it and will lose the premium.

A put option gives the owner/contract holder (the put option buyer) the rigs generally purchased when the underlying stock's price is expected to decline. The purchase of a put option is justified when the investor has bearish expectations. If the price of the underlying decreases, you will want to exercise the option and sell at the strike price, which is higher. Otherwise, he will not exercise it and will lose the premium.

## CHAPTER 2
## NAVIGATING THE OPTIONS MARKET: YOUR FIRST STEPS TO TRADING

Entering the world of trading is a thrilling endeavor that promises financial independence and personal growth. However, any new venture requires careful planning, education, and a strong foundation. Before embarking on your trading journey, you must arm yourself with the knowledge and tools to steer you toward success.

### 1. Define Your Objectives: Setting Clear Goals

Every successful trading journey begins with a clear understanding of your objectives. Are you aiming for short-term profits, long-term wealth accumulation, or a combination? Define your financial goals, risk tolerance, and time horizon. These factors will guide your decision-making and trading strategies, ensuring they align with your aspirations.

### 2. Education is Key: Learn the Basics

Trading is not a guessing game; it's a skill that requires learning and practice. Start by educating yourself about the fundamental trading concepts, including different financial instruments, market dynamics, and trading strategies. Many educational resources are available, from online courses and books to seminars and webinars. A robust knowledge base will equip you with the necessary tools to execute well-informed choices and maneuver through the markets with unwavering assurance.

### 3. Choose Your Trading Style: Find Your Fit

Trading comes in various styles, each catering to different personalities and risk preferences. Whether you're drawn to day trading, swing trading, position trading, or even investing, choosing a style that resonates with you is essential. Your preferred type will dictate your time commitment, the frequency of trades, and the strategies you employ. Remember that finding the right fit may require experimentation and adaptation.

### 4. Select Your Market: Where Will You Trade?

The financial markets offer many choices, including stocks, forex, commodities, cryptocurrencies, etc. Research and identify the market that aligns with your interests and expertise. Each market has unique characteristics and factors influencing its behavior, so thorough research is essential to make informed decisions.

## OPENING A BROKERAGE ACCOUNT AND GAINING ACCESS TO OPTIONS TRADING

Opening an account in a brokerage company is necessary to start investing in the financial markets. Investors and traders cannot trade directly on the markets or exchanges but must do so by opening a brokerage account. If you are determined to invest your money in financial assets, the first step is to open a brokerage account. The same is true if you are willing to become a trader and manage your money and that of your clients in the financial markets.

**What is a Brokerage Account?**
A brokerage account is a contractual arrangement between an astute investor and a duly licensed brokerage firm, wherein the investor can deposit funds with said firm and execute investment orders through the esteemed brokerage. The investor is the proud owner of the assets in the brokerage account and typically needs to report any capital gains arising from the performance as part of their disposable income.

There are several different types of brokerage accounts and brokerage firms. Investors can choose the type of brokerage account and the broker that best suits their financial needs. Some full-service brokers provide extensive investment advice, charging high fees for their efforts. Most online brokers offer a secure platform where option traders can execute trade orders with competitive prices. Brokerage accounts may exhibit variations in order execution speed, utilization of analysis tools, range of tradable assets, and the level of margin trading accessibility for investors.

**How to open a brokerage account**
**1. Ascertain the appropriate brokerage account classification required for optimal trading execution.**
Your investment objectives will be crucial in determining your most suitable brokerage account. A traditional brokerage account presents an optimal choice for individuals seeking to invest with a focus on short-term goals or building a rainy-day fund without the need for long-term commitment until retirement. When opting for a conventional brokerage account, your broker will likely inquire about your preference between a cash or margin account. If you pursue margin privileges, you can leverage your investments by borrowing funds to purchase shares, utilizing your existing portfolio as collateral. Acknowledging the inherent risks involved in margin investing and the accompanying interest charges on borrowed funds is crucial.

However, an individual retirement account (IRA) is your best option if your goal is to save money for retirement.

**2. Compare Costs and Incentives**
Most of the big discount brokers now offer commission-free trading. If you transfer a sizeable investment account from another broker, they may give you a discount as a thank you. That being said, it is imperative to thoroughly examine the comprehensive pricing structure of each online brokerage firm, mainly if you intend to engage in trading activities beyond stocks, such as options, mutual funds, ETFs, bonds, and the like, as these instruments often have their specific rates.

**3. Take a look at the amenities and services offered.**

Particularly for first-time investors, price is only part of it. In the realm of options trading, while it is indeed advantageous to seek the most favorable price, it is imperative to take into account several additional variables when selecting an option trader:

- Research accessibility – Besides availing themselves of third-party research on companies, numerous traders also provide stock ratings.
- Foreign Trading – Some traders offer you the opportunity to exchange currency within your account, enabling you to participate in trading shares on remote stock exchanges. If you think this is important, ensure the broker you select allows this.
- Fractional Stocks: This is especially critical for novice traders as it enables you to initiate investments in your desired stocks without purchasing an entire share.
- Trading Platforms – The diverse brokerages present many trading software and mobile apps, with the added benefit of some even granting individuals the opportunity to test their platforms before initiating an account.
- Convenience – Certain brokerages provide the opportunity for face-to-face investment advice via an extensive network of regional branches, whereas others do not offer this service.

**4. Deciding on a brokerage firm**

You have compiled your knowledge of prices, fees, and amenities provided by various businesses. It is imperative to carefully evaluate the pros and cons of each brokerage, considering your investment objectives, to select the optimal choice.

**5. Complete the new account application**

When utilizing online brokers, submitting an application to initiate a new account can be executed swiftly and seamlessly. As an option trader, providing various forms of identification, such as your Social Security number and driver's license, is essential for verification. To engage in margin or options trading, it is imperative to complete supplementary documentation and provide the broker with pertinent details regarding your net worth, employment status, investable assets, and investment objectives.

**6. Fund the account**

As an astute option trader, you will be presented with a range of deposit options by your esteemed online broker, which may include:

- A bank transfer is the most efficient way to expedite the deposit of funds into your account. A bank transfer, or interbank transfer, is a swift and efficient method of transferring funds between financial institutions. This transaction is typically executed quickly, ensuring the transfer is completed within minutes.

· Checks: The types of checks brokers accept as deposits, and the available funds vary.

· Asset Transfer – This is a valid funding option if you transfer money or move existing investments from one trader to another.

Lastly, it would be best to remain mindful of your broker's minimum requirements while allocating funds to your newly established account.

# LEARNING ABOUT OPTIONS CHAINS AND INTERPRETING OPTIONS SYMBOLS

Options have their language, and the information can seem overwhelming when you start trading options. When you look at an option chart, it first appears to be rows of random numbers, but option chain charts give valuable security information now and where it might go. Mastering the lexicon of an options chain empowers investors to enhance their knowledge, potentially tipping the scales between profitable gains and potential losses within the options markets.

An option chain has two sections: A call option grants the privilege to initiate a long position by purchasing a share. In contrast, a put option bestows the right to create a short work by selling shares.

- The premium, also known as the option price, represents an investor's upfront cost when acquiring an option contract.
- Also listed is the exercise price of an option, which is the share price at which the investor buys the shares if the option is exercised.
- Options list multiple expiration dates, influencing the first option.

## What is an option chain?

An option chain, or matrix, represents the comprehensive compilation of all existing option contracts for a specific security. Shows all quoted call and put options, their expiration, strike prices, and information about the volume and price of a single underlying asset within a given expiration period. The chain shall be duly categorized based on the expiration date and effectively segmented into calls and puts. The chain shall be duly categorized based on the expiration date and effectively segmented into calls and puts. As a comprehensive quote and price data source, an option chain should be distinct from an option series or cycle. The latter merely signifies the range of strike prices and expiration dates that are currently available.

## Key points

· An option chain is a table showing option quotes for a particular underlying security.

· The options chain matrix is updated in real time. It displays the latest price, trading volume, and best bid and asks for call and put options for various options, typically segmented by expiration date.

· Also included is the exercise price of an option, which is the share price at which the investor buys the share if the option is exercised.

## Understanding Ticker Symbols for Stock Options

The inception of the Ticker Symbols for stock options occurred in 2006 through the collaborative efforts of the OCC and a consortium comprising brokerages, exchanges, and clearinghouses. Known as the Options Symbology Initiative (OSI), this extensive undertaking aimed to enhance the ticker symbols for stock options by comprehensively overhauling the data format. To grasp the reasoning behind the extensive, industry-wide revamp of stock option ticker symbols in 2010, let me provide you with a concise historical background.

The previous five-alpha symbols, also called the OPRA (Options Price Reporting Authority) codes, were implemented during the 1970s and 1980s, when the options market was relatively minor and less intricate. (OPRA, the registered securities information processor, efficiently aggregates and disseminates data feeds of price quotations for options contracts to esteemed financial firms, experienced brokers, and astute traders in the United States.)

Since its official launch in 1973, options trading has experienced significant growth. This growth has been further accelerated by the OCC's mandate in 2010, which introduced the current 21-character naming convention. As a result, the options market has evolved from offering basic contracts to a more intricate and diverse range of products. The market's reach has expanded globally, making it a truly international trading arena. As the options market experienced unprecedented growth, the exchanges developed advanced options that surpassed the capabilities of the five-alpha codes.

In the given Nike illustration, it is evident to even a novice options trader that "NKE220624C00099000" represents a call option for Nike stock with a strike price of $99 and an expiration date of June 24, 2022. These crucial details are consistently conveyed within the ticker symbol, adhering to the standard format.

**1. Root Symbol (six-character maximum):** The initial field corresponds to the ticker symbol of the option's underlying stock. Regarding the Nike option, the ticker symbol for this particular option is NKE, which aligns with the stock symbol. While Nike has a single stock ticker, many opportunities exist on the stock, all denoted by the identical initial letters in the option ticker.

**2. Expiration Date (six digits):** The second part of an option ticker comprises three fields representing the expiration date in the format of year-month-day: (yy)(mm)(dd). In the Nike example, the 220624 following the stock ticker signifies the option's expiration date as June 24, 2022.

**3. Call/Put Indicator (one character) or C/P Indicator (one character):** There exist two varieties of options - calls and puts - and the third segment of the ticker comprises a solitary letter - either C or P - signifying whether the option represents a call (buy) or put (sell) contract for a stock. In the Nike example, the presence of the C following the expiration date signifies that the option is a call.

**4. Strike Price (eight digits):** The strike price, denoted by the fourth section of an option ticker, is consistently represented by eight numbers. It signifies the predetermined price at which the option can be purchased (for call options) or sold (for put options). The strike or exercise price is another term used in options trading. In the Nike above example, the eight digits can be represented as 00099000, indicating a strike price of $99. To accurately interpret the strike price in the option ticker, one must perform a straightforward calculation: divide the eight digits by 1,000 or shift the decimal point three to the left. (For instance, when the option ticker is 00078500, the strike price is $78.50.)

## UNDERSTANDING EXPIRATION DATES AND STRIKE PRICES

All options have an expiration date, after which they cease to exist and have no value. Options can be freely bought and sold until the close of trading on the expiration date. This is one of the fundamental differences between buying an option and buying the underlying asset.

Suppose a person buys Telefónica shares on January 2 at 20 euros and sells them at 23. In that case, they will have earned 3 euros (23-20), regardless of whether Telefónica took one month or ten months to rise from 20 to 23 (Note: to calculate the real profitability of an investment, inflation must always be taken into account). But when you buy a call option, you not only have to guess that Telefónica's shares are going to rise but when they will. For example, suppose someone buys on January 2 a call option on Telefónica with an exercise price of 20 euros and an expiration date of March 25 to earn money with that operation. In that case, Telefónica must be above 20 euros on the aforementioned March 25. If, on the expiration date (March 25), Telefónica trades at 19.95 euros, the buyer of the call will have lost all the money invested in the purchase of that call option and will no longer be able to take advantage of possible increases by Telefónica after the That date.

If on April 10, Telefónica is trading at 23 euros, the person who bought the shares at 20 euros on January 2 will be able to sell them at those 23 euros, earning 3 euros per share. On the other hand, the person who bought the call no longer has anything and cannot obtain any benefit from the Telefónica increase between March 26 and April 10. The same thing happens with put options; you must guess when the stock will go down and when.

The more time left to expiration, the more value the options have. It can be seen that if Telefónica is trading at 18 euros, the Telefónica call options with an exercise price of 20 euros and expiration the next day have almost no value since it is very difficult (although not impossible) for Telefónica to rise from 18 to 20 euros in one day. However, if the expiration date of that option is within one year, its value increases a lot since it is much more likely that Telefónica will rise from 18 to 20 euros in 1 year.

**What is the expiration time?**

The expiration time of an option or other derivative contract is the date and time it is voided. Derivative contracts ending out of the money (OTM) at expiration will lose their value, while in-the-money (ITM) contracts will be valued at their settlement price at expiration. The expiration time holds greater specificity than the expiration date and should not be conflated with the most recent trading activity of the option.

· Expiration time is the precise date and time that derivative contracts cease trading and any obligation or right becomes due or expires.

· Typically, the final trading day for an option is on the third Friday of the expiration month.
- Derivative contracts will specify the exact date and time of expiration.

Time to expiration and expiration date have distinct meanings in the options trading world. Time to end refers to the specific moment when the option contract reaches its expiration and is no longer valid. On the other hand, the expiration date represents the designated timeframe during which the option holder must communicate their intentions regarding the contract. Most options traders only need to be concerned with the expiration date but knowing the expiration time is also helpful.

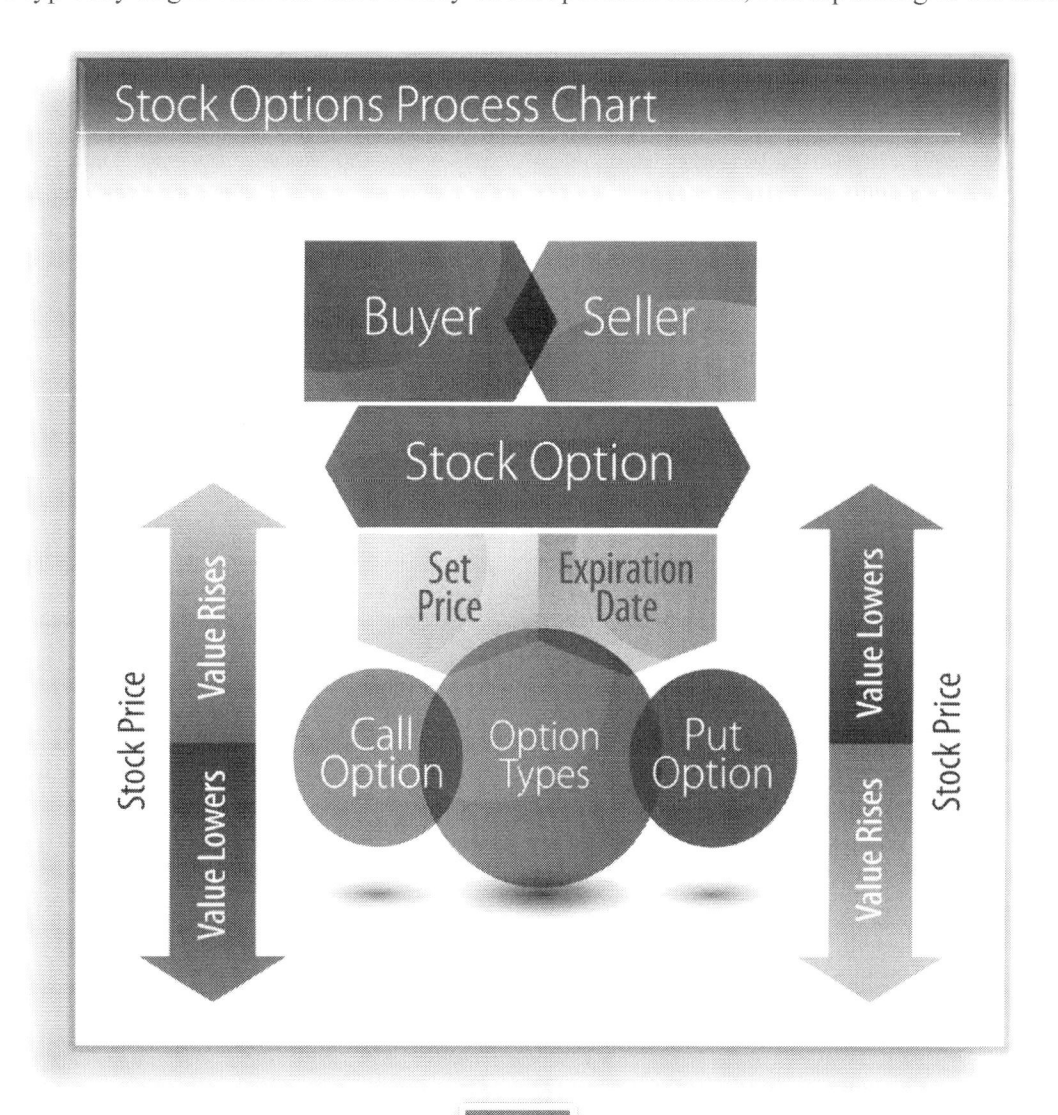

An expiration date in derivatives is the last day in force of an options or futures contract. When option traders initiate long positions, they acquire contracts that grant them the privilege, without any compulsion, to execute the purchase or sale of assets at a prearranged price, commonly referred to as the strike price. The exercise of the option must occur within a specified period, on or before the expiration date. If an investor chooses not to exercise this right, the option expires and loses its value, and the investor loses the money paid to purchase it. The expiration date for US-listed stock options typically aligns with the third Friday of the specified month, corresponding to the month of contract expiry. However, if the third Friday coincides with a holiday, the expiration date is moved to the preceding Thursday. Once an options or futures contract reaches its expiration date, the contract becomes null and void. The last day to trade stock options is the Friday before expiration.

**What is the strike price?**

A strike price, also called an exercise price, represents the price at which a security contract can be exercised, bought, or sold. It is most common in options trading. Options are contracts that give traders the "option" to buy or sell an asset, such as a stock when it reaches a strike price. When used effectively, an option strike price can significantly improve investors' holdings, but it can also seriously hurt returns under certain conditions.

A strike price on a call option represents the price at which the security can be purchased until the expiration date of the contract. In contrast, the strike price of a put option determines the price at which an agreement can be sold during the contract's life.

When the strike price on a call option is below the stock market price, the contract is considered to be traded "**in the money**." However, if the strike price rises above the stock market value, the agreement trades "**out of the money**." Since option investors aim to buy securities below the stock market value, there is no point in buying when the option trades **at the money**.

# CHAPTER 3
## CALL AND PUT OPTIONS REVEALED: THE POWER OF CHOICE

In financial markets, options provide a unique opportunity to harness the power of choice. These versatile instruments, called-and-put options, unlock strategic possibilities beyond traditional trading.

### The Basics of Call and Put Options: Defining Choice

At their core, call and put options give traders the right, but not the authority, to buy (call) or sell (put) a specific underlying asset at a predicted price, known as the strike price, within a certain timeframe. This framework opens doors to strategic maneuvering, as traders can tailor their approach based on market expectations, risk tolerance, and profit objectives.

Acquiring a call option (long position) grants you the privilege, without the compulsion, to initiate the purchase of an underlying asset at a prearranged price. The buyer incurs a cost, referred to as a premium, in exchange for this privilege. In addition to the strike price, the expiration date is predetermined in options trading. This date signifies the duration until the call option buyer holds the right to purchase.

The put buyer can sell a share at the strike price for a period. For that right, the buyer of the put option pays a premium. If the underlying price experiences a decline below the strike price, the option shall possess intrinsic value. The buyer can either sell the option for a profit (this is what many put option buyers do) or exercise the option.

### DIVING DEEPER INTO CALL OPTIONS, THEIR FEATURES, AND PROFIT POTENTIAL

### Call Options

Call options grant purchasers the privilege to acquire security at a prearranged price, whereas Put options bestow purchasers to vend a deposit at a reserved price. With the call option, you have the right (but not the obligation) to buy the security within a certain period.

By purchasing a call option, you want the asset to rise in price. Given the potential future purchase of shares at the prevailing price, one could engage in a profitable transaction by promptly acquiring and selling the shares in the event of a price increase. Please be aware that the purchase of options entails the payment of a premium, as previously indicated. You can think of the premium as an initial payment on your shares or other principal assets. The options contract you get will lapse at some point– at which point you can renew them. Options generally must be renewed weekly, monthly, or quarterly.

### Features of Call Options

**1. Right to Buy:** A call option gives the holder (buyer) the right, but not the responsibility, to buy a specified quantity of the underlying asset at the predetermined strike price within a specified time frame. The seller of the call option (writer) is compelled to sell the principal asset if the buyer exercises the option.

**2. Expiration Date**: Call options have a limited lifespan, as they expire on a specific date. After the expiration date, the call option becomes worthless, and the right to buy the underlying asset at the strike price no longer exists.

**3. Strike Price:** The preset price at which the principal asset can be bought upon exercising the call option. It is set when the option is created and remains fixed throughout its life.

**4. Premium:** The call option buyer compensates the seller with a premium, representing the expense incurred to acquire the privilege of purchasing the underlying asset. The premium represents the maximum potential loss for the buyer, as it is the most they can lose if the option expires worthless.

**5. Profit Potential:** The profit potential of a call option is theoretically unlimited. As the price of the principal asset rises above the strike price, the call option's value increases, allowing the holder to profit from the price appreciation.

**Profit Potentials of Call Options**

The profit potential of a call option depends on the price movement of the principal asset and the option's intrinsic value. The equity value of a call option is determined by taking the positive disparity between the asset's current market value and the price at which it is exercised. Call options allow investors to profit from upward price movements in the asset without owning the asset itself. Understanding the profit potential of call options is crucial for options traders and investors seeking to leverage price appreciation opportunities.

**1. In-The-Money (ITM) Call Options**

An in-the-money call option is one in which the underlying asset's current market price is higher than the option's strike price. For example, if the principal stock trades at $120, a call option with a strike price of $100 is considered in-the-money.

**Profit Potential:** The profit potential of an in-the-money call option is determined by its intrinsic value, which is the difference between the principal asset's current market price and the strike price. As the underlying asset's price rises, the intrinsic value of the call option increases proportionally. The option holder an exercise the option, acquiring the asset at the lower exercise price and executing a sale at the higher market price, thereby capturing a profit equivalent to the intrinsic value.

**For example:** If the underlying stock trades at $120 and the call option's strike price is $100, the intrinsic value is $120 - $100 =$20 per share.

If the option holder has ten call option contracts (each representing 100 shares), the total profit potential would be 10 x $20 = $2000.

**2. At-The-Money (ATM) Call Options**

An at-the-money call option is one in which the underlying asset's current market price equals the option's strike price.

**For example**: If the asset stock trades at $100, a call option with an exercise price of $100 is considered at-the-money.

**Profit Potential**: The profit potential of an at-the-money call option is dependent on the underlying asset's price movement above the strike price. For every increase in the underlying asset's price above the strike price, the call option's value rises accordingly. However, once the option becomes in-the-money, there is intrinsic value. The profit potential is realized when the underlying asset's price moves above the strike price, allowing the call option holder to sell the option at a premium.

### 3. Out-of-The-Money (OTM) Call Options

An out-of-the-money call option is one in which the underlying asset's current market price is lower than the option's strike price.

**For example**: If the asset stock trades at $80, a call option with an exercise price of $100 is considered out-of-the-money.

**Profit Potential** The profit potential of an out-of-the-money call option is contingent on the underlying asset's price rising above the exercise price before the option's expiration date. Until the option becomes in-the-money, there is no intrinsic value, and the option's value is solely based on market expectations and time decay.

## UNDERSTANDING PUT OPTIONS AND THEIR ROLE IN PORTFOLIO PROTECTION

### What Is a Put Option?

A put option, also known as a "put," is a derivative contract that grants the option holder the right, but not the authority, to engage in a short sale or sell a predetermined quantity of an underlying security at a predetermined price during a specified period. The predicted price at which the put option buyer can sell the asset security is the exercise price or striking price. Options are traded on diverse underlying assets, encompassing stocks, currencies, bonds, commodities, futures, and indexes. In contrast to a call option, a put option bestows upon the holder the right to exercise the sale of the underlying security at a predetermined price, either on or before the option contract's expiration date. **Portfolio Protection** Financial markets are inherently volatile, and asset prices can experience significant fluctuations due to various factors such as economic events, geopolitical tensions, and unexpected news. The volatility in the market can pose significant risks to your portfolio, potentially resulting in substantial losses. Portfolio protection strategies aim to minimize these risks by implementing measures that buffer against adverse market movements.

### The Mechanics of Put Options for Portfolio Protection

Incorporating options into your investment strategy primarily aims to hedge against downside risk. Let's explore how put options work in the context of portfolio protection:

1. **Risk Mitigation**: When you purchase put options on assets within your portfolio, you acquire the right to sell those assets at a predetermined strike price. This becomes particularly valuable in bearish market scenarios or during periods of heightened volatility.

2. **Diversified Protection**: A diverse array of assets, such as individual stocks, exchange-traded funds (TFs), and stock market indices, can be encompassed by putting options. This

flexibility allows you to tailor your protection strategy to different components of your portfolio.

3. **Effective Hedging**: As the value of your underlying assets decreases, the value of your put options increases. This inverse relationship provides a hedge against losses in your portfolio, helping offset potential declines.

4. **Preserving Capital**: Using put options strategically can protect a significant portion of your investment capital. This protection prevents substantial losses and preserves your ability to capitalize on future market opportunities. Portfolio protection is a critical aspect of maintaining a resilient investment strategy. Put options offer a potent mechanism to shield your investments from potential downturns and volatility. You can confidently navigate the markets by effectively integrating options into your portfolio, knowing you have a strategic defense against adverse market movements.

## REAL-LIFE EXAMPLES ILLUSTRATING HOW CALL AND PUT OPTIONS ARE USED IN THE MARKET

When diving into the exciting world of options trading, it's natural to wonder how these financial instruments are implemented in real-life situations. Let's explore some practical examples that shed light on how traders and investors use call-and-put options in the market.

**Example 1: Call Options Buying - Capitalizing on a Bullish Outlook**

Imagine you're closely following a tech company, XYZ Inc., and you're convinced their groundbreaking new product will propel their stock price skyward in the coming months. You're optimistic about XYZ Inc.'s future and see an opportunity to profit using call options. You opt to initiate long position by acquiring a call option contract, conferring upon you the privilege to procure shares of XYZ Inc. at a predicted price, known as the strike price, within or before specified date, referred to as the expiration date. Paying a small premium upfront expose, you toa larger position in the underlying stock. Fast forward a couple of months, and your instincts prov correct. XYZ Inc. announces exceptional quarterly earnings and the stock price shoots up. With your call option, you can buy shares at the agreed-upon strike price, even if the market price exceeds it. By engaging in this strategy, you can capture the premium discrepancy between the prevailing market price and the predetermined strike price, amplifying your potential gains in contrast to simply possessing the underlying stock.

**Example 2: Put Option Buying - Protecting Against a Bearish Market**

Let' say you're eyeing a pharmaceutical company, ABC Pharma, and your research indicates that their upcoming drug trial results might disappoint, leading to a potential decline in the stock price to protect yourself from potential losses, you decide to purchase a put option contract. This contract allows you to sell ABC Pharma shares at a predetermined price on or before expiration. You're betting that the stock will drop below the strike price. Sure enough, ABC Pharma announces discouraging trial results, and the stock price takes a nosedive. With your put option in play, you can sell the shares at the agreed-upon strike price, shielding yourself from the losses other investors may incur.

**Example 3: Covered Call Strategy - Generating Income from Your Stock Holdings**

Suppose you're already holding shares of DEF Corporation, and you expect the stock to remain relatively steady or experience slight growth in the short term. You spot an opportunity to generate additional income through a covered call strategy. In this scenario, you sell call option contracts against your existing DEF Corporation shares. By engaging in this strategy, you are effectively entering into a contractual agreement to sell your shares at an established price, known as the strike price, if the option buyers choose to exercise their options. As the covered call writer, you receive premium from the buyers of these call options, which provides an immediate cash infusion into our portfolio. If the stock price remains below the price of the strike throughout the option's lifespan, the buyers won't exercise their options, and you'll keep both your shares and the premium. his strategy can enhance your overall returns, even in a slightly bullish market environment.

in conclusion, these real-life examples demonstrate how call-and-put options can effectively amplify gains, hedge against potential losses, and generate additional income. However, it's crucial to remember that options trading involves risks and requires careful consideration.

## CHAPTER 4
## MAKING YOUR FIRST OPTIONS TRADE: A STEP-BY-STEP ADVENTURE

### GUIDE WALKTHROUGH OF PLACING A SIMPLE OPTIONS TRADE ON A BROKERAGE PLATFORM

Welcome to the exhilarating world of options trading! By now, you've acquired the foundational knowledge to embark on your first actual options trade. Don't worry; we're here to be your trusted guide o this exciting adventure. Let's walk through placing a simple options trade on your chosen brokerage platform.

Before we begin, make sure you've set up your brokerage account. If you haven't already, take a few minutes to open an account with a reliable brokerage that offers options trading services. Once you're al set, it's time to dive in!

**Step 1: research and Identify the Opportunity**
Before you make any trade, it's essential to do your homework. Research and identify a stock or ETF that you believe will make a significant move in the near future. Check out the latest financial news, analyze company reports, and stay updated on market trends to make an informed decision.

**Step 2: Determine Your Strategy**
Now that you have your eye on a potential opportunity, it's time to choose your options trading strategy Are you feeling bullish and expecting the stock to rise in value? Or are you bearish and anticipate a price decline? Your outlook will determine whether you'll be buying call or put options. **Step 3: Select the Right Option Contract**
With your strategy in place, it' time to select the appropriate option contract. Look for options with expiration dates that align with your trading timeline. Additionally, ensure that the strike price suits your expectations of the stock's price movement.

**Step 4: Placing the Trade on our Brokerage Platform**
Now comes the exciting part—lacing your trade! Log in to your brokerage platform and navigate to the options trading section. enter the stock symbol or select the ETF on which you wish to trade options. Choose whether you want to buy a call or put option, depending on your chosen strategy. Then, select the expiration date and strike price from the available options chain.

**Step 5: Review and Confirm** Before you click that "Submit" button, double-check all the details of your options trade. Verify the stock symbol, option type, expiration date, strike price, and the number of contracts you wish to trade. Ensuring accuracy at this stage is crucial. You've taken a significant leap into options trading following this step-by-step guided walkthrough. Remember, practice makes perfect, so keep learning, honing your skills, and seeking device from experienced traders or financial advisors when needed.

**GRASPNG THE CONCEPT OF MARKET MAKERS AND BID-ASK SPREADS**

Market makers play a pivotal role in the bustling realm of options trading. These individuals or firms facilitate the buying and selling of options contracts by providing liquidity to the market. Think of them as the intermediaries, standing ready to buy or sell options at all times, ensuring a continuous flow of trades.

But how do market makers make a profit? This is where bid-ask spreads come into play. When trading options, you'll notice two key prices—the bid and the ask prices. The bid price represents the maximum price at which a buyer is eager to acquire an options contract, whereas the asking price signifies the minimal cost at which a seller is willing to transact. Here's where the magic (and profit) happens for market makers. They generate profits by leveraging the spread between the bids an ask, representing the disparity between the buying and selling prices. As option traders, market makers present bids to purchase options at the bid price and offer to sell them at the asking price. hey profit from the spread, compensating for facilitating liquidity and assuming the associated risks.

For example, if the bid price for an options contract is $2.50, and the asking price is $2.70, the bid-ask spread is $0.20. This means that the market maker earns $0.20 per contract traded.

But wait, how does this affect you as a trader? The bid-ask spread is essential because it represents an immediate cost to enter or exit a trade. When buying options, you'll pay the higher ask price; when selling, you'll receive the lower bid price. This spread can impact your potential profits and losses. Wider bid-ask spreads can eat your returns, so it's essential to be mindful when choosing your options contracts. Highly liquid options with narrow bid-ask spreads are generally preferred as they offer better pricing and execution.

As you delve deeper into options trading, remember that bid-ask spreads may vary depending on the options' liquidity, market conditions, and the underlying asset. It's always a good idea to compare bid-ask spreads across different strikes and expiration dates to find the most favorable prices for your trades. You can confidently navigate the options market with a solid understanding of market maker and bid-ask spreads. Consider bid-ask spreads when making your trades, and seek highly liquid options to optimize your trading experience.

Now that you have a solid grasp of market makers and bid-ask spreads, it's time to understand how these factors impact your trading decisions.

**Understanding the Impact on Profits and Losses:**

The bid-ask spread directly affects your potential profits and losses in options trading. When initiating a purchase of an options contract, one enters the trade at the asking price, which is marginally higher than the bid price. Similarly, when you sell an options contract, you do so at a slightly lower bid price than the asking price. The bid-ask spread differential gives rise to the initial expense referred to as the "spread cost." To be profitable in a long position, the underlying asset's price must move beyond the cost of the spread plus any other trading expenses, such as commissions. For example, if you buy a call option for $3.00 (the asking price) and the bid price is $2.80, the bid-ask spread is $0.20. To break even on the trade, the underling asset's price must rise above $3.20 (the cost of the spread plus the ask price) by expiration. By understanding market makers and bid-ask spreads and employing effective strategies to manage costs, you're on your way to becoming a savvy options trader. Remember, practice and continuous learning are the keys to success in this exciting and dynamic market.

## TIPS FOR MANAGING THE TADE AND MONITORING ITS PERFORMANCE

Trading is an art that requires the ability to enter a position and the skill to manage it effectively. Once you've initiated a trade, whether it's in stocks, options, or any other financial instrument, your journey has just begun. Managing the trade and monitoring its performance are crucial aspects that can make all the difference between success and disappointment. Here are some invaluable tips to help you navigate this essential phase of your trading adventure.

**1. Set Clear Goals and Exit strategies:**

Before entering any trade, set clear objectives for your goal. Define your profit targets and determine the maximum acceptable loss. A well-defined exit strategy helps you avoid emotional decision-making during volatile market conditions.

**2. Stay Informed and Be Flexible:**

Keep a pulse on the financial markets and the underlying assets you're trading. News, earnings reports, and economic events an impact your options trade. Maintain flexibility and remain ready to adapt your trading approach in response to emerging market data.

**3. Use Stop Loss Orders:** Protect your capital by utilizing stop-loss orders. These orders automatically trigger a sale when the option price reaches a predetermined level. Stop losses can help limit potential losses and are especially useful when you can't actively monitor the market.

**4. Implement Trailing Stop:**

Use trailing stops to lock in aims as your options trade becomes profitable. Trailing stops move with the option's price, maintaining a certain percentage of profits below the current market price. This allows you to capture additional profits if the market continues to move in your favor.

**5. Keep a Trading Journal:** Maintain a detailed trading journal to record your trades, strategies, and thoughts behind each decision. Regularly reviewing your trading journal is crucial for identifying patterns, strengths, and areas of improvement in your trading approach.

**6. Avoid Overtrading:**

resist the temptation to trade excessively. Excessive trading can lead to impulsive decisions and increased transaction costs. Stick to your trading plan and avoid making trades out of boredom or frustration.

in conclusion, managing trades and monitoring performance require diligence, discipline, and a systematic approach. By setting precise levels, adhering to your trading plan, and staying informed about market conditions, you increase your chances of making well-informed decisions and achieving your trading objectives. Remember that trading is a continuous learning and adaptation journey; these tips will serve as your guiding principles. If you have enjoyed this book so far feel free to leave a review.

# GLOSSARY

**Asset:** An asset is anything you own that you expect to make or save you money in the future. It can be owned by a company, an organization or an individual. In other words, an asset represents the value of ownership that can be converted into cash.

**Bearish:** Bearish options strategies are employed when the options trader expects the underlying stock price to move downwards.

**Bullish:** Bullish options strategies are simply policies that are adopted by several traders when they expect to see a rise in asset price

**Brokerage:** Brokerage is the activity of buying and selling foreign money, shares in companies, and option trades for other people.

**Exercise price:** The exercise price is the price at which an underlying security can be purchased or sold when trading a call or put option, respectively. It is also referred to as the strike price and is known when an investor initiates the trade.

**Finance:** Finance is a term for matters regarding the management, creation, and study of money and investments.

**Hedging:** Hedging is an advanced risk management strategy that involves buying or selling an investment to potentially help reduce the risk of loss of an existing position.

**Investment:** An investment involves putting capital to use today in order to increase its value over time. An investment requires putting capital to work, in the form of time, money, effort, tc., in hopes of a greater payoff in the future than what was originally put in.

**Investors:** An investor is a person or organization that puts money into financial schemes, property, etc. with the expectation of achieving a profit.

**Leverage:** Leverage is when one uses borrowed funds (debt) for funding the acquisition of assets in the hopes that the income of the new asset or capital gain would surpass the cost of borrowing

**Options:** An option is a contract giving the buyer the right—but not the obligation—to buy (in the case of a call) or sell (in the case of a put) the underlying asset at a specific price on or before a certain date.

**Portfolios:** A portfolio is a collection of financial investments like stocks, bonds, commodities, ash, and cash equivalents, including closed-end funds an exchange-traded funds (ETFs).

**Premium:** A premium is a price paid for above and beyond some basic or intrinsic value.

# **REFERENCES**

*D Propagación de Oso - Invatatiafaceri.ro*. 19 Nov. 2022, invatatiafaceri.ro/es/diccionario-financier/propagacion-de-oso/?expand_article=1. Accessed 13 Aug. 2023.

Chen, Full Bio Fllow LinkedIn Follow Twitter James, et al. "Betting on a Modest Drop: The Bear Put." *Investopedia*, www.investopedia.com/terms/b/bearputspread.asp.

Royal, James. "What Is Options Trading? A Basic Overview." *Bankrate*, 22 June 2023, www.bankrate.com/investing/what-is-options-trading/.

# BOOK 2

## "OPTIONS UNLEASHED: MASTERING ESSENTIAL STRATEGIES FOR BEGINNERS"

# TABLE OF CONTENTS

- CHAPTER 1 .................................................................................................................................. 3
- LONG AND SHORT CALL OPTIONS: BULLS AND BEARS ON THE MOVE ...................................... 3
  - UNDERSTANDING LONG CALL OPTIONS FOR BULLISH POSITIONS AND PROFIT POTENTIAL ................. 3
  - EXPLORING SHORT CALL OPTIONS FOR INCOME GENERATION AND RISK MANAGEMENT .................. 6
  - PRACTICAL SCENARIOS WHERE LONG AND SHORT CALLS CAN BE APPLIED ....................... 8
- CHAPTER 2 .................................................................................................................................. 9
- LONG AND SHORT PUT OPTIONS: TAMING THE BEARISH TERRAIN ........................................... 9
  - LEVERAGING LONG PUT OPTIONS FOR BEARISH POSITIONS AND PORTFOLIO PROTECTION ............. 10
  - UTILIZING SHORT PUT OPTIONS FOR GENERATING INCOME AND ACQUIRING STOCKS ..................... 12
  - REAL-LIFE EXAMPLES TO ILLUSTRATE LONG AND SHORT PUT STRATEGIES ......................... 13
- CHAPTER 3 ................................................................................................................................ 15
- UNCOVERING COVERED CALL STRATEGY: YOUR JOURNEY TO INCOME GENERATION ........................... 15
  - MASTERING THE COVERED CALL STRATEGY FOR CONSISTENT INCOME ............................................ 16
  - UNDERSTANDING THE RISK-REWARD PROFILE AND POTENTIAL TRADEOFFS .................................. 18
  - CASE STUDIES DEMONSTRATING THE IMPLEMENTATION OF COVERED CALL ................................. 20
- REFERENCES ............................................................................................................................. 23

# CHAPTER 1
## LONG AND SHORT CALL OPTIONS: BULLS AND BEARS ON THE MOVE

Call options are like supercharged tickets to potential profits in the stock market. They grant us the right, but not the obligation, to buy (long call) or sell (short call) an underlying asset, such as a stock or ETF, at a specific price within a set timeframe.

Let's begin with the bullish side, the long call option! When you feel optimistic about a particular stock's future, you can buy a long call option to express your bullish outlook. Here's how it works: Imagine you're super enthusiastic about ABC Corp.'s growth prospects, and its stock is currently trading at $50 per share. Anticipating a further surge, you initiate a bullish strategy by purchasing a long call option at a strike price of $55, set to expire in a few months.

Now, here's the magic: If ABC Corp.'s stock were to surpass $55 and soar to, let's say, $65 per share before the option's expiration, you would have the opportunity to exercise your call option and acquire the stock at the predetermined strike price of $55, subsequently selling it in the market at the prevailing price of $65. Boom! You just pocketed a $10 profit per share (minus the option contract cost). But keep in mind that the clock is ticking! The expiration date is crucial, and the longer you wait, the less time value your option has. So, it's essential to be mindful of time decay and have a clear exit plan.

Now, on to the bearish side—the short call option! If you believe a stock's price will plummet, you can take a bearish stance by selling a call option. Sounds risky, right? Well, it comes with a higher level of risk but also the potential for juicy rewards.

Here's the deal: You decide to open a short position on a call option for XYZ Corporation with a strike price of $60, even though the underlying stock currently trades at $55 per share. If XYZ Corp.'s stock stays below $60 until the option's expiration, you keep the premium you received from selling the call option. But if the stock shoots above $60, you could be forced to sell the shares at that price, even if they're worth more in the market.

Both long and short call options come with their risks and rewards. The long call allows you to profit from a stock's rise without owning it, while the short call can help you generate income but requires careful risk management.


## UNDERSTANDING LONG CALL OPTIONS FOR BULLISH POSITIONS AND PROFIT POTENTIAL.

Alright, let's start with the basics. A long call option is a straightforward and bullish strategy. Initiating a long call option position exemplifies a trade where you bear a cost in return for the potential, yet not the obligation, to purchase the principal asset at a fixed price, commonly referred to as the striking price, within a specified timeframe referred to as the expiration date. This type of trade occurs when you enter into a transaction in which you incur a cost in return for the potential, but not the obligation, to buy the underlying asset. You engage in a long-call option position when you enter such a deal. The beauty of a long call option lies in its potential for unlimited profit. Here's how it works: If one holds a bullish outlook on a specific stock or ETF, the recommended approach would be to initiate a long position by purchasing a call option with a strike price below the prevailing market price. As the underlying stock price surpasses the strike price, the value of your long call option appreciates. And guess what? You can participate in all that upside movement without actually owning the stock!

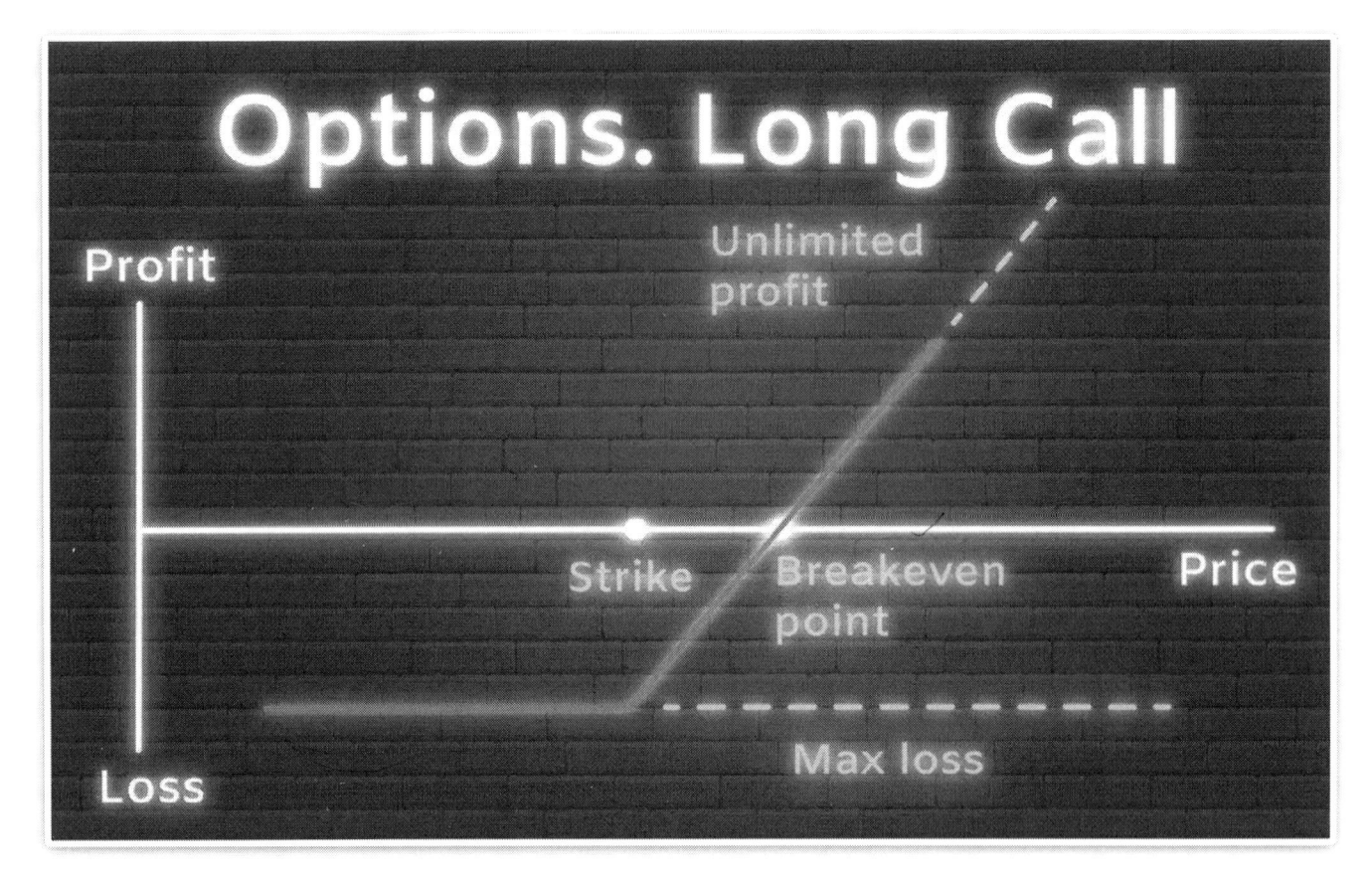

**GRAPH ILLUSTRATING A LONG CALL OPTION**

Let's illustrate this with an example. You are assuming a bullish stance on XYZ Corp., with its stock currently trading at $50 per share. You initiate a bullish position by purchasing a long call option with a strike price of $55 and a three-month expiration.

Now, let's imagine the underlying stock price of XYZ Corp. undergoing a significant surge, soaring to $65 per share before the option's expiration date. Since your strike price is $55, you now have the right to buy the stock at $55 and immediately sell it in the market at $65. Voila! You just pocketed a $10 profit per share (minus the option contract cost).

But hold on, there's one crucial thing to note—time is not your ally with long call options. As the expiration date approaches, the option's time value erodes, and its price may decrease, even if the underlying stock price remains stagnant or moves slightly against your bullish view. So, having a clear plan and being mindful of time decay when trading long call options is essential.

Traders choose long-call options to express a bullish view on a particular stock or ETF. This strategy allows you to benefit from the stock's potential upside without owning the shares.

**Here's How It Works:**
**1. Choosing the Right Option Contract:** When bullish on a specific stock, you look for an appropriate long-call option. This implies opting for a strike price below the prevailing market price of the stock. If the underlying stock price surpasses the strike price, your long call option experiences an increase in value, potentially allowing you to capitalize on the disparity.
**2. Leveraging Unlimited Profit Potential:** The most enticing aspect of a long call option is its unlimited profit potential. As the stock price moves higher, the value of your long call option increases. There's no ceiling on how much you can earn from this strategy—the sky's the limit!
**3. Reduced Capital Outlay:** Another advantage of long-call options is that you don't need to tie up a substantial amount of capital as you would when buying the actual stock. The cost of a long call option is significantly lower than buying the equivalent number of shares of the underlying asset.
Now, let's illustrate the profit potential of long call options with an example:
As an options trader, you envision a bullish outlook on XYZ Corp., with its stock currently priced at $50 per share. You opt to initiate a long call position, selecting a strike price of $55 and a three-month expiration period. After a brief interval, the underlying stock price of XYZ Corp. underwent a substantial upswing, soaring to $65 per share before the option's expiration date. Since your strike price is $55, you now have the right to buy the stock at $55 and immediately sell it in the market at $65. You just pocketed a $10 profit per share (minus the option contract cost).

**Risks and considerations to keep in mind:**
**1. Time Decay:** While long call options offer significant profit potential, time is not your ally. As the expiration date approaches, the option's time value erodes, and its price may decrease, even if the underlying stock price remains stagnant or moves slightly against your bullish view.
**2. Selecting the Right Timeframe:** Choosing the right expiration date is essential. Too short, and you may need to give the stock more time to move in your favor; too long, and the option's time value may erode significantly.
**3. Having an Exit Strategy:** It would help to have a clear exit strategy to manage long call options effectively. Define your profit targets and decide when to cut your losses if the trade goes against you. It's crucial to stick to your plan and avoid making impulsive decisions.
**4. Risk Management:** While the profit potential of long call options is enticing, remember that options trading involves risks. Managing your positions carefully and avoiding overexposing yourself to a single trade is essential.
In conclusion, long call options offer an excellent opportunity for traders with a bullish outlook to participate in potential upside movements with reduced capital outlay. Understanding the risks and implementing sound risk management practices are vital to optimizing the profit potential of this strategy.

EXPLORING SHORT CALL OPTIONS FOR INCOME GENERATION AND RISK MANAGEMENT

When you sell a call option on a stock you don't own, that's called a short call option. It might sound intimidating, but don't worry—I'll break it down for you.

**Income Generation:**

The primary goal of using short-call options is to generate income. Here's how it works: Based on your analysis, you have a bearish outlook on the stock's potential for significant price appreciation in the near term. Consequently, you decide to engage in a strategy known as selling a call option with a strike price above the prevailing market price. As an options trader, you can receive a premium from the call option buyer in exchange for your agreement. Suppose the underlying stock price remains below the designated strike price until the expiration date of the opportunity. In that case, you will retain the premium received as a profitable outcome, while the vote will expire without any intrinsic value. Sweet, right? You just made money from the time decay and the stock not moving in the expected direction.

So, short-call options are like a dance—you enjoy collecting premiums as long as the stock behaves, but you must be prepared to handle the situation if things go against you.

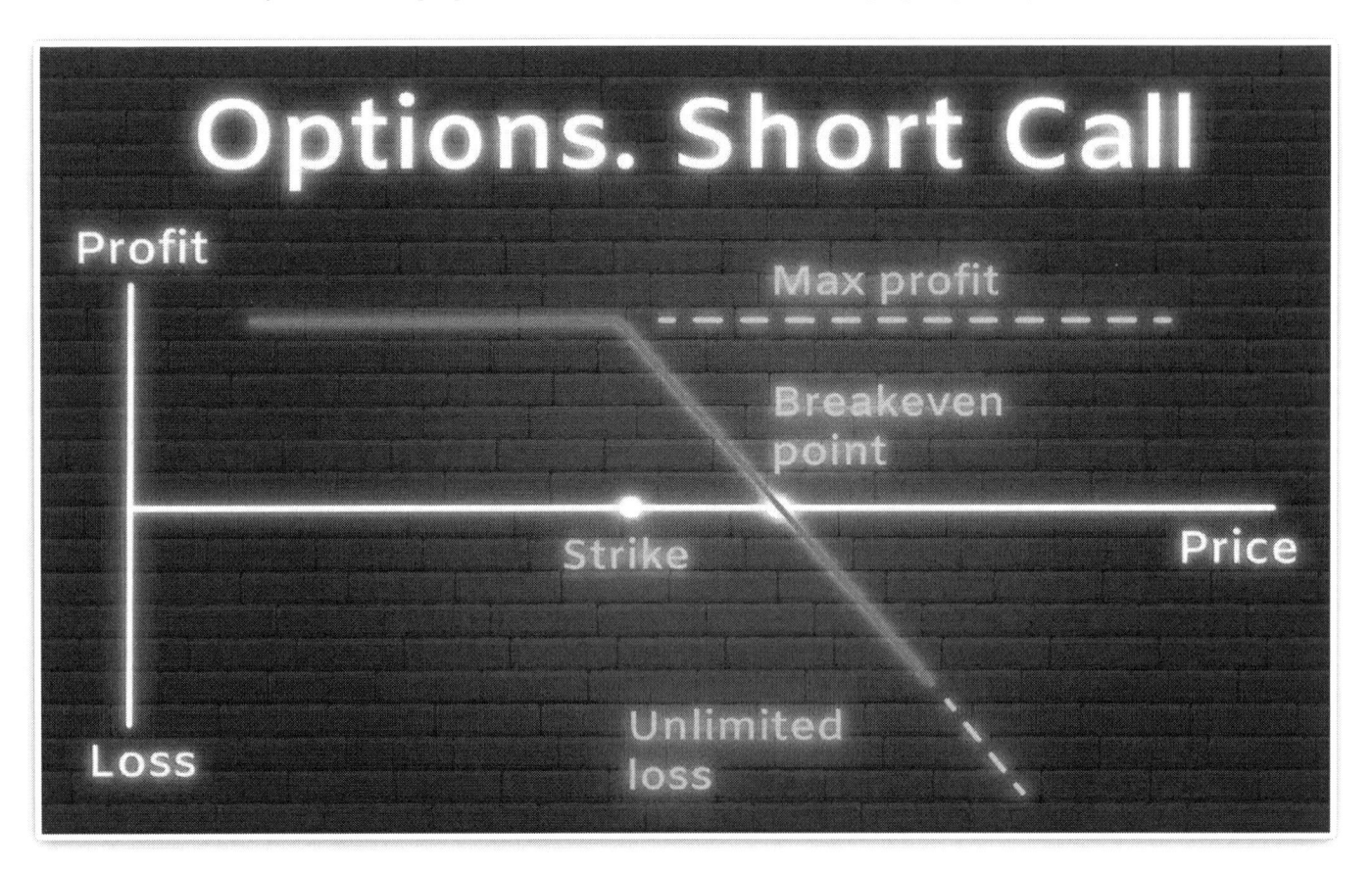

**GRAPH ILLUSTRATING A SHORT CALL OPTION**

**Risk Management:**
As with any options strategy, risk management is vital when dealing with short-call options. Since your potential losses are theoretically unlimited (as the stock price can keep rising), it's essential to have a plan in place. One way to manage the risk is to be selective with the stocks you choose for short-call options. Pick stocks you believe are less likely to experience significant price increases. You can also consider setting up a stop-loss order to protect yourself. A stop-loss order can be utilized to automatically repurchase the short call option if the stock price surpasses a pre-established threshold—this strategic move aids in curtailing potential losses.

And remember, practicing sound risk management is the key to success in any options trading strategy.

**Exploring Short Call Options for Income Generation and Risk Management**

**1. Selecting the Right Strike Price and Expiration Date:** When selling a short call option, choosing the right strike price and expiration date is crucial. Setting the strike price higher than the underlying stock's current market price should be your goal. However, you should ensure that there is still a fair likelihood for the stock to reach that level.

The expiration date should also align with your outlook for the stock's movement. If you anticipate limited price movement in the short term, choosing a closer expiration date might be preferable, as it maximizes the time decay in your favor.

**2. Understanding Assignment Risk:** As an options trader who has taken the position of selling a short-call option, you must be aware of the potential risk of being assigned the obligation to sell the underlying stock at the predetermined strike price. This is commonly referred to as assignment risk in the options trading world. The occurrence is plausible if the call option holder elects to exercise their privilege to purchase the underlying stock from your position.

To manage assignment risk, be prepared to fulfill your obligation if the option gets exercised. If you're uncomfortable holding the stock, consider using a covered call strategy, where you already own the principal stock and sell call options against it. This limits your downside risk, as you're already holding the stock you might be obligated to sell.

**3. Setting Stop-Loss and Take-Profit Levels:** A well-defined exit plan is essential for any options strategy, including short-call options. Determine your desired profit target and set a stop-loss level to protect yourself from excessive losses. For example, you might close the short-call position and buy back the call option if the stock price rises above a certain threshold. This can help you avoid further losses if the stock experiences upward momentum.

**4. Assessing Implied Volatility:** Implied volatility plays a pivotal role in the determination of options pricing. As a seller of short-call options, high implied volatility works in your favor, increasing the premium, you receive when selling the option. On the other hand, if implied volatility is low, the premium you receive may be less attractive. Assess the implied volatility of the options you're selling to optimize your income potential.

## PRACTICAL SCENARIOS WHERE LONG AND SHORT CALLS CAN BE APPLIED

Now that we've grasped the ins and outs of long and short call options, let's dive into the exciting part—how to apply these strategies in the real world practically. Get ready to uncover practical scenarios where long and short-call options can be your ultimate trading tools.

**Scenario 1: Bullish on a Stock, Limited Capital**

Imagine you've done your research and feeling super bullish about a particular stock, but you don't want to put all your hard-earned money into buying the shares. This is where the long call option comes to the rescue. Buying a long call option allows you to participate in the stock's potential upside without owning the shares outright. It's like riding the bull without being tied to it. Plus, long call options offer unlimited profit potential—so if the stock skyrockets, you ride high on those profits.

**Scenario 2: Generating Income, Hedging Your Bets**

You own some shares of a stock that will stay relatively flat in the near term. You don't expect significant price movements, but you would be okay with making extra cash while you wait. Enter the short call option. You collect a surcharge from the option buyer by selling a short-call option against your shares. If the stock price stays lower than the strike price until the option expires, you can keep the premium as a profit and hold it until it expires. It's like getting paid to wait. But here's the hedge part—since you're obligated to sell the shares if the stock price rises above the strike price, you're protected from potential losses if the stock decides to surprise you and shoot up.

**Scenario 3: Neutral on a Stock, Expecting Limited Movement**

Sometimes, you might not strongly believe a stock's direction. You believe it will stay within a narrow price range for a while. This is where a combination strategy can come into play. You can create an iron condor by selling a short call option and a short put option, with strike prices above and below the current stock price. This way, you collect premiums from both options and as long as the stock stays within that range until expiration, you keep those premiums as profit.

**Scenario 4: Earnings Season Excitement:**

Earnings season can be a rollercoaster ride for stocks. You might anticipate some big moves, but you're still determining which direction the stock will take. In this case, you can use a long straddle strategy. This strategy involves initiating a position by purchasing both a long call option and a long-put option with identical strike prices and expiration dates. You're betting on volatility, not direction. If the stock moves significantly, you profit from the winning option and let the losing option expire worthless.

# CHAPTER 2
## LONG AND SHORT PUT OPTIONS: TAMING THE BEARISH TERRAIN

Have you ever wondered how some savvy investors make their moves when they sense the price of a particular asset is about to take a tumble? Well, one of their secret weapons is the short-put spread strategy!
Here's how it works: Imagine you expect the price of a stock or any other underlying asset to drop in the near future. You use a short-put spread to take advantage of this bearish outlook. Now, what's a short put spread? It involves buying and selling options, and they share the same expiration date. The trick is that these put options have different strike prices. So, you buy a put option with a higher strike price, which is "in-the-money" (ITM), meaning it has some intrinsic value. Simultaneously, you sell an additional put option featuring a lower strike price, positioning it as "out-of-the-money" (OTM) and devoid of intrinsic value.

Buying the higher-priced ITM put and selling the lower-priced OTM results in a net debit. The cost of the ITM put is partially offset by the cash you get from selling the OTM put. However, the thrilling aspect lies in the potential for the trader to realize a profit should the underlying asset's price conclude below the strike price of the out-of-the-money (OTM) put option upon expiration. The real benefit comes from the higher intrinsic value of the ITM put, which acts as a cushion against any losses from the sold OTM put.

Now, let's talk about the math involved. The potential net profit achievable through this strategy is the spread between the strike prices of the two put options, subtracting the initial cost (or net debit) incurred to establish the space.
**Profit = Strike price of the long-put option - Strike price of the short put option - Expenses**

So, why do traders love the short-put spread strategy? Well, it's a smart move when they're moderately bearish on an asset. It allows them to profit from a potential drop in price while keeping some control over their risk with the combination of ITM and OTM puts. But remember that all trading strategies come with risks. Potential losses may be encountered if the underlying asset's price surpasses the strike price of the out-of-the-money (OTM) put option upon expiration. However, the maximum loss is limited to the initial net debit you paid to set up the spread.
So, there you have it—the short put spread, a cool strategy that can help you navigate the world of bearish markets with a bit more confidence and control.

LEVERAGING LONG PUT OPTIONS FOR BEARISH POSITIONS AND PORTFOLIO PROTECTION

A common way to protect a portfolio is by purchasing put options. The owner of a put option has the right, but not the obligation, to sell the principal asset at a specific price (known as the striking price) on a particular date. This right is distinguished from the responsibility. By buying put options on the assets that are in the portfolio, you buy protection against possible falls in the prices of those assets. This strategy is called a Protective Put.

Let's say you have a diversified portfolio that includes stocks from multiple companies. If you are concerned about a possible decline in the value of these shares, you can buy put options on those shares. You will be able to restrict the amount of money you lose by purchasing put options and then exercising those options if the stock price drops below the exercise price of the put options. Exercising the put options will allow you to sell the shares at a fixed price.

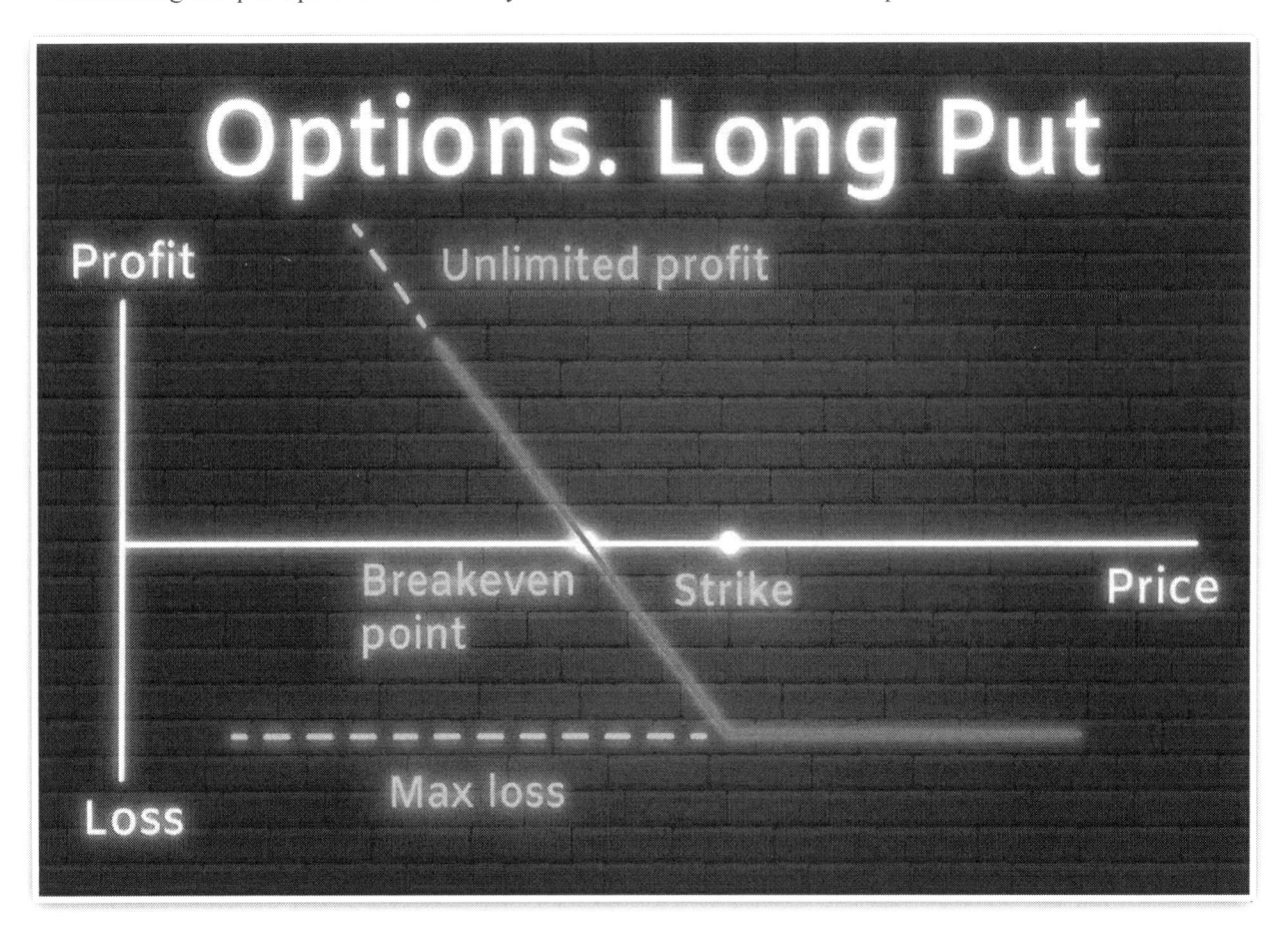

**GRAPH ILLUSTRATING A LONG PUT OPTION**

A long-put option is like an insurance policy against falling prices. Here's how it works: You buy a long-put option for a specific stock. This allows you to sell that particular stock before the option's expiration date at a specific price, referred to as the strike price. You are not required to sell the stock at the predetermined price, but you have the right to do so. Now, assuming the underlying stock price does indeed decline below the strike price before the expiration of the option. This is where the volatility unfolds. One potential strategy is to initiate a long position by purchasing the underlying stock at the prevailing market price, then executing a short work by selling it at the higher strike price. This approach allows for capturing the price differential as a profitable gain. You capitalize on the price drop without owning the stock until you exercise the option.

But wait, there's more! The allure of long-put options lies in their ability to restrict potential losses to the premium invested in purchasing the option. It's like knowing the maximum amount you're risking upfront, which is pretty cool, right?

Now, let's talk about portfolio protection. We all know the market can be unpredictable, and prices can sometimes take an unexpected nosedive. That's when long-put options come to the rescue!

Imagine you have a well-curated portfolio of stocks you believe in, but the market mood starts sour. Don't fret! You're creating a safety net by strategically using long put options on the individual stocks in your portfolio.

If any of your stocks take a tumble, the gains from your long-put options can offset some losses, providing you with protection. It's like having a shield to defend your portfolio from sudden market blows.

Remember, long-put options can be a potent tool for bearish positions and safeguarding your hard-earned investments. It is imperative to grasp the inherent risks and potential rewards associated with options trading while customizing your approach to align with your market outlook and risk tolerance.

**Protect your investment portfolio with a single put option.**

Purchasing put options on market indexes, such as the S&P 500, is yet another common and effective approach for hedging risk. These options help protect your portfolio against a general market downturn. If the market experiences a significant decline, putting options on the index may increase in value, offsetting losses in the portfolio. In addition to buying put options, another popular protection strategy is creating option spreads. An option spread involves the combination of call options and put options to limit risk and the cost of protection. By combining different options, a price range can be created in which the portfolio is protected against adverse movements. It is important to note that protecting a portfolio with options involves costs. The purchase of options entails the payment of premiums, which are the price of the options. These premiums will reduce the potential returns of the portfolio and must be considered when evaluating the hedging strategy.

Financial options offer an effective way to protect a portfolio against adverse market movements. Buying put options on individual assets or market indices, as well as creating option spreads, are common strategies to protect a portfolio. However, it is important to consider the costs associated with buying options and carefully assess the risk-reward ratio before implementing any hedging strategies. Possessing a solid understanding of financial options and consulting with experts to make well-informed and suitable decisions to safeguard your investment portfolio is crucial.

## UTILIZING SHORT PUT OPTIONS FOR GENERATING INCOME AND ACQUIRING STOCKS

So, imagine this scenario: you've had your eye on a particular stock for a while, and you'd love to own it, but it's just a tad too pricey at the moment. Don't worry; short-put options might be the key to making your dream a reality.

Here's the breakdown: You initiate a put option sale for the desired stock, and as a result, you obtain a premium from the buyer of the option. Woah, getting paid upfront? That's cool.

Now, let's break it down: By engaging in the sale of the put option, you are assuming the responsibility of potentially acquiring the underlying stock from the option purchaser at the predetermined strike price, should they decide to exercise the option before or upon expiration. Alternatively, you are proposing the stock at a particular price, the strike price.

You might wonder, "Why on earth would I want to buy the stock if I'm bearish?" Here's the twist: You only want to buy the stock if its price drops below the strike price, also known as "being assigned."

But guess what? If the stock continues to trade at a price higher than the strike price until the option's expiration date, the buyer won't exercise it, which means you get to keep the premium you were paid. It is similar to receiving payment in exchange for the willingness to purchase the stock at a discount potentially. Now, let's talk about generating income. Selling short-put options can be an excellent strategy for bringing in some extra cash. You can regularly sell put options and collect the premiums that come with them as long as you are satisfied with taking ownership of the underlying stock at the price at which the option is struck.

This can be particularly effective in a range-bound or mildly bullish market, where you anticipate the stock to maintain stability or experience slight upward movement. And remember, even if the stock gets assigned to you, you still get to buy it at a price below the current market value.

Naturally, akin to any options trading approach, there exist inherent risks. In the event of a significant downward movement in the stock, you may be obligated to purchase it at a price exceeding the prevailing market value. So, choosing stocks you genuinely want to own and using proper risk management is essential.

Short-put options are a fantastic way to generate income and acquire your favorite stocks at a discount. It's a strategy that requires careful consideration and understanding of the underlying stocks, but with the right approach, it can add a valuable tool to your trading arsenal.

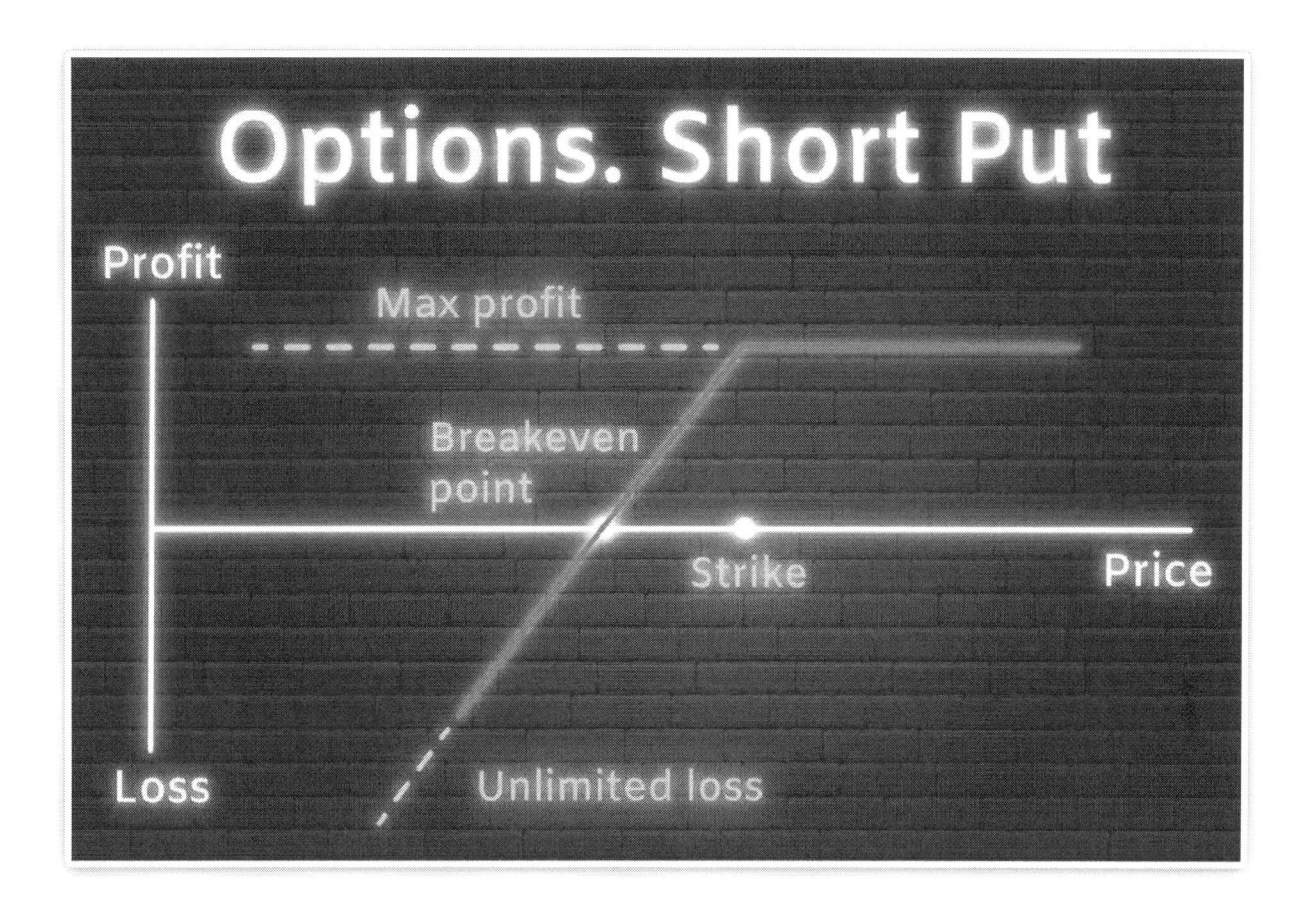

**GRAPH ILLUSTRATING A SHORT PUT OPTION**

REAL-LIFE EXAMPLES TO ILLUSTRATE LONG AND SHORT PUT STRATEGIES

**Long Put Strategy: Betting Against a Stock**
You're keeping a close eye on Company XYZ and notice some concerning signs in their financials. You suspect the stock might take a hit in the near future, and you want to profit from this downward movement. The long-put strategy is a critical player in this scenario. You opt to initiate a long-put position on Company XYZ, selecting a strike price of $50 and a three-month expiration period. The put option is trading at a premium of $3 per share.

Fast forward three months, and your intuition proves correct! Company XYZ faces some challenges, and its stock price drops to $40. You have decided to put your put option to use and sell the underlying stock at the predetermined strike price of $50. This decision was made possible by the fact that you possess a put option. Thanks to the put option, you buy the shares at $40 in the market and immediately sell them for $50. You've made a $7 profit per share ($50 strike price - $40 stock price - $3 premium paid) without owning the stock until you exercised the option.

**Short Put Strategy: Generating Income and Acquiring Stocks**

Imagine you've been eyeing a tech company called TechCo Inc. for a while now. You believe the stock's future looks bright, but the current market price is too steep for your liking. However, you're open to owning the stock at a lower price if the opportunity arises. The short put strategy is being executed on TechCo Inc. by selling a put option with a strike price of $100 and a one-month expiration. The premium collected for the set option is $5 per share.

Now, two things can happen:

a. TechCo's stock stays above $100 by expiration: In this case, the option buyer won't exercise the option, and you get to keep the $5 premium as income.

b. TechCo's stock drops below $100 by expiration: The option buyer exercises the option, and you're obligated to buy the shares at $100 per share. But you were open to owning the stock at a lower price. So, you acquire the shares at a discounted price, thanks to the premium you received.

# CHAPTER 3
# UNCOVERING COVERED CALL STRATEGY: YOUR JOURNEY TO INCOME GENERATION

Welcome to the exciting realm of covered call strategy, where we'll explore a powerful tool for generating income in the options market. Get ready to uncover the secrets of this strategy, as it brings a whole new level of income potential to your trading journey.

So, what's a covered call, and how does it work?

Picture this: You own a particular stock you believe has potential, but it still needs to skyrocket. Your content with holding onto the stock, but why not make extra money while you wait for it to rise?

That's where the covered call strategy swoops in to save the day! Here's how it goes: You decide to write (sell) call options against the stock you already own. The right to exercise the call option rests with the holder. Even so, the holder is under no obligation to purchase 100 shares of the principal stock at the set price (often referred to as the strike price) within a predetermined period (the expiration date), provided that they satisfy several parameters that have been predetermined. You might think, "Wait, why would I sell options against my precious stock?" Well, fear not, my friend! The "covered" in covered call means you have the stock (the underlying asset) to back up the call options you're selling. It's like having insurance for the calls you wrote.

Here's the magic of covered calls: You receive a premium (money) from selling those call options. And guess what? That premium is yours to keep, no matter what happens.

Now, two things can happen next:

1. The stock's price remains below the strike price until expiration: The call options won't get exercised by the buyers. You keep the stock and the premium you received from selling the calls. Double win.

2. The stock's price rises above the strike price before expiration: The call options may get exercised, and the buyers will buy your shares at the strike price. You keep the premium but say goodbye to the shares at the strike price. Well, that's alright. You made a profit from the premium, and your stock reached a level where you were willing to part with it.

Sounds pretty awesome. Covered calls present an excellent opportunity to generate income, particularly when anticipating limited short-term upward movement in the stock's price.

But, as with any strategy, there are considerations to consider. Make sure you choose stocks you're comfortable holding and be aware of potential assignment risks. Also, remember to select strike prices and expiration dates that align with your market outlook and risk tolerance.

**What is a covered call?**
A covered call is a strategic financial transaction wherein the call options writer possesses an equal quantity of the underlying security. To achieve this, an option trader with a bullish position on an asset initiates a covered call strategy by selling call options on the same support to generate a consistent income stream. Their extended position effectively hedges the investor's bullish stance on the underlying asset, allowing the seller to fulfill their obligation of delivering the stock if the buyer exercises the call option.

- A covered call is a popular option strategy used to generate income in the form of option premiums.
- Investors expect only a small increase or decrease in the underlying stock's price over the option's life when they make a covered call.
- To execute a covered call, an investor who is long an asset writes (sells) call options on that same asset.
- Covered calls are frequently utilized by individuals with a long-term outlook on the underlying security, anticipating limited price appreciation shortly.
- This strategy suits investors who believe the underlying price will not move much in the short term.

MASTERING THE COVERED CALL STRATEGY FOR CONSISTENT INCOME

Another possibility is to use this strategy on a recurring basis, at each expiration, on our stock list. The objective would be to obtain the maximum possible profit due to the sale of the SC. Therefore, in this case, we would not do SC OTM but ATM, where the extrinsic value is greatest. Using it this way, we would be willing to be assigned since that would be the main purpose. If someone wants to maximize the strategy, they should look for stocks where the implied volatility of their options is high, although the risk will also be higher. Ivolatility.com is an excellent site for stocks with high IVs, usually with upcoming events (earnings, FDA reports, or similar).

The covered call strategy offers a fantastic opportunity for options traders to generate consistent income while holding on to their preferred stocks. Mastering this strategy involves careful stock selection, strategic timing, and a thorough understanding of risk management. By staying disciplined, flexible, and patient, traders can unlock the potential of covered calls to create a reliable income stream and enhance their overall trading success.

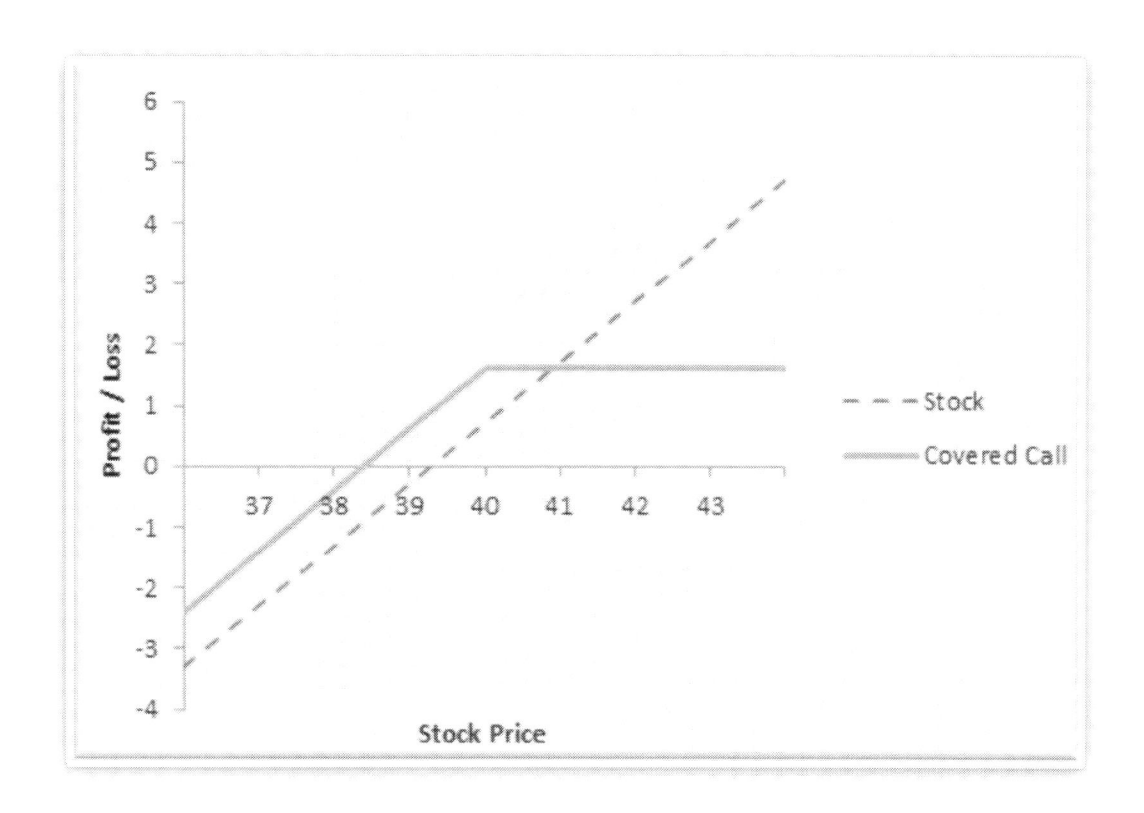

**GRAPH ILLUSTRATING A COVERED CALL**

**Steps and factors involved in mastering the covered call**
**1. Selecting the Right Stocks:** The first step in mastering covered calls is to choose the right stocks to apply this strategy. It's essential to pick stocks the trader is comfortable holding for an extended period. Stocks with strong fundamentals, stable earnings, and a positive outlook are preferred choices. Additionally, diversifying the covered call positions across different sectors and industries can help spread risk and ensure a more balanced portfolio.
**2. Timing and Market Conditions:** Timing is critical in the options market, and covered calls are no exception. Traders should look for opportunities to write covered calls when they believe the stock's price will remain relatively stable or experience only moderate fluctuations. If the trader anticipates significant price movements or major events that could impact the stock, it may be best to avoid writing covered calls during such periods.
**3. Strike Price Selection:** The choice of strike price plays a vital role in the effectiveness of the covered call strategy. Options traders often opt for a strike price slightly above the prevailing market price of the underlying stock. This allows them to capture additional upside potential if the stock rises while still earning a premium from the call options. It is crucial to strike a balance between setting the strike price too high, which may lead to the options remaining unexercised, and setting it too low, which may result in the stock being sold below its market value.
**4. Expiration Dates and Time Horizon:** Selecting the appropriate expiration dates is essential for a successful covered call strategy. Traders should consider the time horizon of their investment

thesis and choose expiration dates that align with their expectations for the stock's performance. Monthly or quarterly expirations are common choices, allowing traders to adjust their positions more frequently if needed.

UNDERSTANDING THE RISK-REWARD PROFILE AND POTENTIAL TRADEOFFS

**Risk reward concept**

Risk reward is a general tradeoff that underlies almost anything from which a return can be generated. Any time you invest money in something, there is a risk, big or small, that you won't get your money back. – that the investment will fail. If you take that risk, you expect a return to compensate for potential losses. Theoretically, the higher the risk you should take by holding the investment, the lower the risk and the less you should get on average.

**DIAGRAM ILLUSTRATING A RISK-REWARD RATIO**

**Determining your risk choice**

Given the many investment options available, how does an astute investor ascertain their risk tolerance? Everyone is different, and it's hard to create a consistent model that applies to everyone, but here are two important things to consider when deciding how much risk to take:

**1. Time horizon:** Before investing, you should always determine how long you need to invest your money. If you have $20,000 to invest today but need it in a year for a down payment on a new house, investing money in high-risk stocks isn't the best strategy. In options trading, the higher the risk associated with an investment, the higher its level of volatility or price fluctuations. If your time horizon is relatively short, you may be compelled to execute a sale of your securities at a substantial loss. With an extended time horizon, option traders have a more significant opportunity to recover from potential losses, thus enabling them to exhibit a theoretically higher tolerance for increased risks. For example, if that $20,000 is for a lakeside cabin you plan to buy in 10 years, you could invest the money in high-risk stocks. Because? Because more time is available to recoup losses, you're less likely to be forced to sell the job too soon.

**2. Finance:** Another essential factor in determining your risk tolerance is determining how much money you stand to lose. This may not be the most optimistic investment method, but it is the most realistic. By investing money that you can't lose or can afford to be tied up for a certain period, you won't be pressured to sell any investment due to panic or liquidity problems. The more money you have, the more risk you can take. Compare, for example, a person with a net worth of $50,000 to another with a net worth of $5 million. If you both invest $25,000 of your net worth in securities, a decline will significantly impact the person with the lower net worth than the person with the higher net worth.

**Risk-Reward Ratio**

A fundamental principle in options trading is to establish a minimum risk-reward ratio that is attainable and in line with the success rate of your trading strategy. As a general rule of thumb, know that if you wait too long for deeper entry, you may miss out on some trades, but if they do trigger, the result will be a much better risk-reward ratio, with a higher success rate. Good risk-reward discipline will help you trade with greater efficiency, a higher level of success, less stress, and faster conviction as to whether or not your trade was successful.

**Risk-Reward Dynamics of Covered Calls**

**1. Risk-Reward Profile:**
Like all trading strategies, covered calls have their unique risk-reward profile.
**Reward:** The primary reward in the covered call strategy is the premium you receive from selling the call options. This premium is yours to keep, regardless of what happens next. If the stock's price remains below the strike price until expiration, the call options won't get exercised, and you get to keep the premium as pure profit.

**Risk:** Now, here's the catch. If the stock's price soars beyond the strike price of the call options you sold, the call options might get exercised. In this scenario, you'll have to say farewell to your beloved shares and sell them at the strike price. But don't worry! The premium you received earlier remains in your possession, providing a cushion against potential losses if you sell the stock below its current market value.

**2. Potential Tradeoffs:**

**Tradeoff 1 - Income vs. Stock Appreciation:**

The covered call strategy's main focus is income generation from the premiums. However, you're capping your stock's upside potential by writing covered calls. If the stock's price rises significantly, you might miss out on higher profits compared to holding the stock without writing calls. It's a classic risk-reward balance – you're getting consistent income but sacrificing some potential stock appreciation.

**Tradeoff 2 - Limited Downside Protection:**

Yes, you have some downside protection thanks to the premium you received, but it could be better. The premium may not fully offset the losses if the stock's price plummets. Remember that covered calls provide partial downside protection, but you're not entirely immune to market downturns.

**Tradeoff 3 - Opportunity Cost:**

Opportunity cost is the cost of forgoing the potential gains from alternative strategies. While enjoying those premium payments from covered calls, you might wonder what could have been if you didn't write those calls and the stock made a significant upward move. It's essential to weigh this opportunity cost against the steady income you're generating.

In conclusion, the covered call strategy comes with its risk-reward profile and tradeoffs. You're earning consistent income from the premiums and limiting some of the stock's upside potential. It's a balancing act between income generation, downside protection, and potential opportunity costs.

CASE STUDIES DEMONSTRATING THE IMPLEMENTATION OF COVERED CALL

The covered call strategy is one of the most popular and versatile approaches for income generation. Exploring real-life case studies becomes imperative as we delve into the heart of mastering covered calls. These case studies offer a practical glimpse into the world of covered call implementation, shedding light on the successes, challenges, and potential tradeoffs that traders may encounter.

**Case Study: Bob's Blue-Chip Bliss**

Meet Bob, a seasoned investor with a penchant for blue-chip stocks and a thirst for consistent income. Bob owns 500 shares of the tech giant XYZ Inc., a company he firmly believes in for its strong fundamentals and potential growth. The covered call strategy catches his attention as he contemplates his next move.

Step 1 - Stock Selection:
Bob meticulously assesses various candidates and settles on XYZ Inc. as his ideal covered call pick. With a long-term bullish outlook on the stock, he used it as the foundation of his covered call strategy.

Step 2 - Writing the Call Option:
With XYZ Inc. trading at $100 per share, Bob proceeds to sell five call options contracts, each representing 100 shares, with a strike price of $110 and an expiration date three months from now. The reward? A juicy premium of $3 per option, amounting to a total premium income of $1,500.

Step 3 - Monitoring and Flexibility:
As the covered call period unfolds, XYZ's stock price inches upward, gradually reaching $115. This price surge places the call options Bob sold into the in-the-money territory, and he faces an intriguing decision. Should he hold onto his beloved XYZ shares and let them potentially be called away at $110, or does he buy back the call options and retain them while locking in profits?

**Outcome:**

Bob chooses to seize the opportunity and buys back the call options at a premium cost of $5 per option, resulting in a total premium cost of $2,500. By doing so, he ensures that he retains his cherished XYZ shares, which have appreciated from $100 to $115 during the covered call period. After considering the premium cost, Bob's net profit from the trade amounts to $1,500 ($2,500 premium income - $2,500 premium cost).

**Key Takeaways:**

Bob's case study highlights the delicate art of flexibility in covered call trading. By monitoring the performance of his position and being agile in his decision-making, Bob navigated the dynamic options market and secured a respectable profit. The covered call strategy rewarded him with consistent income while allowing him to retain his stock and capitalize on its appreciation potential.

Implementing covered call strategies can lead to consistent income and strategic portfolio management. Remember, each trade is a learning opportunity, and with patience, discipline, and a firm grasp of market dynamics, you, too, can master the art of covered calls and unleash their potential in your journey to financial prosperity.

# GLOSSARY

**Expiration date:** The expiration time is the precise date and time at which derivatives contracts cease to trade and any obligations or rights come due or expire.

**ETF:** Exchange traded fund options are standardized put and call options on underlying exchange traded funds (ETFs). ETFs are securities representing ownership in portfolios of assets designed with an objective to generally correspond to the price and yield performance of individual indexes.

**Intrinsic value:** The intrinsic value represents the difference between the current price of the underlying security and the option's exercise price, or strike price. Essentially, intrinsic value exists if the strike price is below the current market price in regard to calls and above for puts.

**Long call:** A long call option is, simply, your standard call option in which the buyer has the right, but not the obligation, to buy a stock at a strike price in the future.

**Short call:** A Short Call means selling of a call option where you are obliged to buy the underlying asset at a fixed price in the future.

**Long put:** A long put is a position when somebody buys a put option. It is in and of itself, however, a bearish position in the market. Investors go long put options if they think a security's price will fall. Investors may go long put options to speculate on price drops or to hedge a portfolio against downside losses.

**Short put:** A short put is when a trader sells or writes a put option on a security. The idea behind the short put is to profit from an increase in the stock's price by collecting the premium associated with a sale in a short put.

**Risk-Reward Ratio:** The Risk-to-Reward ratio is used to weigh a trade's potential profit (reward) against its potential loss (risk). The R/R ratio is used by stock traders and investors to determine the price at which they will exit a trade, regardless of whether it generates a profit or a loss.

# REFERENCES

"1.3 Long Put | the Four Basic Options Strategies | InformIT." *Www.informit.com*, www.informit.com/articles/article.aspx?p=2425214&seqNum=4.

Auquan. "Bull or Bear, Long or Short — Basic Trading Terms." *Auquan*, 23 Aug. 2017, medium.com/auquan/bull-or-bear-long-or-short-basic-trading-terms-d855ebd0eb0b.

Martin, Mike. "Bullish vs Bearish and Long vs Short Explained." *Projectfinance*, 10 Nov. 2021, www.projectfinance.com/bullish-vs-bearish-long-short/.

"Options: Calls and Puts." *Corporate Finance Institute*, 18 May 2015, corporatefinanceinstitute.com/resources/derivatives/options-calls-and-puts/.

Royal, James. "What Is a Covered Call?" *Bankrate*, 17 Feb. 2023, www.bankrate.com/investing/covered-call-options-strategy/.

Seabury, Chris. "Profiting in Bear and Bull Markets." *Investopedia*, 20 Apr. 2023, www.investopedia.com/articles/stocks/09/profit-in-bear-bull-markets.asp.

"Using Covered Calls - Fidelity." *Www.fidelity.com*, www.fidelity.com/learning-center/investment-products/options/beyondgenerating-income-covered-calls.

"What Is a Covered Call Strategy?" *CI Global Asset Management*, 3 Feb. 2023, www.cifinancial.com/ci-gam/ca/en/expert-insights/articles/what-is-a-covered-call-strategy.html.

Yegge, Mark. "The Top Covered Call Strategies for Maximizing Your Passive Income." *Www.linkedin.com*, 12 May 2023, www.linkedin.com/pulse/top-covered-call-strategies-maximizing-your-passive-income-mark-yegge.

# BOOK 3

## "OPTIONS NAVIGATOR: SAILING THROUGH ANALYSIS FOR BEGINNERS."

# TABLE OF CONTENTS

CHAPTER 1 .................................................................................................................................. 3

UNDERSTANDING DELTA AND GAMMA: THE SAILING WIND .................................................... 3

    GRASPING THE CONCEPT OF DELTA AND ITS SIGNIFICANCE IN OPTIONS PRICING ............... 5

    EXPLORING GAMMA AND ITS ROLE IN MEASURING OPTIONS' PRICE SENSITIVITY ............... 7

    APPLYING DELTA AND GAMMA TO MAKE INFORMED TRADING DECISIONS ...................... 10

CHAPTER 2 ................................................................................................................................ 12

UNRAVELING THETA AND VEGA: THE RHYTHMS OF TIME AND VOLATILITY .......................... 12

    UNDERSTANDING THETA AND ITS EFFECT ON TIME DECAY IN OPTIONS .......................... 12

    ANALYZING VEGA AND ITS IMPACT ON OPTIONS PRICING DURING MARKET VOLATILITY ................. 16

    REAL-LIFE EXAMPLES OF HOW THETA AND VEGA INFLUENCE OPTIONS ........................... 18

CHAPTER 3 ................................................................................................................................ 19

BASIC OPTIONS ANALYSIS: MAPPING YOUR PROFIT AND LOSS SCENARIOS .......................... 19

    EVALUATING POTENTIAL PROFITS AND LOSSES USING SIMPLE OPTIONS STRATEGIES ...................... 20

    IDENTIFYING BREAK-EVEN POINTS AND RISK-REWARD PROFILES ..................................... 22

    USING OPTIONS ANALYSIS TO MAKE WELL-INFORMED TRADE PLANNING DECISIONS ..................... 24

GLOSSARY ................................................................................................................................. 26

REFERENCES .............................................................................................................................. 27

# CHAPTER 1
## UNDERSTANDING DELTA AND GAMMA: THE SAILING WIND

In the exciting realm of options trading, mastering the concepts of Delta and Gamma is akin to learning the intricacies of the tides before setting sail on the open sea. Just as a skilled sailor must comprehend the ebb and flow of the ocean currents, a savvy trader must grasp the dynamics of Delta and Gamma to navigate the ever-changing market waters.

**Delta: The Velocity of Change**

Imagine you're steering a ship, and Delta is your compass, guiding you on how your option's value will change with every tick of the underlying asset's price. Delta quantifies an option's price change relative to a one-point movement in the underlying security. The range for call options is 0 to 1, indicating the potential increase in value as the underlying asset fluctuates. On the other hand, put options range from -1 to 0, signifying the possible decrease in value with the underlying asset's fluctuations.

A Delta of 0.5 implies that for every $1, the underlying asset's price rises, and your call option's value should increase by $0.50. For put options, a Delta of -0.5 indicates that for every $1 the underlying asset's price climbs, your put option's value should decrease by $0.50. Understanding Delta's impact enables you to anticipate and react to price changes, enhancing your trading decisions.

**Gamma: The Accelerator of Change**

Picture yourself adjusting your ship's sails to harness the wind's power. Gamma is like that sail, amplifying the impact of Delta. It measures how much Delta changes with every $1 move in the underlying security's price. A higher Gamma suggests that Delta will change rapidly with even small price movements, while a lower Gamma indicates a slower shift.

Gamma is essential because it highlights the potential for rapid profits or losses. High Gamma can mean more substantial gains and increased vulnerability to sharp losses. Therefore, it's crucial to consider Gamma when constructing options strategies, mainly if you're targeting short-term market movements.

**The Symbiotic Relationship**

Delta and Gamma share a symbiotic relationship that seasoned traders exploit to their advantage. Gamma is the driving force behind the changes in Delta, effectively making Delta dynamic. As the underlying security's price fluctuates, the Delta of an option adjusts in response, influenced by Gamma's influence. This dynamic interplay empowers traders to fine-tune their strategies in real-time, adapting to evolving market conditions.

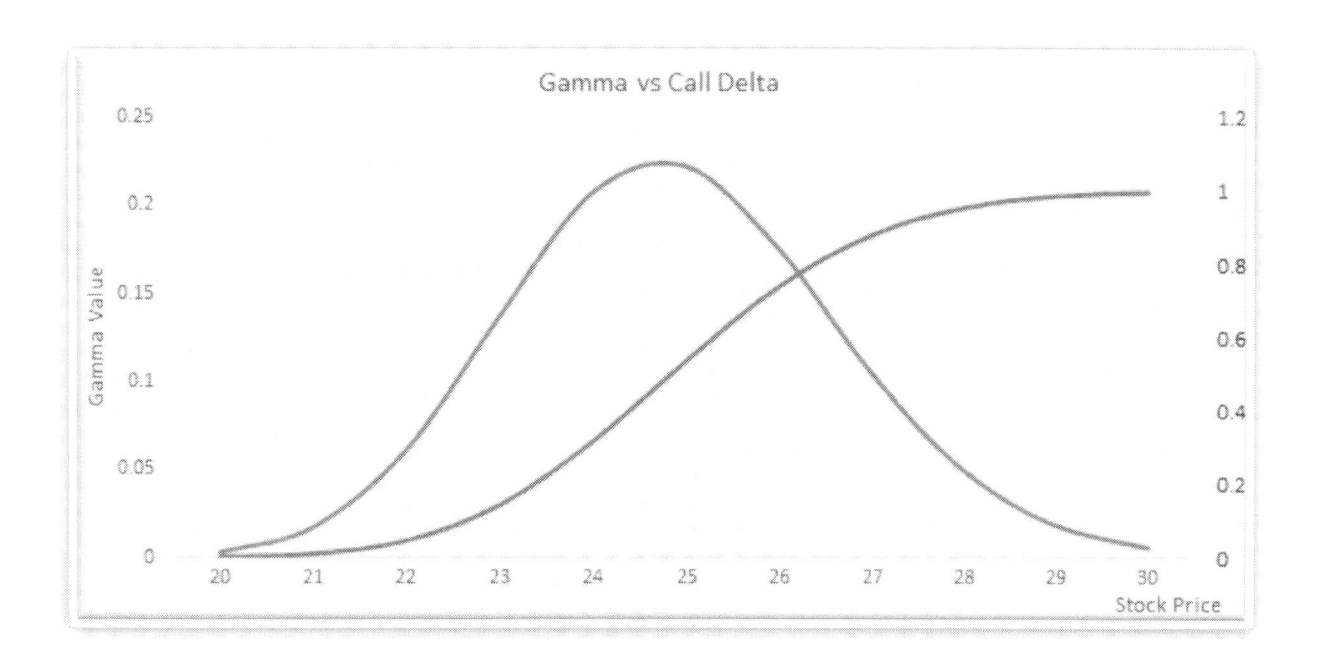

## GRAPH ILLUSTRATING THE SYMBIOTIC RELATIONSHIP BETWEEN GAMMA AND DELTA

**Examples**

Picture yourself as the proud owner of a call option boasting a Delta of 0.6 and a Gamma of 0.08. In the event of a $1 increase in the underlying stock price, the option's Delta could rise to 0.68 due to the positive Gamma. This demonstrates how Gamma accelerates the change in Delta, enhancing your potential gains as the stock price increases.

Conversely, a put option with a Delta of -0.4 and a Gamma of 0.06 could experience a Delta change to -0.46 if the underlying asset's price drops by $1. The negative Gamma amplifies the option's loss potential as the stock price falls.

In the dynamic realm of options trading, comprehending the intricacies of Delta and Gamma is akin to skillfully navigating a vessel amidst the perpetual ebb and flow of the market. Delta serves as your compass, guiding you on how option values change with underlying asset prices, while Gamma acts as the accelerator, magnifying Delta's shifts. Equipped with this valuable insight, you can fine-tune your trading strategies to navigate the ever-changing market conditions, executing astute choices that leverage the oscillations and undulations of the financial landscape. Just as a skilled sailor navigates the open waters, a proficient trader navigates the complex landscape of options with an eye on Delta and Gamma, harnessing their power for successful trading adventures.

## GRASPING THE CONCEPT OF DELTA AND ITS SIGNIFICANCE IN OPTIONS PRICING

In the intricate world of options trading, where many factors drive strategies and decisions, understanding Delta is a foundational skill that can significantly influence your trading success. Delta, often called the "holy grail" of options Greeks, is not just a Greek letter but a dynamic metric that plays a crucial role in options pricing and risk management.

**Delta**

Delta is the Greek letter that tells us how much the price of our option or strategy will move based on the underlying movement. The delta value ranges from 0.0 to 1.0 for Calls options and from 0.0 to -1.0 for Puts options. In both cases, options were bought since options sold take the opposite sign.

For example, if my option has a delta of 0.6, that means my option will go up $0.60 for every $1.0 the underlying goes up. In the chain of options, the values of the Greek letters are found in unitary format, but if we introduce a contract, the Delta of 0.6 would be 60; if we introduce 10 contracts, we would have 600 deltas, and so on. The greater the Delta, the greater the benefit we will obtain if the movement accompanies it, and the greater the loss will be if the underlying goes against our Delta. If we were to make a ranking of importance, Delta would be the most important Greek since it is directly affected by the share price movement.

**The Essence of Delta**

Delta is the rate of change in an option's price for a $1 change in the underlying asset's price. It gives traders insights into how their options' values fluctuate as the market moves. Delta ranges between -1 and 1 for put and call options, respectively. A Delta of 0.5 on a call option means that for every $1 increase in the underlying asset's price, the option's value is expected to rise by $0.50.

Delta reflects an option's directional exposure. A positive Delta indicates that the option's value moves with the underlying asset's price. At the same time, a negative Delta suggests the option's value moves inversely to the underlying asset's price.

**GRAPH ILLUSTRATING A DELTA OPTION AGAINST STOCK PRICE**

**Significance of delta in Options Pricing**

Delta is the cornerstone of options pricing models, with the Black-Scholes model being a prime example. This model uses Delta as a primary input to calculate an option's theoretical value. The Delta of an option influences its premium, providing traders with a tangible measure of an option's sensitivity to market movements.

For instance, if you're bullish on a stock, a call option with a higher Delta can offer substantial profit potential as the stock price rises, given that the option's value will increase significantly for every dollar the stock appreciates. On the flip side, if you're bearish, a put option with a higher Delta offers similar advantages in a downward-moving market.

**Delta and Hedging Strategies**

Delta is a powerful tool for risk management and hedging. It allows traders to create positions that offset the directional exposure of their portfolio. For instance, if you hold a portfolio of stocks concerned about a potential market downturn, you can purchase put options with negative Deltas. These puts will increase in value as the stock market declines, offsetting losses in your stock portfolio.

**Dynamic Nature of Delta**

Delta is not static; it changes based on various factors, including the underlying asset's price, time to expiration, and implied volatility. As an option approaches expiration, its Delta becomes more fixed, behaving like the corresponding stock position. However, when an option is "at-the-money" or "near-the-money," Delta tends to be highly sensitive to underlying asset price changes.

In the complex arena of options trading, understanding Delta is akin to having a compass that guides your decisions in response to market shifts. It's not just a theoretical concept but a real-world indicator that influences options pricing, risk management, and strategies. By gaining a deep understanding of Delta's significance and influence on options pricing and your trading portfolio, you arm yourself with a formidable tool to navigate the intricacies of the financial market with enhanced confidence and precision.

## EXPLORING GAMMA AND ITS ROLE IN MEASURING OPTIONS' PRICE SENSITIVITY

In the dynamic world of options trading, where even the slightest market movements can significantly impact profits and losses, understanding the concept of Gamma becomes essential. Gamma, also known as the "accelerator" in the world of options trading, is a crucial factor determining the speed at which an option's Delta changes in response to fluctuations in the underlying asset's price. As an advanced options metric, Gamma is a powerful tool, traders use to fine-tune their strategies and manage risk effectively.

**What is Gamma?**

Gamma ($\Gamma$) is an option risk metric that describes the rate of change of an option's Delta per one-point movement in the underlying asset's price. Therefore, Gamma measures how the rate of change in an option's price will change with fluctuations in the underlying price. The larger the range, the more volatile the option price will be. Gamma is a crucial metric that quantifies the curvature of a derivative's worth about the underlying asset. It is one of the Greek options, alongside Delta, Rho, Theta, and Vega. These are utilized to evaluate the risk inherent in option portfolios. Gamma, the illustrious first derivative of the Delta, is a vital tool in the noble pursuit of quantifying the dynamic nature of an option's price about its profound proximity to the sacred realms of in-the-money or out-of-the-money status. The Delta will exhibit changes in response to fluctuations in the underlying asset. If the Delta of an option is +40 with a range of 10, a $1 increase in the underlying price would result in the option's Delta increasing to +50.

When the option being measured is well in or out of the money, the Gamma is small. The range is maximum when the option is close to or in the money. Gamma is also larger for options with short expirations than for longer-term options. The range is important because it accounts for convexity issues when engaging in option hedging strategies. In option trading, certain portfolio managers or traders may find themselves immersed in extensive securities portfolios, necessitating a heightened level of precision in hedging. You can use a third-order derivative called "color." Color measures the rate of change in Gamma and is vital in maintaining a gamma-hedged portfolio.

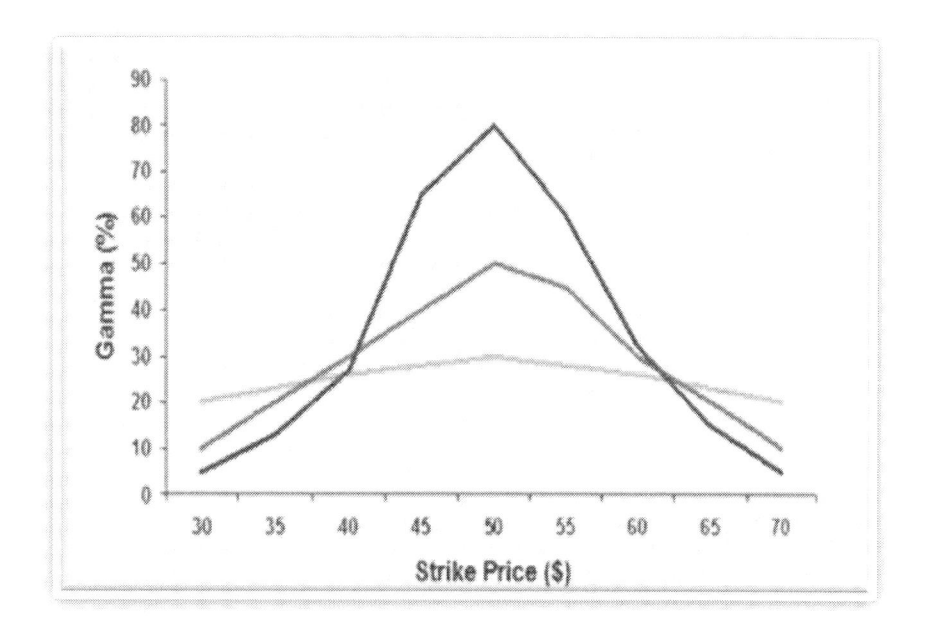

**GRAPH ILLUSTRATING A GAMMA OPTION AGAINST STOCK PRICE**

Gamma measures the rate of change of the Delta for every one-point increase in the underlying asset. It is invaluable in helping traders predict changes in an option's Delta or overall position. The range will be wider for at-the-money options and progressively narrower for in-the-money and out-of-the-money options. Unlike Delta, Gamma is always positive to be long for both call and put options.

- Gamma is the rate of change of an option's Delta based on a single point movement in the delta price.
- Gamma is at its highest when an option is in the money and at its lowest when it is further out of the money.
- The range is also higher for options closer to expiration than options with a later date, other things being equal.
- The range is a crucial factor in assessing the impact of underlying asset movements on option pricing.
- Delta-gamma hedging immunizes an options position against movements in the underlying asset

## The Essence of Gamma

Gamma is a crucial metric in options trading as it quantifies the rate of change of an option's Delta in response to a $1 movement in the underlying asset's price. While Delta indicates an option's price movement concerning the underlying asset, Gamma provides insights into how quickly Delta changes. Gamma is always positive for both call and put options and ranges between 0 and 1.

In simple terms, Gamma highlights the rate of change of an option's sensitivity to market fluctuations. If Delta is the "directional indicator," Gamma is the "sensitivity gauge." A higher Gamma indicates increased responsiveness of an option's Delta to fluctuations in the underlying asset's price.

## Significance in Options Trading

Gamma's significance is multifold, particularly in options strategies and risk management.

1. **Dynamic Nature of Delta:** As the underlying asset's price moves, an option's Delta changes due to Gamma. This dynamic nature becomes especially relevant when assessing how a position will react to market fluctuations.

2. **Impact on Profits and Losses:** Gamma is crucial in understanding a position's potential profits or losses. When an option has a high Gamma, its Delta can change significantly with small price movements in the underlying asset. Depending on market direction, this can lead to rapid profit accumulation or substantial losses.

3. **Managing Risk:** Gamma aids traders in managing risk by allowing them to assess how positions might evolve. For instance, a trader can use Gamma to anticipate the potential impact of an adverse market movement and adjust their positions accordingly.

4. **Options Strategies:** Gamma plays a vital role in constructing options strategies. Strategies that involve dynamic adjustments and quick reactions to market movements, such as scalping or day trading, benefit from high Gamma positions.

## Gamma and Implied Volatility

It's crucial to note that Gamma is not constant. It varies based on factors like time to expiration and implied volatility. Generally, options with longer expirations have higher Gamma because they have more time for their Deltas to change. Additionally, Gamma tends to be higher for at-the-money options compared to deep-in-the-money or out-of-the-money options.

## What is Gamma used for?

Given the transient nature of an option's delta measure, traders rely on the range to obtain a more precise understanding of how the option's Delta will fluctuate over time in response to variations in the underlying price. Delta measures the option price's responsiveness to underlying asset price changes.

The range decreases, approaching zero, as an option becomes more profitable, and the Delta approaches one. The range also approaches zero the more an option gets out of the money. The range is at its highest point when the price is on offer.

Calculating the range is complex and requires financial software or spreadsheets to find an exact value. However, the following demonstrates a rough range calculation. Let's analyze a call option on an underlying stock with a delta of 0.40. If the stock's value experiences a $1.00 increase, the option's value will rise by 40 cents, and its Delta will undergo a corresponding adjustment. Following the $1 upward movement, let us consider the option's Delta of 0.53. The delta differential of 0.13 can be viewed as an estimated gamma measurement.

All long options have a positive range, while all short options have a negative range.

**How Gamma Impacts Option Prices**

Gamma has a significant impact on the prices of options. When Gamma is high, small movements in the underlying asset's price can cause significant changes in the option's price. This effect is particularly pronounced for options with short maturities. When Gamma is low, the option's Delta changes more slowly in response to price movements, which means the option's price is less sensitive to underlying asset price changes. Gamma can also affect the implied volatility of options. When Gamma is high, market participants may need to adjust their hedges more frequently, which can lead to a higher demand for options and, therefore, higher implied volatility. Conversely, when Gamma is low, market participants may need to adjust their hedges less frequently, leading to lower demand for options and, therefore, lower implied volatility.

APPLYING DELTA AND GAMMA TO MAKE INFORMED TRADING DECISIONS

Now that we've grasped the significance of Delta and Gamma let's navigate through the real-life applications that empower us to make sound choices in the tumultuous sea of options.

**Application 1: Risk Management in Delta**

Indeed, the formidable Delta quantifies an option's price responsiveness to fluctuations in the underlying asset. As traders, it becomes our compass to gauge risk and set sail confidently. We must consider the Delta of our positions when we embark on our trading journey.

**Scenario:**

Let's say we've purchased a call option on XYZ Inc. with a delta of 0.6. This means that for every $1 change in XYZ's stock price, our option's price will move to approximately $0.60. With a higher delta, our position becomes more exposed to the ups and downs of the underlying stock.

**Trading Decision:**

If we seek a conservative approach, we might opt for options with lower delta values to limit potential losses. Conversely, if we're searching for more significant profit potential and can handle higher risk, we may set sail with options with higher delta values.

**Application 2: Riding the Gamma Waves**

Gamma measures the sensitivity of an option's Delta to movements in the underlying stock price. It helps us understand how Delta may fluctuate, empowering us to navigate through changing market conditions.

**Scenario:**

Suppose we've sold a put option on ABC Corp. with a gamma of 0.04. This implies that if a $1 change in ABC's stock price, the option's Delta will experience a 0.04 increase.

**Trading Decision:**

By monitoring Gamma, we can anticipate how quickly our position in Delta will change with market movements. If we expect minimal fluctuations, we may confidently ride the waves of a stable delta. However, in a volatile market, we must be vigilant and make timely adjustments to our sails to stay on course.

**Application 3: Hedging Strategies with Delta and Gamma**

Delta and Gamma enable us to deploy powerful hedging strategies, offering protection.

**Scenario:**

We hold a portfolio of stocks and are concerned about potential market downturns. We can use options to hedge against losses.

**Trading Decision:**

Using Delta, we identify the appropriate number of put options to purchase to offset potential losses in the portfolio. Additionally, monitoring Gamma allows us to adjust our hedge as market conditions change, ensuring our protective measures stay effective.

In conclusion, applying Delta and Gamma in options trading equips us with the skills of seasoned navigators. As we make informed decisions based on these essential concepts, we navigate confidently through uncertain waters, capturing opportunities and guarding against risks. If this book has helped you in any way so far feel free to leave a review for this book.

# CHAPTER 2
# UNRAVELING THETA AND VEGA: THE RHYTHMS OF TIME AND VOLATILITY

**Theta: The Rhythms of Time**

Imagine Theta as the rhythmic beat of a drum, setting the pace of your options' time decay. Every day that passes, your options lose a little bit of value, like the gentle waves eroding the shore. But don't let it dampen your spirits! Understanding Theta empowers you to make savvy decisions. As time sails on, your options' value gradually diminishes. But fear not! Theta doesn't discriminate. It affects all options, whether they're calls or puts. So, consider the ticking clock when crafting your strategies. Be mindful of Theta's impact on your positions when you're out on the open sea of trading. If you're aiming for quick profits, short-term options might be your vessel of choice. But for longer voyages, consider options with a more extended expiration date to minimize the impact of Theta's rhythmic beat.

**Vega: Riding the Waves of Volatility**

Vega, the surging waves of market volatility! As the ocean's tides rise and fall, so does Vega, influencing your options' prices as market volatility ebbs and flows. But fret not, Vega's not your adversary – it's your ally in crafting weatherproof strategies. When the market experiences turbulence, Vega rises like a mighty tide, causing option prices to surge. But Vega recedes when the waters are calm, and option prices follow suit. Understanding Vega enables you to ride these waves to your advantage. When you sense a storm brewing in the market, consider trading options with higher Vega to amplify your potential profits. But in times of tranquility, opt for options with lower Vega to minimize costs. As a skilled navigator, let Vega be your guiding light in turbulent seas.

Understanding Theta and Vega is your compass in the vast ocean of options trading. Embrace Theta's rhythmic beat of time and ride the waves of Vega's volatility to make informed trading decisions. Armed with this knowledge, you're well-equipped to navigate through the ups and downs of the market with confidence.

## UNDERSTANDING THETA AND ITS EFFECT ON TIME DECAY IN OPTIONS

**Theta: Definition and explanation**

Theta is the amount by which the option price will decrease at the end of a calendar day, given the same stock price and volatility level. Theta is specified with a negative number because the elapsed period causes the time value to decrease. The value of Theta is not linear, especially when the strike (underlying value of an option) is close to the money. The closer the expiry date approaches, the more the theoretical depreciation increases. Therefore, the expiration indicated by Theta tends to be gradual at first and accelerates as the expiration date approaches. Understanding when you want to find the best time to buy or sell options is essential. On the expiry date, an option no longer has any time value and is only calculated at its intrinsic value if the underlying asset is in-the-money.

Theta is based on calendar days rather than exchange days since option pricing models also consider weekends. So, options tend to expire seven days in five trading days, with some of the weekend's time decay already factored into the price on the previous Thursday and Friday. At-the-money strikes have higher Theta than in-the-money and out-of-the-money strikes. For at-money (and also near-money) strikes, time value decay is exponential and not (nearly) linear as with out-of-the-money and in-the-money strikes.

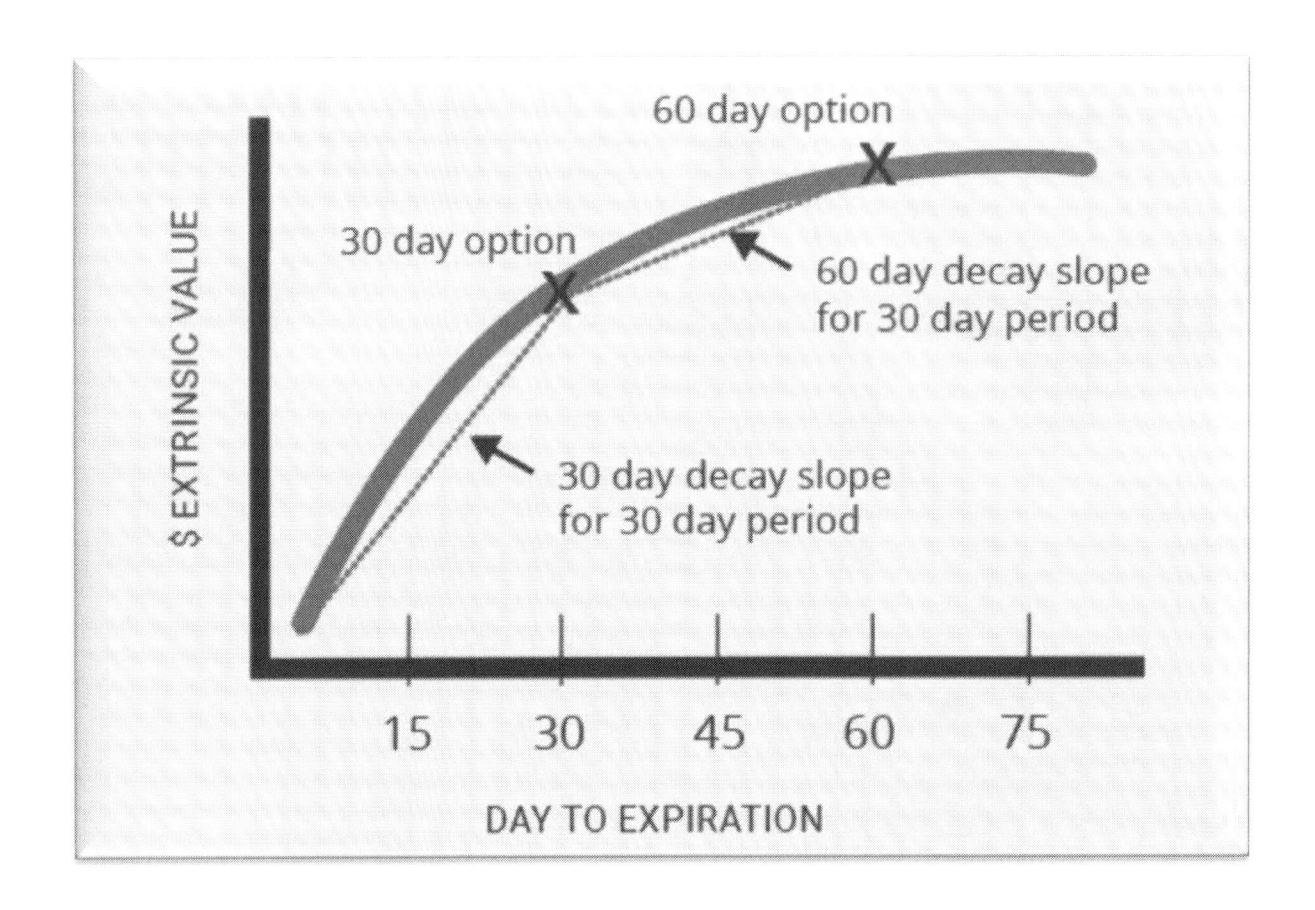

**GRAPH ILLUSTRATING THETA, A TIME DECAY IN OPTION**

Theta, also known as time decay, quantifies the sensitivity of an option's price to the passage of time. It is commonly referred to as Theta or the erosion of time value. Theta, also known as time decay, quantifies the rate at which an option's value erodes as it nears its expiration date, assuming no changes in other factors. For instance, if a trader has a long position in an opportunity with a theta of 0.6, it is anticipated that the option's value will decline by $0.60 per day, assuming no other factors change.

As an options trader, it is essential to note that the theta value tends to approach zero as an option gets closer to being in the money. Long call and put options exhibit a negative theta, indicating that time decay works against the value of these options. Conversely, short call and put options demonstrate a positive theta, implying that time decay favors the importance of these options. Like a fine-tuned instrument, options exhibit an intensified time decay as they draw closer to their expiration date. In the realm of options trading, it is essential to note that an asset's Theta will always be zero if its price remains unaffected by the passage of time. Theta is about time erosion on the option premium. Purchased options give an option investor the right to buy or sell stock until the option's end date. If the option value changes by an amount different from its Theta, that result is due to the influence of the Delta, Vegas, or both metrics. Theta is always negative on long positions as the time value decreases daily. In the case of short positions (option is sold, short position), the Theta is correspondingly positive.

Calls and puts on underlying with higher implied volatility have larger (i.e., more negative) theta values than those with lower volatility because more time values can decay due to the higher implied volatility. Call options tend to have higher theta values than put options.

**Time Decay Unveiled**

Time decay, represented by Theta, is where an option's value erodes as it gets closer to its expiration date. Every day that passes reduces the option's extrinsic value, particularly for options that are out of the money or at the money. In-the-money options are less affected by time decay because they have intrinsic value that offsets some decay.

Theta is generally negative for long positions (e.g., buyers of options) and positive for short positions (e.g., sellers of options). As an option nears its expiration date, its Theta experiences a rise due to heightened time decay. For example, an option with a high Theta of -0.05 indicates that its value is expected to decrease by $0.05 per day due to time decay.

**Effect on Options Pricing**

Theta's effect on options pricing is particularly significant in the context of various trading strategies.

- **Long Options:** Traders who hold long positions in options face the challenge of time decay eroding the option's value; as expiration approaches, value erosion increases, especially for options that are out of the money. Traders need to be mindful of this factor when buying options and consider strategies to counteract the negative impact of time decay.
- **Short Options:** For traders who sell options, Theta can work in their favor. Trading options with high Theta allows traders to capture time decay as profit. Short-term selling strategies, like covered calls or cash-secured puts, rely on Theta to generate income over time.

**Effect of Theta on Options Trading**

1. The effect of an elapsed period on option value is measured by the sensitivity ratio known as Theta. This is influenced by the strikes' moneyness, the time until expiry, and the implied volatility of the underlying asset. Using Theta as a key influencer, we can adjust our trading plans to be consistent with our personal risk threshold and view of the overall market.

2. Measurement of daily loss of value: When an out-of-the-money call option is purchased, the premium paid for the option is only the time value. After all, out-of-the-money options have no intrinsic value. When, on the expiry date, the option has no intrinsic value, then it is not exercised, and it expires without value.

3. From the time of purchase until maturity, the value undergoes a slow erosion at the beginning, which accelerates over time.

Theta measures an option's daily loss in value due to the passage of time.

4. Theta, therefore, represents how much value the option loses per day. The closer an option is to expiration, the faster the option will lose value over time. Fortunately, it's easy to explain. If two options have the same strike price but have two different expiration dates, the loss in value will be higher per day for the short-term option than for the longer-term option. From about a month before expiration, this value exponentially evaporates from the option.

Theta, the harbinger of time decay, is an integral aspect of options trading that cannot be ignored. Recognizing its effects on options pricing and incorporating it into trading strategies is vital for success. Whether it's devising strategies that harness time decay or actively managing positions to offset its impact, traders who grasp the nuances of Theta can navigate the temporal waters of options trading with greater confidence and efficiency.

ANALYZING VEGA AND ITS IMPACT ON OPTIONS PRICING DURING MARKET VOLATILITY

Vega emerges as a crucial player in the dynamic realm of options trading, where factors like time, price, and volatility intersect. Vega, the volatility factor, encapsulates the option price's responsiveness to fluctuations in market volatility. Understanding Vega and its impact is essential for traders seeking to navigate the intricate landscape of options pricing, especially during heightened market volatility.

**Vega**

Vega measures the impact of implied volatility fluctuations on an option's value. In other words, the option's volatility sensitivity is a crucial factor to consider. Vega quantifies the impact on an option's price resulting from a 1% shift in the underlying asset's volatility. If an opportunity possesses a Vega of 0.2, its value will fluctuate by $0.20 for each 1% alteration in the underlying asset's volatility. The heightened volatility of the underlying asset augments the likelihood of the help attaining extreme values. This enhances the intrinsic worth of an option on said underlying asset.

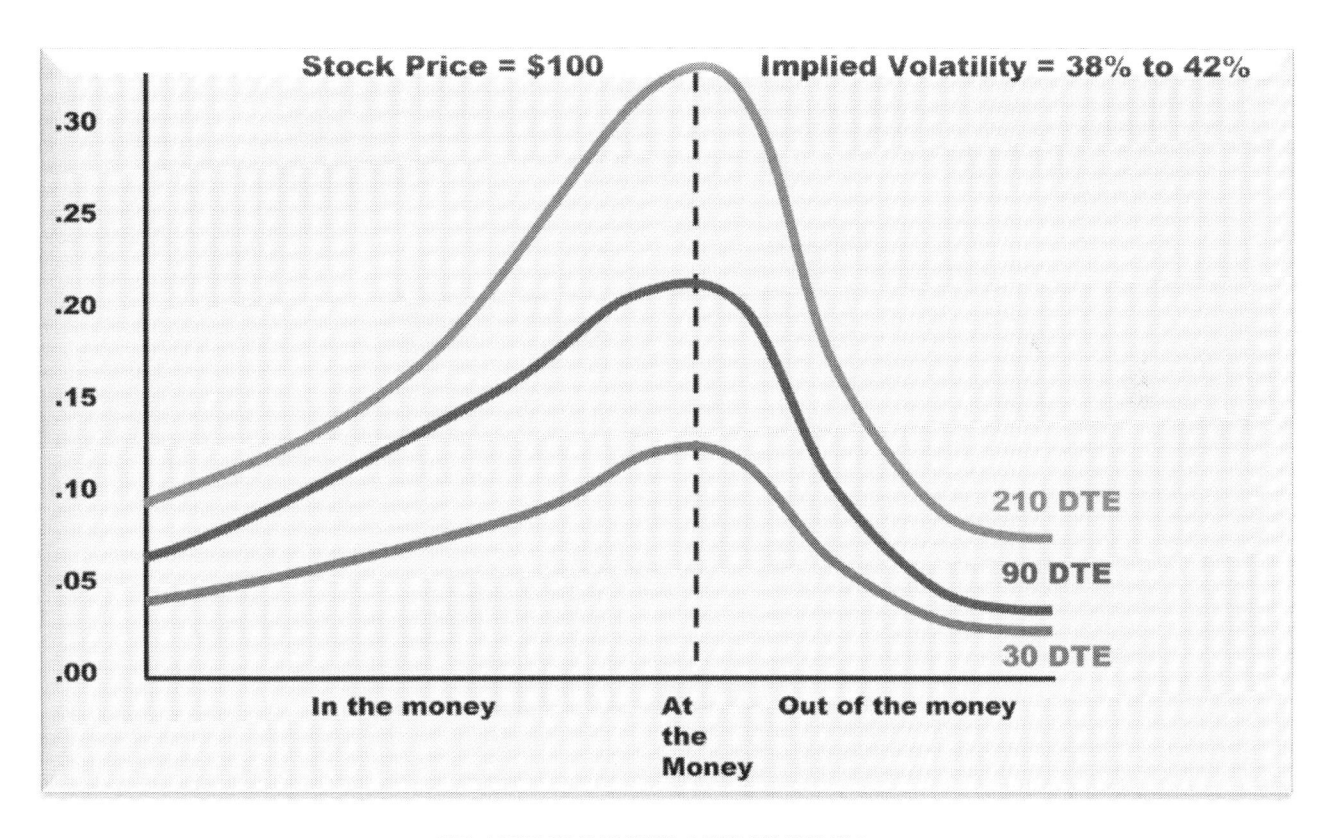

**GRAPH ILLUSTRATING VEGA**

Conversely, a decrease in volatility has a negative impact on the price of an option. The Vega is higher on at-the-money options with a longer time to expiration. An interesting point is that there is no Greek letter called Vega. Multiple theories exist elucidating this term's inclusion within the cohort of Greek letters that articulate the perils associated with options.

The rate of change of our option price also depends on the respective implied volatility, denoted by the letter Vega. As volatility increases, an option becomes more expensive; if it decreases, the price falls.

The most important thing about the option Greek Vega:

- Rate of change of option price depending on volatility
- As volatility increases, the option price becomes more expensive
- If volatility decreases, the option price becomes cheaper
- The longer the remaining term, the larger the Vega
- The Vega is the biggest when it comes to ATM options

Vega is always given as a percentage and adds or subtracts this value from the option price, depending on whether volatility is rising or falling. An option's price falls as volatility decreases due to Vegas. Vega specifies the extent to which the option price changes if the underlying asset's volatility (e.g., a share) rises or falls by one percentage point. Long calls and long puts have a positive Vega. They thus benefit from an increase in volatility.

On the other hand, short calls and short puts have a negative Vega. You benefit from a decrease in the volatility of the underlying asset. Vega quantifies the impact of changes in implied volatility on an option's value.

**Volatility's Impact on Options**

In the context of options trading, volatility pertains to the magnitude of price swings observed in the underlying asset. High volatility indicates significant price swings, while low volatility suggests a more stable price movement. Vega quantifies the influence of changes in volatility on an option's value. As market conditions shift and volatility increases or decreases, options react accordingly, and Vega measures this responsiveness.

**Understanding Vega's influence is vital for various aspects of options trading:**

- **Implied Volatility:** Implied volatility reflects the market's expectations of future price volatility. When implied volatility rises, Vega increases, contributing to a rise in option prices. Conversely, when implied volatility drops, Vega decreases, leading to a decline in option prices.

- **Options Strategies:** Vega's impact is felt across multiple options strategies. Strategies like straddles and strangles, which involve trading both call and put options, often benefit from increases in volatility. These strategies capitalize on the potential for significant price movements.

**Navigating Market Volatility**

During periods of market volatility, understanding and analyzing Vega is paramount:

1. **Hedging Strategies:** Traders often use options to hedge against adverse price movements in their portfolios. In times of heightened volatility, options with higher Vega values can serve as effective hedges, offering increased protection as potential price swings rise.

2. **Options Pricing:** Vega becomes particularly significant when assessing options prices. Traders must consider the intrinsic and extrinsic values of options and the influence of volatility changes on those values.

3. **Adjustment Techniques:** Volatile market conditions may prompt traders to adjust their options positions. Understanding Vega helps traders make informed decisions about when and how to adjust positions to manage risk effectively. Vega on-the-money, out-of-the-money and in-the-money options

Vega navigates traders through the intricate terrain of market volatility. Recognizing its impact on options pricing empowers traders to make well-informed decisions that align with their strategies and risk management goals. As volatility fluctuates, Vega provides a lens through which traders can anticipate and respond to changes in options prices, ensuring that their trading journeys remain on course.

## REAL-LIFE EXAMPLES OF HOW THETA AND VEGA INFLUENCE OPTIONS

**Example 1: The Time Decay Dance with Theta:**

Imagine you hold a call option on a company's stock with a current price of $100 and an expiration date set for one month from now. Your option has a theta of -0.03, meaning it loses $0.03 in value daily due to time decay. With all other factors constant over the next ten days, your option's value will decrease by $0.30 ($0.03 x 10 days).

**Takeaway:** As time passes, options with shorter expiration dates will lose value more rapidly due to Theta, making them suitable for short-term traders seeking quick profits.

**Example 2: The Volatile Ride of Vega:**

Let's say there's an impending earnings report for the company whose stock you hold options. Anticipating increased market volatility, you notice that your option's Vega is 0.15. After the earnings report, the stock experienced a surge in volatility, causing Vega to increase to 0.25.

**Takeaway:** Higher Vega indicates that your option's price is more sensitive to changes in volatility. When market uncertainty spikes, options with higher Vega can experience substantial price swings, presenting opportunities for significant gains or losses.

**Example 3: Vega's Impact on Option Premiums:**

Suppose you're considering two options on different companies, each with a strike price of $50. Option A has a vega of 0.10, while Option B has a 0.30. Both options have the same expiration date and other identical factors. As market volatility increases, Option B's price will experience a larger increase compared to Option A.

**Takeaway:** Options with higher Vega can amplify price changes in response to volatility, offering the potential for greater profits during periods of increased market uncertainty.

# CHAPTER 3
## BASIC OPTIONS ANALYSIS: MAPPING YOUR PROFIT AND LOSS SCENARIOS

Trading in the world of options is akin to embarking on a high-stakes adventure – navigating the unpredictable waters of the market, seizing opportunities, and weathering storms. But every seasoned trader knows that preparation is vital, and understanding how to evaluate potential profits and losses using simple options strategies is your compass to success.

**Picture this:** You've set your course for the open seas of options trading, ready to navigate the unpredictable waters of the market. But how can you steer your ship toward potential profits while avoiding treacherous rocks? The answer lies in mastering the art of evaluating potential gains and losses using simple options strategies. Let's journey through real-life experiences to unveil the secrets of successful trading.

**Sailing with Covered Calls: A Real-Life Tale**

Imagine holding a stock that you believe will grow steadily but not dramatically. Covered calls can be your compass in this scenario. This strategy entails engaging in a covered call strategy by selling a call option on a stock position, generating additional income. Imagine holding a long position in Company XYZ, with an underlying stock price of $50 per share. A short position is established through the sale of a call option with a price of $55. If the stock rises to $55 or higher, the option may be exercised, and you'll sell your shares at a higher price. Your profit includes the stock's appreciation and the premium you received for selling the call.

**Navigating the Storm with Protective Puts**

Now, consider the stormy weather of market volatility. Protecting your portfolio becomes paramount. Enter protective puts – your insurance against potential losses. Let's say you own shares of Company ABC, valued at $60 each. Concerned about potential downside risk, you initiate a long put position at a strike price of $55. If the stock plunges, the put option gains value, helping offset your losses. Your potential loss is limited to the put option's cost, allowing you to weather the storm more confidently.

**Sailing into Opportunities with Long Calls**

Sometimes, market waves present promising opportunities. You've been researching Company DEF and believe it's about to experience a significant price surge. A long-call strategy might be your ticket to ride that wave. You initiate a long call position with a strike price of $40, establishing a bullish outlook on the underlying stock priced at $35. If the stock's value rockets past $40, your call option becomes more valuable, potentially allowing you to sell it at a profit. However, if the stock doesn't reach the strike price, your loss is limited to the premium you paid for the option.

EVALUATING POTENTIAL PROFITS AND LOSSES USING SIMPLE OPTIONS STRATEGIES

In the dynamic world of financial markets, the allure of potential profits is often accompanied by the ever-present specter of potential losses. Traders are akin to sailors navigating through the tumultuous waters of uncertainty, seeking strategies that promise gains and shield against the perils of financial storms. Enter the realm of options, where sophisticated instruments provide a powerful toolkit to evaluate, strategize, and ultimately manage potential profits and losses.

**The Landscape of Potential Profits and Losses**

Options trading offers a unique advantage—the ability to design strategies that align with specific market outlooks and risk tolerances. This flexibility allows traders to not only seek profit opportunities but also to calculate potential losses with precision. By understanding and quantifying these potential outcomes, traders can make well-informed decisions grounded in

reality rather than speculation.

**The Language of Strategies: Calls and Puts**

Two fundamental options strategies, calls, and puts, form the bedrock of options trading. Calls allow traders to acquire an underlying asset at a prearranged price (strike price) during a designated period (expiration). Puts, conversely, grants the option to execute a sell order for an underlying asset at a predetermined price within a specified timeframe.

Evaluating potential profits and losses using these strategies entails comprehending the interplay of variables such as the strike price, premium paid, and the underlying asset's price movement. By exploring different scenarios, traders can glean insights into the trade's potential profitability and the extent of potential losses.

**Calculating Potential Profits**

The potential profitability of options trading is contingent upon the disparity between the prevailing market price of the underlying asset and the designated strike price while also considering the premium that has been paid. For instance, in a call option, if the underlying asset's market price rises significantly above the strike price, potential profits can be substantial. On the flip side, in a put option, potential gains materialize when the underlying asset's market price experiences a substantial decline below the strike price.

**Mapping Potential Losses**

Understanding potential losses is equally crucial, as it safeguards traders against unexpected adverse market movements. The maximum potential loss is confined to the premium paid in all options. In contrast, the total possible loss in put options is restricted to the difference between the strike price and zero minus the premium paid.

## IDENTIFYING BREAK-EVEN POINTS AND RISK-REWARD PROFILES

In the exhilarating world of trading, where risk and reward dance in a delicate balance, understanding break-even points and risk-reward profiles is akin to wielding a compass that guides traders through the labyrinth of profit and loss. These concepts are vital instruments for options traders, enabling them to plot their trajectory, evaluate possible scenarios, and execute well-informed choices that align with their investment goals. With the ability to unveil the intricate dynamics of trade scenarios, identifying break-even points and risk-reward profiles emerges as a cornerstone of strategic trade planning.

**Decoding Break-Even Points: Where Gains and Losses Converge**

Picture yourself on the precipice of a new trade; the excitement mingled with a hint of apprehension. You've placed your bets, but when will your efforts translate into gains? This is where the concept of break-even points comes to the fore. Imagine it as the fulcrum on which your trade pivots between profit and loss. It's the price level at which the gains offset the initial investment or premium paid. Identifying these points empowers you to gauge the threshold at which your trade shifts from unprofitable to profitable territory.

In real-life terms, think of it as the moment when your ship crosses a threshold, leaving the stormy waters of uncertainty behind and sailing into the calmer seas of profitability. Your analysis of break-even points becomes your tactical tool to decide whether to stay the course or adjust your strategy as market conditions evolve.

**Risk-Reward Profiles: Unmasking the Potential**

Break-even points serve as crucial markers of equilibrium, while risk-reward profiles vividly illustrate potential outcomes and aid traders in evaluating if a trade aligns with their risk appetite. These profiles visually represent the trade's risk and reward dynamics across different price levels of the underlying asset.

A risk-reward profile typically takes the form of a graph, with the x-axis representing the underlying asset's price and the y-axis representing potential gains or losses. The graph reveals crucial information, such as the maximum potential loss, maximum potential gain, and the range within which the trade is profitable.

The risk-reward profile unveils an essential truth: trades with higher potential rewards often entail higher risks. Traders must meticulously analyze these profiles to evaluate whether the potential reward justifies the assumed risk. This analysis facilitates the optimization of trading strategies by providing a clear view of the trade-offs between risk and potential profit.

Identifying break-even points and understanding risk-reward profiles encapsulates the heart of strategic trade planning. It empowers option traders with the capability to navigate the intricacies of the market, evaluate the viability of trades, and execute decisions that align with their risk tolerance and profit goals. While these concepts may seem like numbers on paper, they can transform traders into astute navigators of the financial landscape, capable of charting courses that lead to profitable shores.

## USING OPTIONS ANALYSIS TO MAKE WELL-INFORMED TRADE PLANNING DECISIONS

In the dynamic world of financial markets, where uncertainty and risk are constant companions, making well-informed trade planning decisions is paramount. Options analysis is an exceptional tool in the arsenal of traders and investors, enabling them to effectively navigate the intricate dynamics of the market with enhanced precision and confidence. By employing options analysis, traders can effectively strategize, hedge against risks, enhance potential returns, and create versatile trading plans that adapt to changing market conditions.

One of the primary advantages of options analysis is its ability to accommodate diverse market outlooks. Traders can craft strategies that profit from bullish, bearish, or neutral price movements. For instance, if a trader expects a stock's price to rise, they might employ a straightforward call option strategy. Conversely, if a downward move is anticipated, utilizing put options can provide a protective hedge or speculative opportunity. Moreover, options allow traders to harness volatility by creating strategies that thrive on price swings, a feature particularly valuable during uncertain market conditions.

Crucially, options analysis introduces a level of risk management that can be tailored to traders' risk tolerance and goals. Through meticulous analysis of the potential risks and rewards, option traders possess the ability to strategically assess and execute trades that harmonize with their investment objectives. Moreover, options limit traders' losses, often capping the investment amount to the premium paid for the options contract.

**Options Analysis: Your Strategic Toolkit**

Consider options analysis as your ship's navigation instruments—a sextant for the financial world. It empowers you to dissect the complex interplay of factors that drive market movements. Just as a skilled sailor observes the stars, currents, and winds, a trader analyzes historical price data, implied volatility trends, and economic indicators. Each piece of information is a thread in the tapestry of analysis, guiding you toward the optimal trade planning decision.

Envision yourself as an analyst poring over a treasure map of data. You decipher the Greek symbols—Delta, Gamma, Theta, and Vega—that hold the key to understanding option behavior. Delta guides you through the relationship between option prices and underlying asset movement. Gamma captures the rate of change in the Delta, akin to the shifting currents beneath the surface.

Theta reveals the passage of time's impact on options, while Vega sheds light on the volatility's effect. As a navigator relies on charts and instruments, you use these metrics to forecast potential outcomes.

In conclusion, options analysis is a potent tool that empowers traders to make well-informed trade planning decisions. It offers versatility, risk management, and the ability to adapt to various market conditions. By combining a deep understanding of options mechanics, market trends, and analytical tools, traders can harness the potential of options to create robust trading plans that enhance their chances of success. In the ever-changing realm of markets, options analysis remains an indispensable tool for traders aiming to gain a competitive advantage in the dynamic financial landscape.

# GLOSSARY

**Break-even:** The break-even price is the price in the underlying asset at which investors can choose to exercise or dispose of the contract without incurring a loss.

**Delta:** Delta measures how much an option's price can be expected to move for every $1 change in the price of the underlying security or index.

**Gamma:** Gamma represents the rate of change between an option's Delta and the underlying asset's price. Higher Gamma values indicate that the Delta could change dramatically with even very small price changes in the underlying stock or fund.

**Vega**: Vega is the Greek that measures an option's sensitivity to implied volatility. It is the change in the option's price for a one-point change in implied volatility.

**Theta:** Theta is the decay in an option's time value that occurs as it gets closer to expiration.

**Risk reward:** The Risk-to-Reward ratio is used to weigh a trade's potential profit (reward) against its potential loss (risk). The R/R ratio is used by stock traders and investors to determine the price at which they will exit a trade, regardless of whether it generates a profit or a loss.

**Underlying asset:** The underlying asset is the basic security or investment vehicle on which derivatives operate. Underlying assets can be individual securities, like stocks or bonds, or groups of securities, like in an index fund.

**Volatility:** Volatility is a statistical measure of the dispersion of returns for a given security or market index. In most cases, the higher the volatility, the riskier the security.

# REFERENCES

Ashburn, Doug. "Britannica Money." *Www.britannica.com*, www.britannica.com/money/option-greeks-delta-theta-gamma-vega.

Chen, James. "What Is Gamma in Investing and How Is It Used?" *Investopedia*, 21 Aug. 2022, www.investopedia.com/terms/g/gamma.asp#:~:text=Gamma%20(%CE%93)%20is%20an%20options.

Hall, Mary. "Using the "Greeks" to Understand Options." *Investopedia*, 20 Feb. 2020, www.investopedia.com/trading/using-the-greeks-to-understand-options/.

Hayes, Adam. "Inside the Risk/Reward Ratio." *Investopedia*, 3 May 2023, www.investopedia.com/terms/r/riskrewardratio.asp#:~:text=The%20risk%2Freward%20ratio%20marks.

Summa, John. "Option Greeks: The 4 Factors to Measure Risk." *Investopedia*, 24 Aug. 2021, www.investopedia.com/trading/getting-to-know-the-greeks/#:~:text=Theta%20measures%20the%20daily%20drop.

"Tradeoffs: The Currency of Decision Making." *Farnam Street*, 9 Dec. 2019, fs. blog/tradeoffs-decision-making/.

"What Is Risk-Reward Ratio? | Definition from TechTarget." *WhatIs.com*, www.techtarget.com/whatis/definition/risk-reward-ratio.

# BOOK 4

## " OPTIONS ASCENSION: EMBARKING ON INTERMEDIATE STRATEGIES"

# TABLE OF CONTENTS

CHAPTER 1 .................................................................................................................................. 3

BULLISH STRATEGIES: ASCENDING TO NEW HEIGHTS ............................................................. 3

    UNDERSTANDING BULL CALL SPREADS FOR MAXIMIZING BULLISH VIEWS ........................ 4

    EXPLORING BULL PUT SPREADS FOR INCOME GENERATION IN RISING MARKETS ............. 7

    CASE STUDIES OF SUCCESSFUL BULLISH TRADES USING THESE STRATEGIES ................... 9

CHAPTER 2 ................................................................................................................................ 11

BEARISH STRATEGIES: NAVIGATING MARKET DOWNTRENDS ............................................... 11

    MASTERING BEAR CALL SPREADS FOR BEARISH POSITIONS AND INCOME GENERATION .. 12

    UTILIZING BEAR PUT SPREADS FOR DOWNSIDE PROTECTION AND PROFIT POTENTIAL .... 14

    REAL-LIFE EXAMPLES DEMONSTRATING BEARISH STRATEGIES IN ACTION ..................... 16

CHAPTER 3 ................................................................................................................................ 18

MARKET ANALYSIS FOR OPTION TRADERS: THE COMPASS FOR SUCCESS ............................ 18

    INTRODUCING TECHNICAL AND FUNDAMENTAL ANALYSIS FOR OPTIONS TRADERS ....... 18

    USING CHARTS, INDICATORS, AND FINANCIAL DATA TO MAKE INFORMED TRADING DECISIONS ...... 22

    INCORPORATING MARKET ANALYSIS INTO OPTION STRATEGY SELECTION ..................... 24

GLOSSARY ................................................................................................................................. 26

REFERENCES ............................................................................................................................. 27

# CHAPTER 1
## BULLISH STRATEGIES: ASCENDING TO NEW HEIGHTS

Bullish spreads can be formed by either having a long bid spread or a short sell spread.

A bull spread consists of a call and a put with different strike prices but the same expiration and underlying contract. This strategy pays off in a bull market, also known as the bull market.

**A buy bull spread strategy.**

Before the options expire, a trader anticipates a modest increase in the market.

You would pay three dollars to purchase a 105 call and two dollars to sell a 110 call if the underlying market was trading at 100. You get a premium for selling the 110 call, which equals the price of the 105 option. The spread is one dollar in price overall. This spread's dead-center value is 106. This is the spread fee plus the 105-point strike price.

The best-case scenario is if the market ends at or above 110 because the 105-110 bid spread will leave a $5 profit. This is the maximum spread payout, regardless of where the underlying ends up. If we subtract the dollar from the spread, the total profit on the trade is four dollars. Let's say the underlying has finished at 113. The 105 call will earn the trader $8, but he will have to pay $3 on the 110 call. If the market ends at 130, the 105 call will earn the trader $25, but he will have to pay 20 dollars at call 110.

The worst-case scenario is if the market ends at 105 or above because the 105 and 110 calls expire from the money and are worthless. The trader loses the total cost of the spread, one dollar. If he had bought just the 105 call for three dollars, his loss would be three dollars instead of one.

If the underlying ends at 107.5, the long 105 calls would cost $2.5, and the short 110 calls would expire worthless. The trader's payout of 2.5 minus a dollar spread cost brings him a profit of $1.5. If the trader had bought just the 105 call, his payout would still have been $2.5, but that's less than the three he would have paid for just the 105 call.

We already commented that selling a put differential can also form a bullish differential. Selling a put is another way to be bullish in the market. Remember that if the underlying futures conclude above or at the strike price, you can keep the premium you get from selling the put.

**Selling a put spread.**

Instead of buying the 105-110 bid spread, we can sell the 110-105 ask spread. This would involve selling the 110 puts and buying the 105 puts, thus yielding four dollars with the underlying future trading at 100. The breakeven of the spread is 106 since that is the strike price, 110 minus the credit of the spread, four dollars. Yes, it is the same deadlock as in the bullish buy spread.

Let's see why. If the market ends above 110, the puts expire worthless. Therefore, the trader keeps the net four dollars received when selling the put.

If the market ends at 103, the 110 put is worth seven dollars, and the 105 put is worth two. Therefore, the ask spread has a value of five dollars. The trader has received four and must pay five dollars, which translates to a dollar of losses.

If the market ends at 107.5, the 100 put is worth $2.5, and the 105 put expires worthless. The trader must pay back 2.5 of his four-dollar credit, which leaves a profit of $1.5.

We can see that all three scenarios have the same outcome if we buy a bid spread or sell the ask spread to create a bullish position. Traders still want the market to end above the spread price.

UNDERSTANDING BULL CALL SPREADS FOR MAXIMIZING BULLISH VIEWS

**What is a Bull Call Spread?**

A bull call spread is a strategy created to profit from a constrained rise in a security's price. The technique uses two call options to generate a lower and higher strike price range. Bull call margin helps limit stock ownership losses, but it also limits gains.

- When a trader wagers that a stock will only have a slight price increase, they use a bull call spread as an options strategy.

- The technique uses two call options to generate a lower and higher strike price range.

- The spread of bullish calls may cap your stock ownership losses, but it also caps your gains.

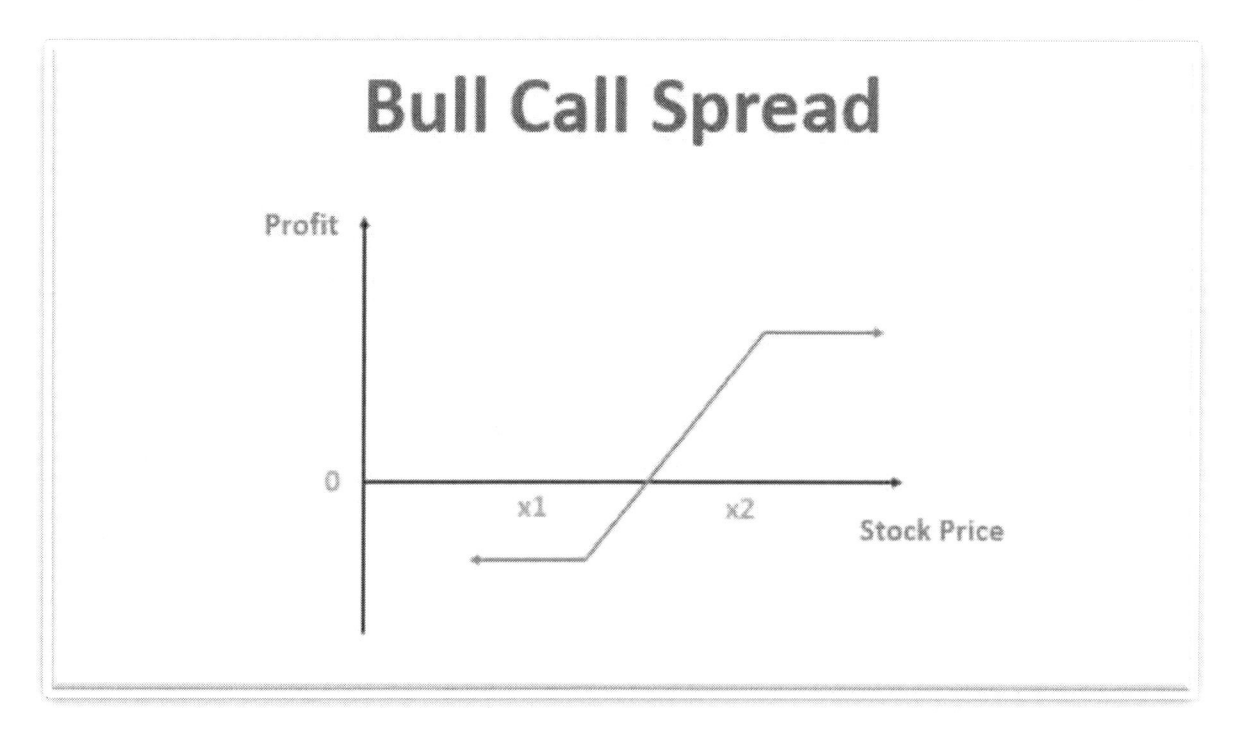

**GRAPH ILLUSTRATING A BULL CALL SPREAD**

**Understanding a Bull Call Spread**

A vertical spread is the bull call spread. In a vertical space, the same number of options on underlying securities with the same expiration date are simultaneously bought and written. However, the strike prices are different. The purchase of the option is what produces the profit should the trade work. The written option reduces the initial cost of the operation but, in turn, will limit the profits.

The bull call spread consists of the following stages that involve two call options.

1. Select an asset that will marginally increase in value over a specific time frame.
2. Purchase a call option with an above-market strike price and a specific expiration date, paying the premium.
3. Premium income can be generated by selling a call option with the same expiration date and a higher strike price than the initial call option.

The premium received for the sale of the call option partially offsets the premium paid by the investor for the purchase of the call option. The cost of the approach, or the net difference between the two call options, is essentially the investor's debt.

The bullish call spread lowers the call option's cost. However, there is a cost associated with it. Stock price gains are also capped, creating a limited range in which the investor can profit. Traders will use the bullish call spread if they believe that the value of an asset will rise moderately. Most of the time, they will use this strategy in times of high volatility.

Due to the lower and higher strike prices, the gains and losses of the bull call spread are constrained. If, at expiration, the stock price falls below the lowest strike price, the first call option purchased, the investor does not exercise the option. The option strategy lapses worthless, and the investor loses the net premium paid at the outset. If they exercise the option, they would have to pay more, the selected exercise price, for an asset that is currently trading at a lower price.

If the share price has risen at expiration and is trading above the higher strike price (the second call option is sold), the investor exercises his first option with the lower strike price. Now, they can buy the shares for less than the current market value.

However, the second call option sold is still active. The options market will automatically exercise or grant this call option. The investor will sell the shares purchased with the lowest first exercise option at the second-highest price. As a result, the gains from the purchase of the first call option are limited to the exercise price of the option sold. The gain is the difference between the lower strike price and the higher strike price less, of course, the net cost or premium paid in advance.

With a bullish spread, losses are capped by reducing risk, as the investor can only lose the net cost of creating the spread. However, the disadvantage of the strategy is that the profits are also limited.

### How is a Bull Call Spread implemented?

Implementing a bull call spread involves choosing the asset that is likely to appreciate slightly over a given period of time. The next step entails executing a call option sale, aligning the expiration date with the original purchase option while concurrently initiating a call option purchase with a strike price exceeding the prevailing market price. The cost of the approach is equal to the net difference between the premiums earned for selling the call and those paid to buy it.

### The benefit of a Bull Call Spread

With a bullish spread, losses are limited, which reduces risk as the investor can only lose the net cost of creating the spread. The net cost is also lower since the premium charged for the sale of the call helps cover the cost of the premium paid to purchase the call. Traders will use the bull option spread if they believe an asset will appreciate enough to justify exercising the long option but not enough when the short option can be exercised.

### Making profits with the Bull Call spread

Due to the lower and higher strike prices, the gains and losses from the bull call spread are constrained. If it expires, the stock price falls below the lowest strike price, the first call option and the investor does not exercise the option. The option strategy expires, and the investor loses the net premium paid at the outset. If they exercise the option, they will have to pay more (the chosen exercise price) for an asset that is currently trading for less.

The investor executes his first option with the lower strike price if it has expired, the share price has increased, and it is trading above the upper strike price, the second put option. Now, they can buy the shares for less than the current market value.

However, the option to buy the second sale is still active. The options market will automatically exercise or assign this call option. The investor will sell the shares purchased with the first lowest exercise option at the second highest exercise price. As a result, the gains made on purchases with first-call options are limited by the exercise price of the option sold. The profit is the difference between the lower and higher strike prices, less the upfront net cost or premium.

By lowering the risk, a bull call spread limits losses such that the investor can only lose the net cost of establishing the space. However, the disadvantage of the strategy is that the profits are also limited.

## EXPLORING BULL PUT SPREADS FOR INCOME GENERATION IN RISING MARKETS

The bull put spread is a derivative strategy that involves writing a put option on a stock to generate premium income while potentially acquiring the stock at a favorable price. One significant risk associated with putting writing is the potential obligation for the investor to purchase the underlying stock at the set strike price, irrespective of the stock's considerable decline below the strike price. Consequently, the investor may encounter an immediate and substantial loss. A bull put spread effectively manages the inherent risk associated with put writing by simultaneously purchasing a put at a lower price. This action reduces the net premium received and decreases the risk associated with the short-put position.

**Bull Put Spread Definition**

A bull put spread entails selling or shorting a set option while concurrently buying another put option (on the identical underlying asset) with an equivalent expiration date but a lower strike price. A bull put spread is a popular strategy among option traders, as it falls under one of the four basic types. The credit received for the short set leg of a bull put spread is typically higher than the debit paid for the long put, resulting in an upfront payment or credit when initiating this strategy. A bull put space, a credit (set) spread, or a short put spread is a strategy used in options trading.

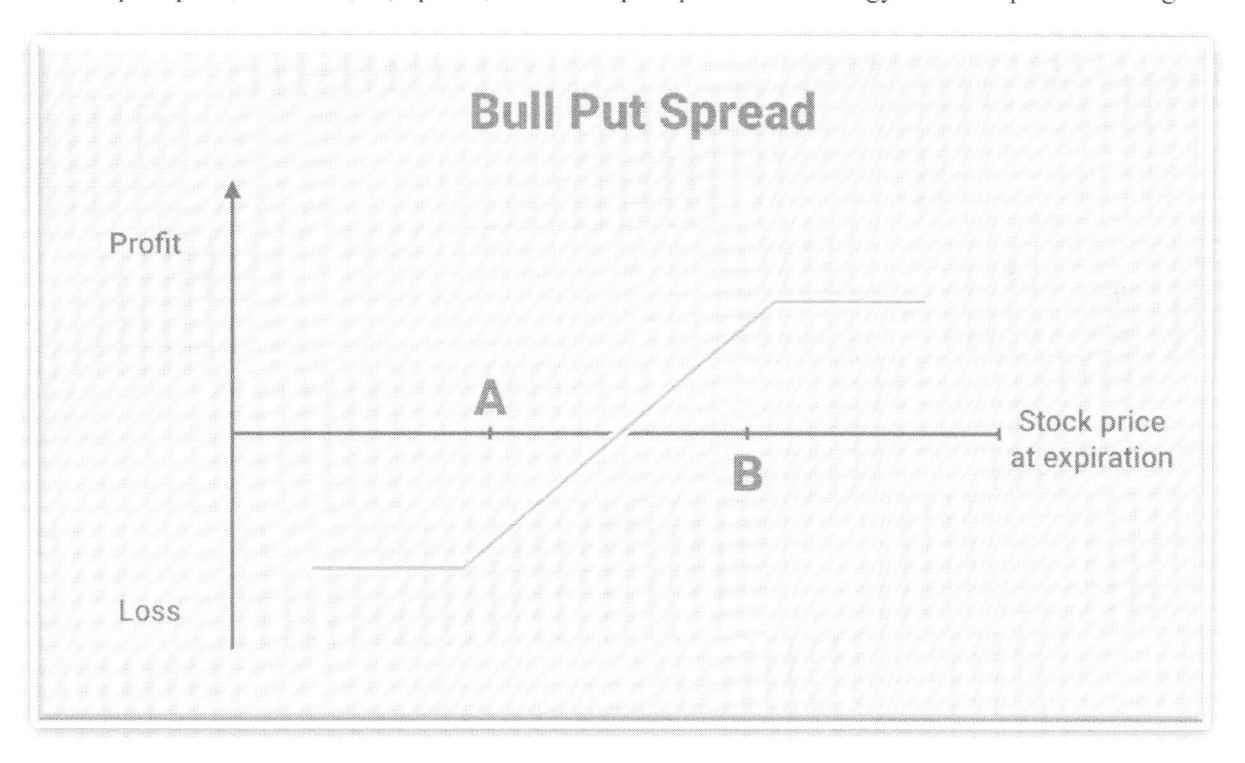

**GRAPH ILLUSTRATING A BULL PUT SPREAD**

**Profiting from a Bull Put Spread**

A bull put spread should be considered in the following situations:

- **To earn premium income**: This strategy is optimal for traders or investors seeking to generate premium income while mitigating risk compared to solely writing puts.

- **To buy a stock at a lesser price**: A bull put spread presents an enticing opportunity to strategically acquire a desired stock at a more favorable and effective price below its prevailing market value.

- **To capitalize on sideways to marginally higher markets**: Selling puts and implementing bullish put spreads are highly advantageous strategies for markets and stocks exhibiting a sideways to marginally higher trading pattern. Another bullish approach, such as purchasing call options or establishing bull call spreads, may not yield optimal results in such market conditions.

- **To generate income in choppy markets**: Selling options can be risky during market downturns due to the increased likelihood of being assigned stocks at potentially inflated prices.

**Profits and Loss from Put Options**

Investors commonly acquire options with a bearish outlook on a particular stock. This implies their anticipation of the stock declining below the option's strike price. The bull spread is strategically crafted to capitalize on an upward movement in the store. Suppose the underlying stock is trading above the strike price at expiration. In that case, the put option will expire worthless as it would not be advantageous for anyone to exercise the option and sell the stock at a lesser price than the current market value. Consequently, the put buyer incurs a loss equivalent to the premium expended.

When an investor is bearish on a stock, they would often purchase put options in the hopes that the stock will decline below the option's strike price. The bull spread, on the other hand, is intended to profit from a stock's increase. Because no one would sell the stock at a strike price below the market price, if the stock trades above the strike at expiration, the put option expires worthless. The investor who purchased the put loses the value of the premium they paid.

**Bull Put Profit and Loss**

The difference between the proceeds from the sold put and the cost of the bought put determines the bull put spread's maximum profit. In other words, the maximum profit is the net credit obtained at the beginning, which can only occur if the stock price closes higher than the higher strike price at expiration.

One potential downside of employing this particular strategy is that it constrains the potential profit that can be realized if the underlying stock significantly surpasses the upper strike price associated with the sold-out option. The investor would collect the initial credit but forego potential future profits.

If the stock price falls below the upper strike within the chosen strategy, the investor may experience a loss as the put option is anticipated to be exercised. A market participant may seek to initiate a short position by selling their shares at this more favorable strike price.

However, the option trader was able to generate a total credit for the strategy at the outset. This credit option offers a protective buffer against potential losses. Once the underlying stock experiences a significant decline, resulting in the complete erosion of the credit received, the trader initiates a loss on the trade.

If the stock price dips below the lower strike put option, resulting in a loss for both put options, the strategy would incur its maximum loss. The maximum loss can be calculated by subtracting the net credit received from the difference between the strike prices.

## CASE STUDIES OF SUCCESSFUL BULLISH TRADES USING THESE STRATEGIES

### Example of a Bull Put Spread

Suppose an options trader holds a bullish outlook on Apple for the upcoming month. Consider the underlying stock's current trading price of $275 per share. To execute a bullish put spread strategy, the trader would:

1. Executes a sell order for one put option with a strike price of $280, expiring in one month, at a premium of $8.50.
2. Buys one put option with an exercise price of $270, expiring in one month, for $2.

The options trader realizes a net credit of $6.50 for the two options, resulting from a $8.50 credit minus a $2 premium paid. Because a single options contract corresponds to 100 shares of the principal asset, the total credit received amounts to $650.

### Scenario 1 Maximum Profit

Assuming a bullish scenario, let's consider the possibility of Apple experiencing an upward movement and reaching a trading price of $300 at the expiration date. The maximum profit is $650, calculated as ($8.50 - $2) x 100 shares = $650. Once the stock surpasses the upper strike price, the strategy no longer generates any further profit potential.

### Scenario 2 Maximum Loss

The maximum loss is realized if Apple's share price is equal to or lower than the low strike of $270. However, the potential loss is capped at $350, which is determined by subtracting the strike price of the $280 put from the strike price of the $270 set and then subtracting the premium received from selling the spread, all multiplied by 100 shares.

Ideally, the options trader seeks the underlying stock to expire above the $280 per share strike price, maximizing potential profits.

**Example of Bull Call Spread Strategy**

Imagine a pharmaceutical company, PharmaHealth Corp., with its stock trading at $50. An investor anticipates a moderate increase and executes the following spread:

Initiate a long position by purchasing a call option at a strike price of $55.

Initiate a short position by selling a call option with a strike price of $60.

**Outcome:** If PharmaHealth's stock rises above $60, the investor's gains are capped, as the short call option limits potential profits. However, the premium from selling the higher strike call option partially offsets the cost of the lower strike call option.

# CHAPTER 2
# BEARISH STRATEGIES: NAVIGATING MARKET DOWNTRENDS

The primary motivation for an investor to initiate a short spread is their anticipation of a moderate decline in the underlying stock's value. Doing so aims to capitalize on this potential decline or safeguard their position. Two primary bearish spread strategies are available for traders: the bear put spread and the bear call spread. Both cases would be classified as vertical spreads.

A bear put margin involves simultaneously buying a put option to benefit from the expected drop in the underlying value and selling (writing) another put option with the same expiration but at a lesser strike price to generate income to offset the purchase cost of the underlying security.

On the contrary, a bear call spread strategy entails the act of selling (writing) a call option to generate income while simultaneously purchasing a call option with the same expiration but at a greater strike price to cap potential upside risk. This strategy results in a total credit to the merchant's account.

Rolling spreads can also involve ratios, such as buying a put to sell two or more puts at less of a strike price than the first. Since it is a spread strategy that pays when the underlying falls, you will lose if the market rises. However, the loss will be limited to the premium paid for the spread.

Traders use this short-spread strategy when they expect the price of an underlying to fall soon. It involves buying and selling put options with the same expiration but different strike prices.

A put option with a greater strike price is bought, and another with a lower strike price is sold. The higher-priced put option is in-the-money (ITM), while the lower-priced put is an out-of-the-money option. This strategy results in a total debit to the trader as the cost of the ITM put is adjusted by the cash flow from the OTM put.

The trader makes a profit if the underlying price ends up being less than the strike price of the out-of-the-money put option. The benefit arises from the higher intrinsic value of the High Price Put. Net profit is, therefore, equal to the strike difference in prices less the spread creation cost.

Profit = Strike price of the long-put option - Strike price of the short-put option - Expenses

## MASTERING BEAR CALL SPREADS FOR BEARISH POSITIONS AND INCOME GENERATION

A bear call spread is a two-step options strategy in which a call option is sold, and the upfront option premium is collected. A second call option with the same expiration date but a greater strike price is simultaneously bought. One of the four fundamental vertical option spreads is a bear call spread. The strike of the sold call (the short call leg) is lower than that of the purchased call (the long call leg); hence, the option premium earned on the first leg is always more significant than the cost incurred on the second leg.

A bear call spread is sometimes called a credit call spread or a short call spread because it results in the receipt of an upfront premium when initiated. Based on an options trader's pessimistic assessment of a stock, index, or other financial instrument, this approach is typically employed to create premium revenue.

Purchasing two call options with different strike prices but the same expiration date results in a bear call spread.

Bear call spreads are seen as having minimal risk and limited reward since they allow traders to limit their losses or generate smaller profits. The strike prices of their call options set the upper and lower bounds of their gains and losses.

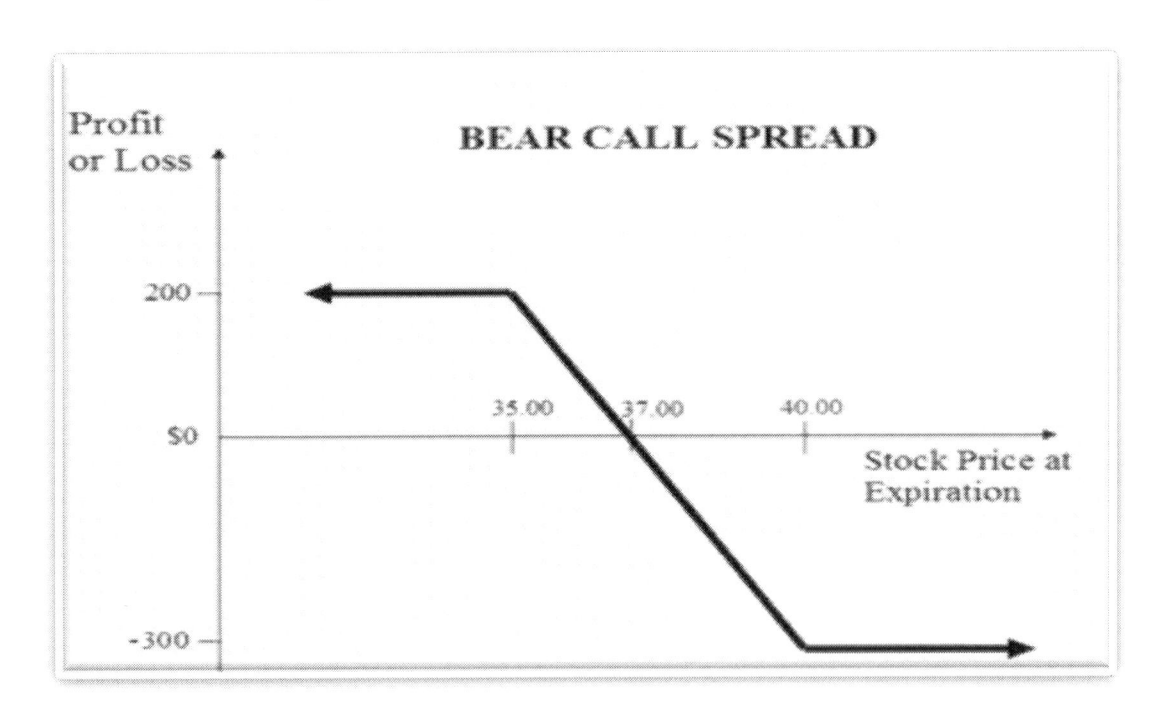

**GRAPH ILLUSTRATING A BEAR CALL SPREAD**

## Profiting from a Bear Call Spread

The risk-mitigation tactic of purchasing call options to cover a short position in a stock or index is comparable to a bear call spread. The maximum profit in a short sale is the difference between the price at which the short sale was executed and zero (the theoretical low to which a stock can decline). In contrast, in a bear call spread, the instrument sold short is a call option rather than a store, limiting the maximum gain to the net premium received.

Therefore, when trading in the following scenarios, a bear call spread should be taken into account:

- **A modest downside is expected:** This is ideal for a trader who foresees a modest stock or index downturn instead of a significant plunge. Why? The trader would be better off using a technique like a short sale, buying options, or starting a bear put spread, where the potential rewards are enormous and not limited to only the premium paid if the anticipation is for a significant decrease.

- **Volatility is high:** A high level of implied volatility results in more premium income. Therefore, even though the bear call spread's short and long legs substantially lessen the impact of volatility, this strategy performs best when volatility is higher.

- **Risk mitigation is required:** The theoretically unlimited loss that could result from the naked (i.e., uncovered) short sale of a call option is theoretically capped by a bear call spread. Remember that the seller must deliver the underlying security at the strike price when selling a call. Consider the possible loss if the value of the underlying security increases by two, three, or ten times before the call's expiration. As a result, even if the long leg in a bear call spread lowers the net premium that the call seller (or writer) can earn, its cost is entirely justified by the significant risk reduction it provides.

**Steps to Master Bear Call Spreads for Bearish Positions and Income Generation:**

**1. Market Analysis:** Before executing a bear call spread, conducting a thorough market analysis is essential. This involves evaluating the underlying asset's current price trend, volatility, and potential catalysts that might drive it lower. Proper analysis helps to increase the probability of success in the trade.

**2. Selecting Strike Prices:** Choose the strike prices for the two call options based on the anticipated price movement of the underlying asset. The sold (lower) call option should ideally be slightly out-of-the-money (OTM) to maximize the net credit received, while the bought (higher) call option acts as a buffer to limit potential losses.

**3. Option Expiration:** Select an expiration date that aligns with your market outlook. A shorter expiration might be suitable if you expect a rapid price decline. A more prolonged expiration can be chosen for a more extended bearish outlook to give the trade more time to develop.

**4. Calculating Potential Profit and Loss:** Understanding the potential profit and loss is crucial. The maximum profit is restricted to the initial net credit. The absolute maximum loss is the difference between the strike prices and the net credit.

Mastering bear call spreads for bearish positions and income generation requires a combination of technical knowledge, market analysis, risk management, and a systematic approach to trading. This strategy offers a controlled way to profit from downward price movements while limiting potential losses.

## UTILIZING BEAR PUT SPREADS FOR DOWNSIDE PROTECTION AND PROFIT POTENTIAL

A bear put spread is a strategy employed by astute investors or traders who anticipate a substantial downward movement in the value of a security or asset. The primary objective is to mitigate the expenses of maintaining the option trade. A bear put spread is executed by buying put options and selling an equal number of puts on the same principal asset with the same expiration date but at a lesser strike price. The potential upside of employing this particular strategy is represented by the disparity between the two strike prices while considering the options' net cost. A put option grants the holder the privilege, yet not the duty, to execute the sale of a predetermined quantity of the underlying security at a certain strike price on or before the option's expiration. A bear put spread, alternatively referred to as a debit set spread or a long-put spread, is a strategy employed by option traders.

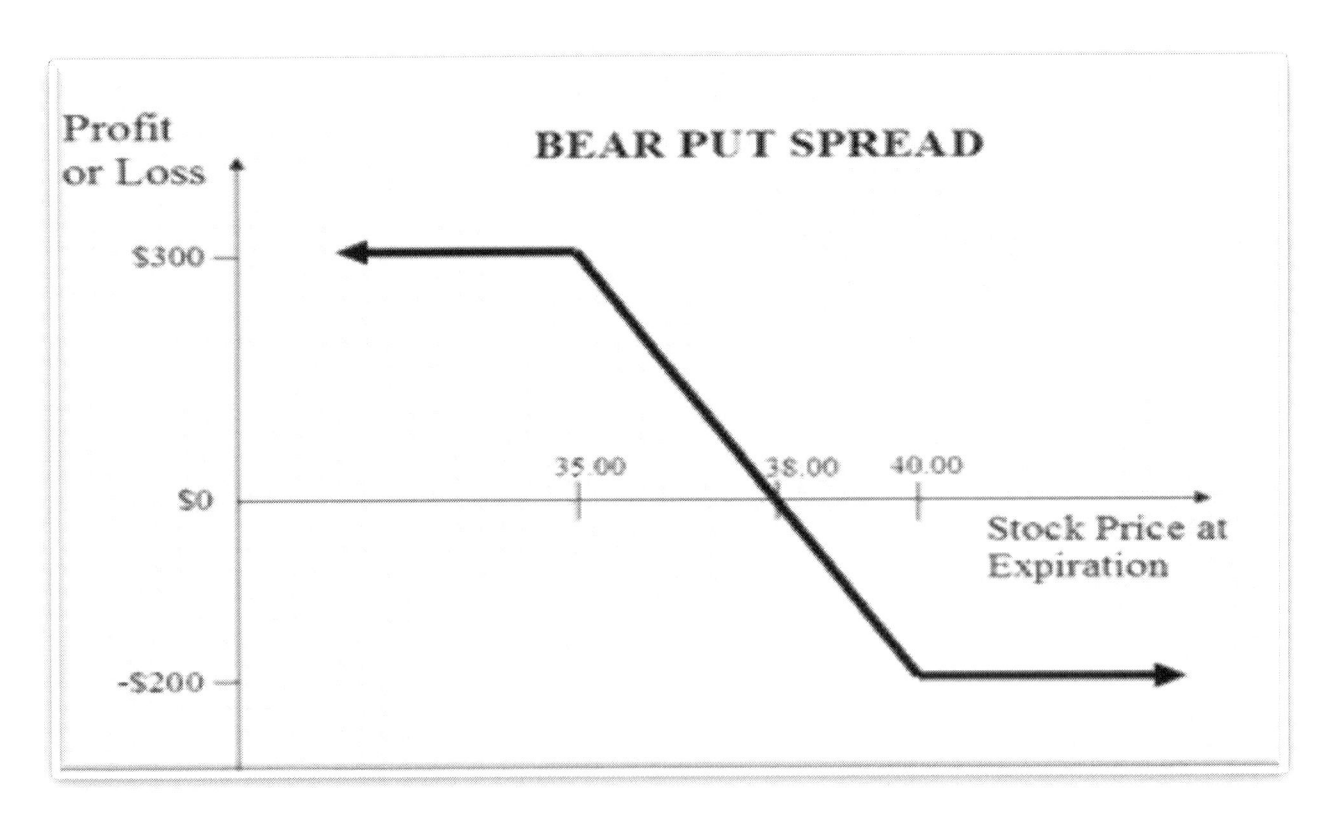

**GRAPH ILLUSTRATING A BEAR PUT SPREAD**

- A bearish investor who seeks to maximize gains while limiting losses will use a bearish spread as part of their options trading strategy.

- Bear put spreads include buying and selling puts for the same asset with the same expiration date but different prices.

- When the price of the underlying securities drops, a bearish spread makes money.

For example, you believe that XYZ Corporation's stock price will likely decline soon. However, you also want to protect yourself from a massive loss if the stock price falls sharply. For example, to create a bear put spread, you may buy a $50 put option and sell a $45 put option with a three-month expiration date.

The maximum loss on this trade is the net premium paid, which would be the difference between the premiums of the two put options. In this example, the premiums are $2.50 and $1.50, respectively. This means that your maximum loss would be $100, which is the cost of buying the $50 put option minus the proceeds from selling the $45 put option.

You can only make money on this transaction if the difference between the two strike prices exceeds the net premium. The highest profit you may make would be $400 less the $100 net premium paid because there are $5 variations between the strike prices.

The bear put spread will start to profit if the p falls below the strike price of the short put option, which in this case is $45. For every dollar the stock price falls below $45, you will make an additional $100 profit. The variation between the two strike prices, less the net premium paid, will cap your profit at $400.

The bear put spread will start to lose money if the price of the stock rises above the strike price of the long put option, which in this case is $50. For every dollar that the cost of the stock rises above $50, you will lose an additional $100. However, your loss will be capped at the net premium of $100.

The bear put spread is a flexible options strategy that can generate potential profits while minimizing downside risk. It is a fantastic choice for investors who anticipate that the price of a principal asset will drop soon but also want to cut their losses if the market swings against them.

**Bear Put Spread: Profit and Loss**

A bearish spread produces a net deficit. The maximum amount a trader can lose on any debit spread, such as the bear put space, is the net debit, sometimes the gross debit. It is the cost of the option with the higher strike price, less the fee of the vote with the lower strike price. It occurs if the principal asset closes at any price higher than the buy-put option's strike price at expiration. Minimal risk entails minimal gain. The difference between the strike prices, less the cost of the put with the higher strike price, is the maximum a trader can make from a bear put spread.

In this scenario, the trader sells the shares at the higher strike price by exercising his higher strike put. If it is profitable, the other set option with a lower strike price is automatically exercised, and the trader buys the stock at the lower strike price. As a result, no net position is built into the underlying stock. Both options expire without being exercised if the stock price exceeds the higher strike price at expiration. If the stock cost is below the higher strike put's expense but not below the lower strike put, the higher strike put is exercised, causing the trader to take a short position in the underlying stock.

Overall, bear put spreads can be a good option for investors who want to protect against downside risk while generating potential profits. However, it is important to understand the risks involved before using this strategy.

REAL-LIFE EXAMPLES DEMONSTRATING BEARISH STRATEGIES IN ACTION

- In 2008, during the financial crisis, many investors used bearish spreads to protect their portfolios from the decline in the stock market. By buying options on puts with greater strike prices and selling put options with a lesser strike price, investors could limit their losses while still generating some profits as the market fell.
- In 2018, during the trade war between the United States and China, many investors used bear call spreads to bet on a decline in the stock market. By buying call options with lower strike prices and selling call options with higher strike prices, investors could profit if the stock market fell.
- In 2020, during the COVID-19 pandemic, many investors used bearish spreads to protect their portfolios from the decline in the stock market. Investors could reduce their losses while making some money when the market went down by buying options on puts with higher strike prices and selling them with lower strike prices.

These are just a few examples of how bearish strategies can be used in real life. It is important to note that these strategies are not without risk, and it is important to understand the risks involved before using them.

Here is a more detailed example of how a bear put spread can be used to protect against downside risk:

- You believe that the stock price of XYZ Corporation is likely to decline soon. However, it would be best to safeguard against suffering a substantial loss if the stock price drops significantly. By purchasing a put option with a $50 striking price and selling a set option with a $45, both of which have a three-month expiration date, you can establish a bear put spread. The maximum loss on this trade is the net premium paid, which would be the difference between the premiums of the two put options. In this example, let's say the premiums are $2.50 and $1.50, respectively. This means that your maximum loss would be $100, which is the cost of buying the $50 put option minus the proceeds from selling the $45 put option.

- You can only profit on this transaction if the difference between the two strike prices exceeds the net premium. The highest profit you may make would be $400 less the $100 net premium paid because there are $5 variations between the strike prices.

# CHAPTER 3
# MARKET ANALYSIS FOR OPTION TRADERS: THE COMPASS FOR SUCCESS

When analyzing the market, an options trader should consider several aspects to make informed trading decisions. First, it is essential to understand the overall market direction to decide whether to be bullish (optimistic), bearish (pessimistic), or neutral about the market. Furthermore, the trader should evaluate the volatility of the market and the underlying stock or asset, as it directly impacts option prices. Looking at specific indicators, company news, and global events can also help anticipate potential market changes or risks. Thorough market analysis forms the basis for developing an appropriate option trading strategy, allowing the trader to respond better to current market conditions.

Before we get into market analysis, let me remind you of a simple truth: Only two forces move a market: supply and demand. They are the common denominator of any economic, political, social, or scientific market event - thus of paramount importance to bulls and bears and their open positions.

Market analysis all have one thing in common: estimating supply and demand. Some can be accurate but must constantly catch up to the price action. By switching between bears and bulls, traders can affect the market they are analyzing. As soon as you open a new trade, it changes again. Therefore, it is imperative to understand that the only way to gain an advantage is to do the best possible market analysis of supply and demand.

## INTRODUCING TECHNICAL AND FUNDAMENTAL ANALYSIS FOR OPTIONS TRADERS

**Technical analysis**

Technical analysis predicts an instrument's price action based on its past price values.

In essence, technical analysts believe that historical and present data provide all the necessary information to evaluate the instrument. Therefore, the graph, price, and volume are treated as self-sufficient sources of information and investigated with mathematical and statistical tools. Trends and patterns play a decisive role, as do the numerous indicators created to adapt to every instrument and market condition.

Technical analysis, therefore, stands in opposition to the fundamental one, but only in appearance. To be more precise, the technical analyst does not see the point of conducting a fundamental type analysis because he believes that the current price value already expresses the result of this study. If the price rises, the sentiment must be bullish; if it falls, it must be bearish.

The technical approach is described for the first time in the well-known theory of Charles Dow at the beginning of the twentieth century. We will focus on the practical deductions that derive from his studies:

- Price action discounts everything: This is by far the most crucial premise, without which any other statement would be worthless. Its meaning is that the price intrinsically reflects the action of any factor capable of influencing its performance, be it of a fundamental, psychological, political, or other nature. It follows that the study of price action is complete and sufficient.

- Prices move following trends: The very purpose of the graphic representation is to appreciate how trends are born and continue. This statement goes hand in hand with another: a trend will continue to follow the same direction until a new force intervenes to change it. It is a re-adaptation of the principle of inertia, which states that the forces acting on the price have a direction and an intensity and are, therefore, vectors. If no force intervenes to stop the price movement, it continues potentially indefinitely.

- History repeats itself: The forces acting on the price are always the same, and the collective psychological mechanisms of market investors do not change. This means that history repeats itself according to similar cycles, which can be divided into well-defined phases: it's all about identifying them correctly. This doesn't mean that the price always follows the same precise points (or there wouldn't be much effort to find trading opportunities), but only that the alternation of primary, secondary, and minor trends characterizes a basic harmony.

The most important element of technical market analysis is its connection to the chart. When you look at a chart, you are already doing technical analysis. The basis of the chart analysis is the Dow analysis by the famous publisher and journalist Charles Dow. Among other things, Dow proposed that the market discounts everything. Simply put, this means that every factor that impacts supply and demand is reflected in price. This, in turn, is displayed in real-time in a chart.

The pure doctrine of technical analysis advocates against studying almost anything but the price chart as unreliable data. But therein lies a weakness of technical market analysis - it only analyzes what has already happened. So, the question for traders is: How can I stay competitive when everything I know is already common knowledge?

**Elements of Technical Market Analysis**

Price action strategies can be understood as a subculture of technical analysis that is growing in popularity. One reason is that price action finds most technical analysis tools, such as technical indicators, unsuitable for giving traders a competitive advantage, even though they agree with the postulates of Dow's theory.

Price action traders conclude "bare" charts, with price action supporting their initial data collection decisions. Everything else is just for support, not for initiating a trade. The foundation of price action trading is the observation that the price is returning to levels where it previously reversed or consolidated, reflecting residual supply and demand.

**What does residual supply and demand mean?**

Institutional traders from banks, hedge funds, and multinational organizations don't chase the market; they care about completing their orders at the desired price. Your market analysis is limited to where the market will be in the next month or year. If the market moves from the level, you were trading today, your orders will not be canceled. They keep their positions open until the market returns.

These remaining open orders skew the market's composition, attracting more orders. Price action strategies are, therefore, primarily used in daily market analysis.

**Use and applications of technical analysis.**

The heart of technical analysis, as mentioned, is still today represented by the Dow theory, which initially applied only to stock markets. Charles Dow was, in fact, with Charles Bergstresser and Edward Jones, the creator of the Dow 30 and the Dow Transport. The former collects the 30 largest-cap blue chip companies listed on the NYSE, while the latter reflects the performance of the 20 largest transportation companies.

Dow believed the indices composed in this way could provide general information on the state of the economy. , thanks to their comparison, it was possible to qualify the validity of the trends. If a rise had followed an increase in one of the two in the other, the analyst would have had confirmation of the effective birth of a bullish trend.

For years, great traders have contributed by developing new indicators, indices, oscillators, and strategies without questioning the foundations laid by Dow. Today, technical analysis is applied to trading any financial instrument with a historical data set: futures, commodities, forex (where it is still the most widely used form of analysis), and any other asset.

**Fundamental analysis tools**

The fundamental analysis relies not on price charts but on evaluating economic data such as the ECB key interest rates, inflation rates, or trade balances. Fundamental analysis is based on the idea that markets first overprice financial instruments but eventually discover the correct price. The period of mispricing thus presents trading opportunities.

Fundamental market analysis does not provide precise entry or exit points for trading. However, it is an excellent tool for predicting long-term price action when used wisely.

A company's financial health is directly related to its stock price. In the case of countries, however, an improved economic situation is not necessarily reflected in comparable growth in the value of the currency. Instead, the relative importance of a currency is fed by several factors such as national monetary policy, economic indicators, technical advances, international developments, or natural disasters.

**Economic theories and raw data of fundamental market analysis**

In addition to market sentiment, some economic theories aim to identify differences between a currency's rate and actual value. Here are some examples:

- Purchasing Power Parity: This assumes that goods should cost the same even after a currency adjustment. If not, there are good trading opportunities.
- Interest Rate Parity: The same as Purchasing Power Parity, but with financial assets instead of goods. Their purchase in different countries should cost the same after the interest rate adjustment.
- Balance of Trade Theory: Refers to a country's balance of trade. The currency will lose value if more goods and services are imported than exported.
- Real Interest Rate: The same as interest rate parity. A currency with a higher interest rate will appreciate against a currency with a lower interest rate because it attracts more investment.
- Asset Market: Similar to the trade balance, except that foreign investment inflows and outflows are calculated. The higher the foreign investment, the more the national currency appreciates.

**Why Choose Fundamental Analysis?**

This type of analysis is ideally suited to traders who want to delve deeply into the financial world. It is less pragmatic than other forms of analysis and takes more time to master than many new traders are willing to invest. However, if applied correctly, it can bring great satisfaction.

Ultimately, market analysis aims to find trading opportunities and avoid surprises that could jeopardize your investments.

Therefore, the more thorough your research and analysis, the less chance you have of being caught off guard. Some of the most famous top traders in the world rely on fundamental analysis, so why not take an example?

It should be noted that, like any other form of analysis, it is not infallible: the market can change drastically in a few minutes, nullifying speculations and overturning the result of operations.

**How do you set up a fundamental analysis?**

If you take the fundamental route, the first thing to do is familiarize yourself with the instrument you intend to trade and study every possible event capable of influencing its performance. It will be essential to find one or more reliable sources to keep up with the news and make sure you follow them daily by subscribing to the newsletters and consulting them.

The fundamental trader's inseparable friend is the economic calendar, which collects reports and upcoming financial events from significant market players. Through observation and study, one must learn which events are relevant to the asset of interest and then discover how to prepare for those events.

## USING CHARTS, INDICATORS, AND FINANCIAL DATA TO MAKE INFORMED TRADING DECISIONS

**Charting**

Charts are a graphically represented sequence of prices. They represent the history of a market. The Y-axis shows the price, and the X-axis shows the time. No matter what trading style you choose - long-term position trading or short-term intraday trading - it all starts with charting. Charting has only been used on Wall Street for over a century. However, documents from the Far East contain price representations in the form of candlesticks from about 300 years ago. They are known as "rice courses" because they were first used in the rice trade.

The most basic tool available to a technical trader is candlesticks. Using candlestick patterns to predict price action is a trading strategy in itself.

In addition to learning the most common chart patterns, it is essential to understand the underlying supply and demand mechanisms. The most famous formations are support and resistance lines, trend channels, triangles, and flags.

Remember that the supporting constructs presented here can never predict future market movements. They can only be used by the trader to understand past price movements better.

**The SPDR S&P 500 (SPY) ETF's bar chart is shown in the following picture. The bars often lengthen during decreases, indicating an increase in volatility. Additionally, more down (red) price bars than up (green) price bars show declines.**

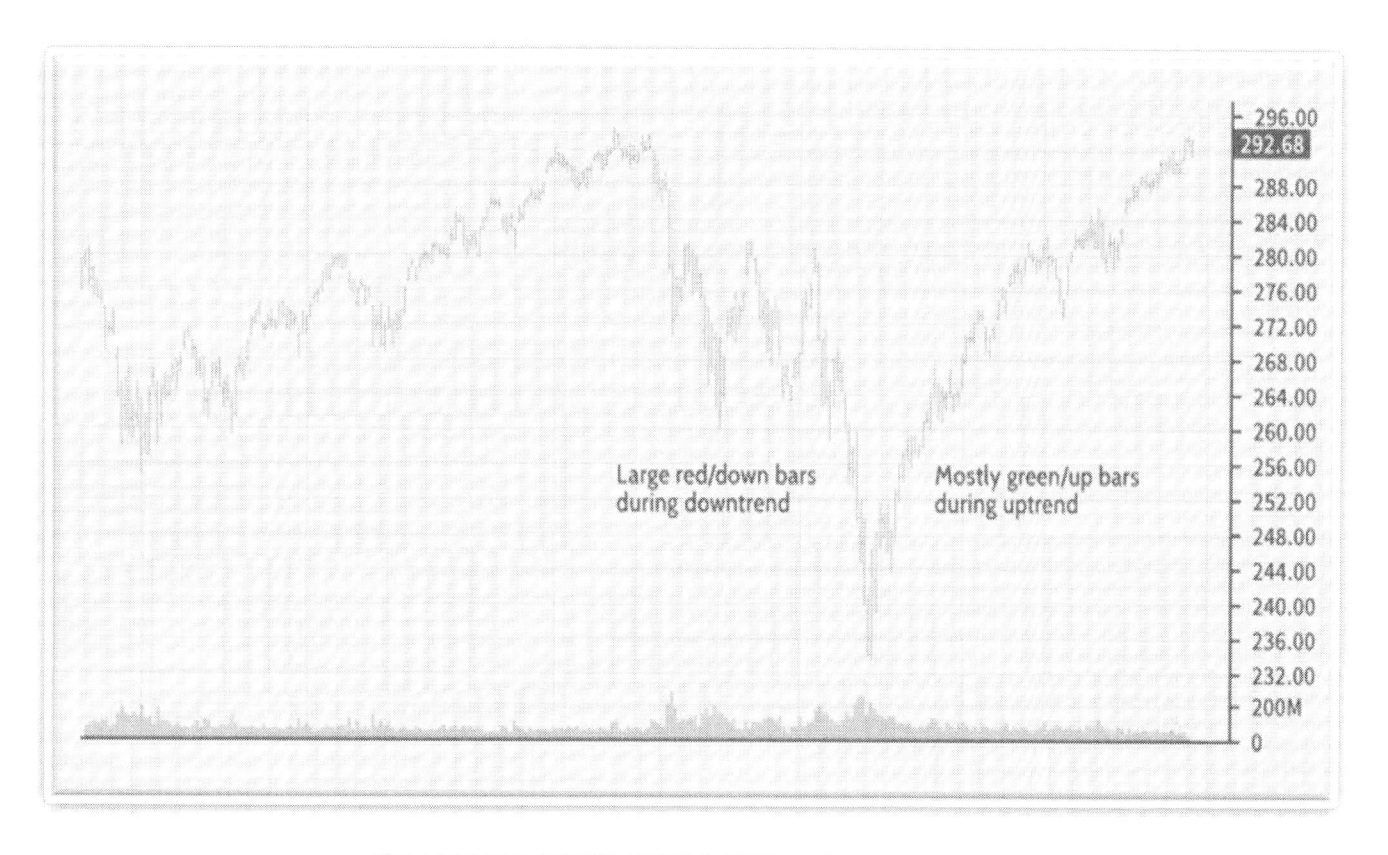

**GRAPH ILLUSTRATING THE USE OF CHART**

**Indicators**

If you have used a trading platform before, you have probably seen a technical indicator. Technical indicators can be divided into two large groups:

- Trend indicators: Moving averages (MA), moving average convergence and divergence (MACD), and average directional index (ADX) are a few examples of these. They indicate the direction and strength of a trend but not always the direction of current price action.

- Oscillators: Relative Strength Index (RSI), Stochastic Indicator or Parabolic SAR. They point to a potential trend reversal.

Finally, there are volume-based indicators. Trading volume has always been understood as the defining factor of supply and demand. However, this cannot be determined precisely on the Forex market because it is not traded on a central stock exchange but OTC (over the counter).

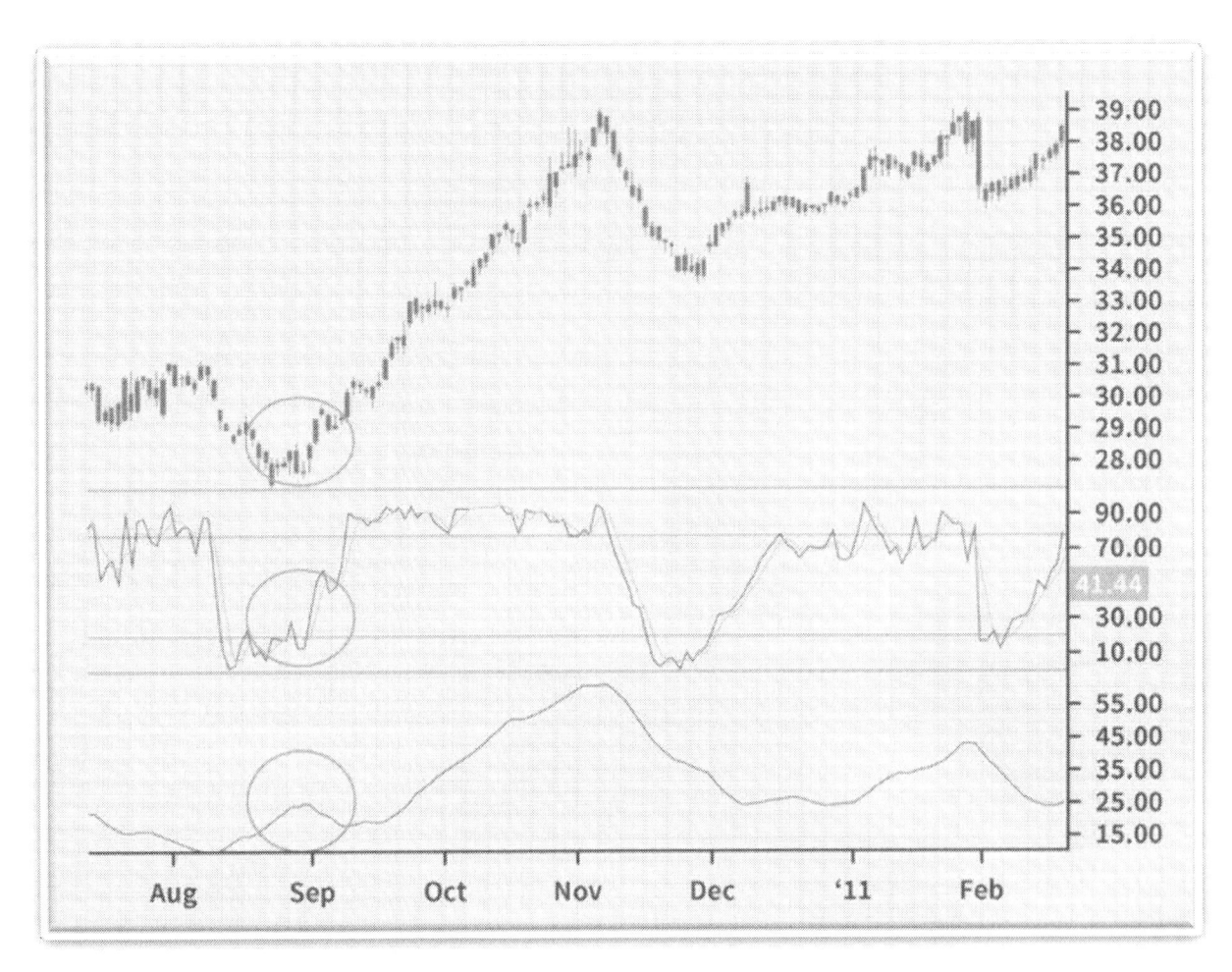

**GRAPH ILLUSTRATING TRADING INDICATOR**

Trading indicators are imperfect. They must catch up to the price and often be reinterpreted after determining the closing price. They are regularly combined with each other to complement each other. Otherwise, they often fall apart. As a beginner, when professional traders advise you to keep your chart simple and clear, they talk about not trusting technical indicators too much. Finally, it is essential to note that trading strategies that rely exclusively on technical indicators offer no competitive advantage.

INCORPORATING MARKET ANALYSIS INTO OPTION STRATEGY SELECTION

Most traders tend to use whatever trading strategy suits them best, whether technical analysis, fundamental analysis, or a mixture of the two. Interest rates, inflation rates, trade balances, market sentiment, and other essential factors can give traders a big-picture view. However, in the short term, financial instruments rarely move in a straight line, which means a lot of short-term price action provides favorable trading opportunities. In this regard, the use of technical market analysis can be very effective.

Whatever analysis method you use, you should always trace your logic to the supply and demand relationship.

**Two types of market analysis can be used for option trading:**

- Technical analysis examines historical price patterns to identify trends and support and resistance levels. Future price changes can be predicted using this information, which can also be used to pinpoint probable trade entry and exit points.
- Fundamental analysis looks at economic factors, company financials, and industry trends to assess the intrinsic value of an asset. This information can be used to determine whether an option is overpriced or underpriced.

By combining the technical and fundamental analysis, you may gain a complete picture of the market and make more educated judgments about your trading options.

Here are some specific examples of how market analysis can be used to select option strategies:

- Technical analysis: If a stock is bullish, consider buying call options. This way, you can profit from the stock's price appreciation without paying the total price.
- Fundamental analysis: If a company is undervalued, consider buying put options. This way, you can profit if the stock price falls below your strike price.
- Combined analysis: If a stock is in a bullish trend and the company is also undervalued, consider buying a straddle. No matter how the market moves, this option strategy allows you to purchase or sell the stock at the predetermined price.

Market analysis is only sometimes perfect. There will always be times when you make a bad trade, even if you do your research. However, by incorporating market analysis into your option strategy selection, you can increase your chances of success.

# GLOSSARY

**Bearish:** Bearish means the ability for prices to go down. Someone can be bearish about either the market as a whole, individual stocks or specific sectors. Someone who believes ABC Corp.'s stock will soon go down is said to be bearish on that company.

**Bullish:** Bullish means an investor believes a stock or the overall market will go higher. A bullish investor is often referred to as a bull, and a bearish investor as a bear.

**Indicator**: Indicators typically refer to technical chart patterns deriving from the price, volume, or open interest of a given security. It's a quantitative tool that is used by traders and investors to predict the future movement of an underlying asset.

**Charts:** Chart is a graph that shows traders and investors the market price of options over a given period. The options chart is essentially a stock chart with options instead of stocks. Traders can monitor options prices in the same way as a stock chart.

**Technical analysis:** Technical analysis as a trading discipline that is used for the evaluation of investments and identification of trading opportunities. It is done by analyzing the trends in statistics that are collected from trading activities such as movement of price and volume.

**Fundamental analysis:** Fundamental analysis is a method of evaluating the intrinsic value of an asset and analyzing the factors that could influence its price in the future. This form of analysis is based on external events and influences, as well as financial statements and industry trends.

**Bear spread:** Bear Spread is a kind of price spread where you buy, call or put options at different strike prices having the same expiration and is used when an investor thinks that a stock price will go down, but it will not go down drastically.

**Bull spread:** A bull spread is an optimistic options strategy designed to profit from a moderate rise in the price of a security or asset.

# REFERENCES

"7 Best Bearish Options Trading Strategies | Motilal Oswal." *Www.motilaloswal.com*, www.motilaloswal.com/blog-details/7-best-bearish-options-trading-strategies/5563.

*BROKERAGE: OPTIONS Technical Analysis for Options Trading a Fidelity Investments Webinar.*

"Bull Market Options Trading Strategies." *Www.optionstrading.org*, www.optionstrading.org/strategies/bullish-market/.

"Bullish Trading Strategies | the Options & Futures Guide." *Www.theoptionsguide.com*, www.theoptionsguide.com/bullish-trading-strategies.aspx.

"Definition and Types of Bullish Options Trading Strategies." *Nirmal Bang*, www.nirmalbang.com/knowledge-center/bullish-options-trading-strategy.html.

experience, Full Bio Akhilesh Ganti is a forex trading expert who has 20+ years of, et al. "Bear Spread Definition." *Investopedia*, 21 Apr. 2022, www.investopedia.com/terms/b/bearspread.asp.

"What Are Bullish Options Strategies?" *5paisa*, 30 May 2023, www.5paisa.com/stock-market-guide/derivatives-trading/what-are-bullish-option-strategies#:~:text=The%20bullish%20spread%20options%20strategy.

# BOOK 5

"OPTIONS ELEVATION: UNLOCKING ADVANCED STRATEGIES AND VOLATILITY TRADING"

# TABLE OF CONTENTS

- CHAPTER 1 .................................................................................................................................3
- BUTTERFLY SPREADS: FINDING BALANCE IN YOUR TRADES.................................................3
  - UNDERSTANDING LONG BUTTERFLY SPREADS FOR BALANCED STRATEGIES.................5
  - EXPLORING SHORT BUTTERFLY SPREADS FOR TARGETED SPREADS FOR TARGETED MARKET SCENARIOS.......................................................................................................................8
  - REAL-LIFE EXAMPLES SHOWCASING BUTTERFLY SPREADS' EFFECTIVENESS .......................9
- CHAPTER 2 ...............................................................................................................................11
- CALENDAR SPREADS: TIME AS YOUR TRADING ALLY.............................................................11
  - LEVERAGING LONG CALENDAR SPREADS FOR TIME-BASED TRADES ..................................12
  - UTILIZING SHORT CALENDAR SPREADS FOR VOLATILE MARKET CONDITIONS....................14
  - APPLYING CALENDAR SPREADS EFFECTIVELY IN DIFFERENT MARKET SCENARIOS............15
- CHAPTER 3 ...............................................................................................................................17
- TRADING VOLATILITY WITH STRADDLES AND STRANGLES ..................................................17
  - MASTERING LONG STRADDLE STRATEGY FOR CAPTURING ..................................................18
  - UNDERSTANDING SHORT STRADDLE AND STRANGLE FOR RANGE-BOUND MARKET STRATEGIES......20
  - REAL-LIFE USE CASES OF VOLATILITY TRADING WITH STRADDLES AND STRANGLES..........22
- GLOSSARY .................................................................................................................................24
- REFERENCES .............................................................................................................................25

# CHAPTER 1
# BUTTERFLY SPREADS: FINDING BALANCE IN YOUR TRADES

Options traders commonly employ butterfly spreads as strategic trading techniques. Remember that an option is a financial derivative that derives value from an underlying asset, like a stock or commodity. Option contracts allow buyers to buy or sell the underlying asset on a specific expiration or exercise date. The essence of the butterfly spread is a strategy that encapsulates the importance of finding equilibrium in your trades.

As noted above, a butterfly spread combines a bullish and bearish spread. This strategy employs a neutral approach by utilizing four option contracts with identical expiration dates yet varying strike prices:

- A higher strike price
- An exercise price to the offer
- A lower strike price

The options with the highest and lowest strike prices are the same distance from at-the-money options. If at-the-money options have a strike price of $60, the upper and lower options must have strike prices equal to dollar amounts above and below $60. At $55 and $65, for example, since these strike prices are both from $5 to $60.

Put or call options can be used for a butterfly distribution. Combining options in various ways will create different types of butterfly spreads, each designed to benefit from volatility or low volatility. A spread strategy can be defined by its profitability or profit and loss profile perspectives.

Picture a butterfly in flight - a harmonious symphony of wings moving in sync, maintaining perfect equilibrium. Similarly, a butterfly spread involves a carefully constructed combination of options contracts to balance risk and reward. This strategy is designed for a specific purpose: to profit from minimal price movement in the underlying asset.

**What is a Butterfly Spread?**
First of all, the term butterfly spread refers to the spine and wings of the butterfly when they are fully open. In investing terms, the column is the asset's current price, and each wing is the fixed area of risk and reward. Thus, a butterfly spread will use three strike prices: the lowest, the current, and the highest. .When you initiate a long position in a stock, you incur the cost of acquiring the right to execute a call option or a put option on an underlying asset at a predetermined strike price within a designated time frame. A butterfly spread strategy encompasses a quartet of four call options, four put options, or a blend of both.

**The Anatomy of a Butterfly Spread**
A butterfly spread involves using three strike prices and two expiration dates simultaneously. It consists of two call options and one put option, all with the same expiration date. The central strike price forms the body of the butterfly, while the two outer strike prices create the wings. The strategy is named after its visual resemblance to a butterfly's wings.

**Consider this real-life scenario:** Imagine a stock you believe will experience only modest price fluctuations soon. Instead of traditional directional bets, a butterfly spread offers an alternative approach. You could simultaneously buy one call option with a lower strike price, sell two call options with a middle strike price, and buy one call option with a higher strike price.

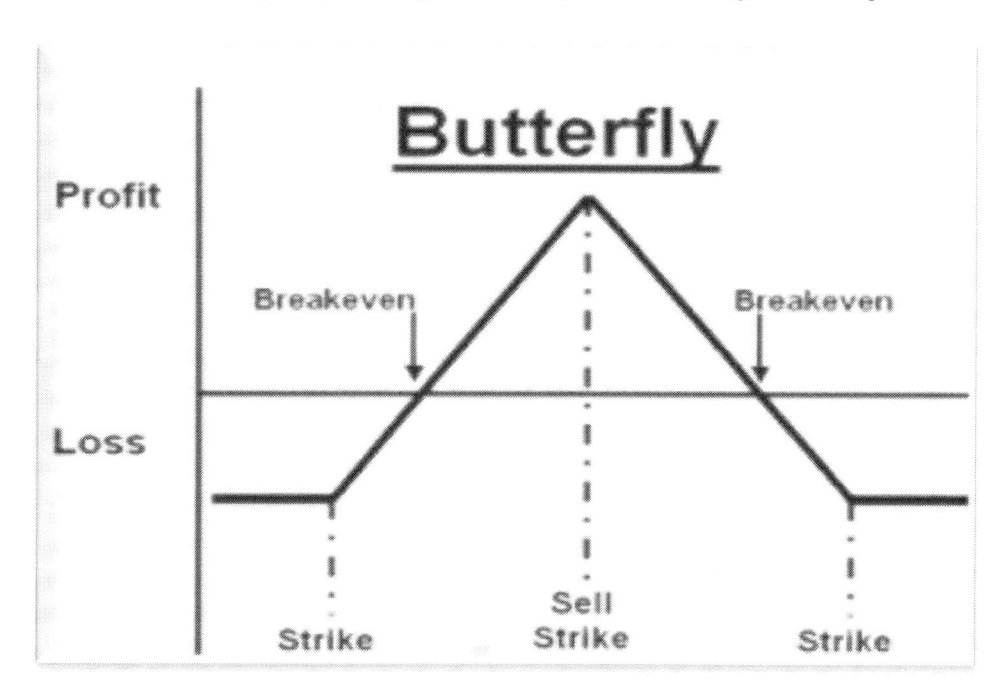

**GRAPH ILUSTRATING A BUTTERFLY SPREAD**

**How to Use the Butterfly Spread in Trading?**
When analyzing butterfly spreads, there are two main issues to consider in relation to the expected movement of a stock or index:
- **Minimum volatility:** Suppose you believe that a stock or index will experience minimal volatility over a given period. In that scenario, one could employ long-call and long-put butterfly spreads as strategic options to establish a position. A debit will be associated with implementing this strategy but will represent your maximum potential loss. The potential profit can be determined by calculating the potential gains upon opening the position.
- **Expected volatility:** Anticipate bullish or bearish volatility in a specific stock or index. It considers implementing a short-call butterfly spread or a short-put butterfly spread. Since you are buying at-the-money call/put options, there is no intrinsic value, only time value. Therefore, moving in the "right" direction will maximize your profits.

**Simplifying Butterfly Spreads**
The key to making a profit or loss on any butterfly spread revolves around the intrinsic value and time value of an option. The disparity between the strike price and the underlying stock or index's

current market price determines an option's intrinsic value. For example, if you had the option to buy the S&P 500 at 4,200 and the option expired with the index at 4,300, the intrinsic value would be 100. Since the option expired, there is no time value. However, if, for instance, you initiated a three-month option position, at the moment of initiation, the cost would encompass both intrinsic value and a component of time value, which will gradually diminish as the expiration date draws near.

You'll find that at-the-money options are more popular and generally have a higher degree of time value included in the option price. This is simply a matter of supply and demand: the higher the demand, the higher the option price. Therefore, time value is often described as the premium.

UNDERSTANDING LONG BUTTERFLY SPREADS FOR BALANCED STRATEGIES.

The butterfly spread is a neutral strategy involving simultaneously using a bull and bear spread. There are three strike prices involved in a butterfly spread. These spreads have limited risk and may include a call or put option. A long call extension is a trade used by an investor who does not believe that the price of an asset will stray much from its current price.

**A long-term butterfly spread** is another type of option spread that results in a position for an investor who does not expect the price of an asset to stray much from its current price. This trade involved selling two put options at or near the current market price and buying one at the money put option and one out of the money put option. In both cases, the maximum gain at expiration occurs at the strike price of the short or put options. The maximum loss occurs above or below the exercise prices of the purchased options. The formula for the maximum loss for the long-call butterfly is as follows:

**Maximum profit = Strike price of short call options - Strike price of long call option at the lowest strike price - Premium plus commissions paid for the trade at the beginning**

The maximum profit is attained when the underlying asset's price coincides with the strike price of the short-call options upon expiration.

The breakeven point for the long call butterfly can occur at two prices at expiration:
- **Upper breakeven point = highest long call strike price - net premium and commissions paid lowest Breakeven Point = Lowest Long Call Option Strike Price + Net Premium and Fees Paid**

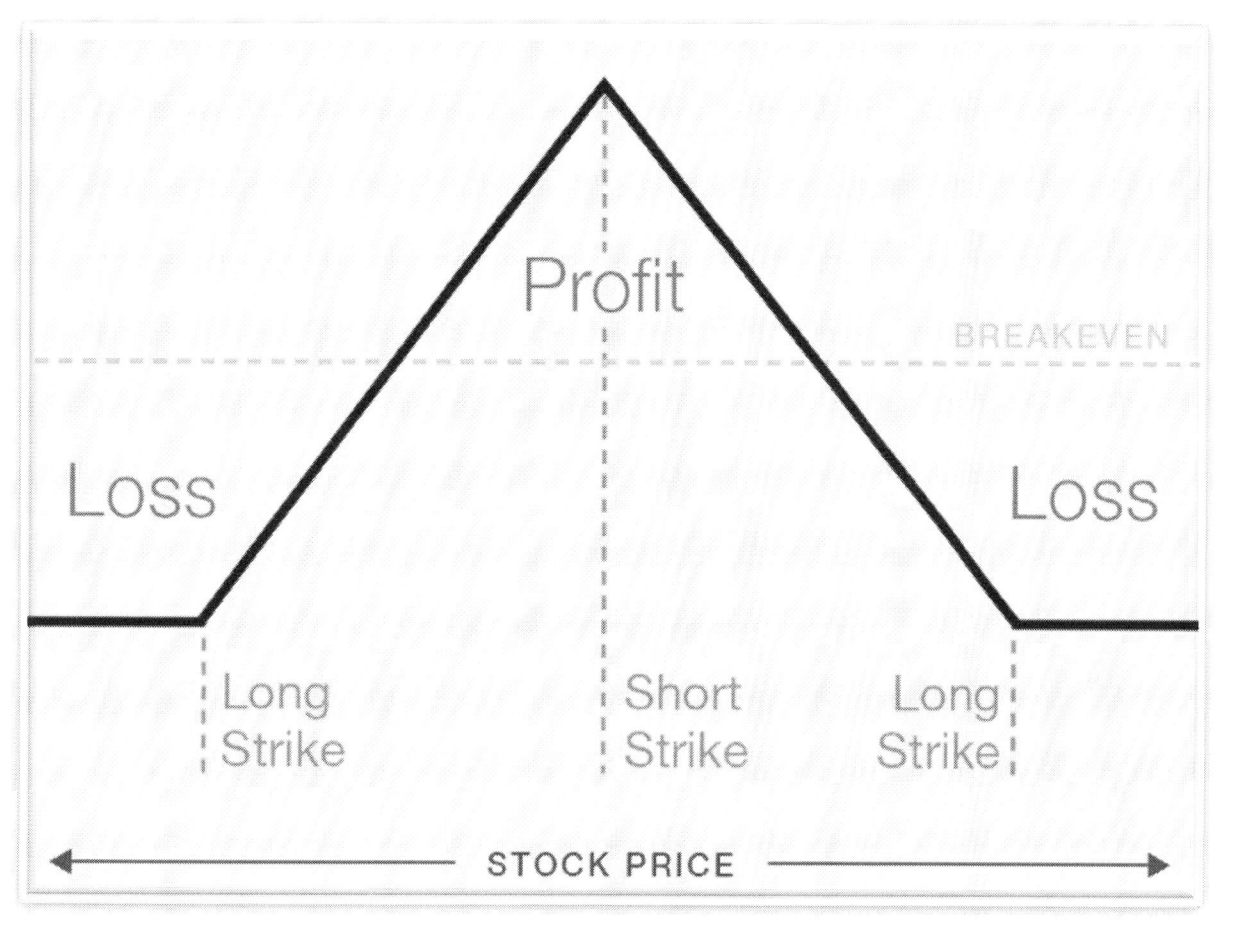

**GRAPH ILUSTRATING A LONG BUTTERFLY SPREAD**

**Long Call Butterfly Spread Example**

Let's say Verizon (VZ) shares are trading at $60. An investor believes it will move slowly in the next few months. The decision has been made to implement a long call butterfly spread to generate profit if the price remains current. The investor has written two call options on Verizon with an exercise price of $60 and purchased two additional ones at $55 and $65.

In this scenario, the investor earns the most profit if Verizon shares are priced at $60 at expiration. If the price of Verizon is below $55 or above $65 at expiration, the investor will incur their maximum loss. This loss is calculated by subtracting the gains from selling the two intermediate strike options from the cost of purchasing the two lateral call options (higher and lower strikes).

If the underlying asset's price is between $55 and $65, you could take a loss or a profit. However, the premium paid to enter the position is critical. It costs $2.50 to enter the location. Based on this, the position would suffer a loss if Verizon's price is below $60 minus $2.50. The statement above holds if the underlying asset is valued at $60 with an additional $2.50 at expiration. In this scenario, the position will be deemed successful if the underlying asset's price falls between $57.50 and $62.50 at expiration.

The present scenario does not include commission costs, which may be incurred when engaging in multiple options trades.

**How do you build a long butterfly extension?**

The long-put butterfly spread involves initiating a position by purchasing an out-of-the-money set option with a lower strike price, simultaneously selling (writing) two at-the-money puts, and finally buying an at-the-money put option with a lower strike price. Like the long-call butterfly strategy, this position exhibits its maximum profit potential when the underlying asset is maintained at the strike price of the intermediate options.

The maximum profit equals the highest exercise price, less the exercise price of the put option sold, less the premium paid. The maximum trade loss is limited to the initial premiums and commissions paid.

**When to use the long butterfly spreads.**

It is recommended to use it when it is predicted that the share price will move very little and close to the central strike on the expiration date. Also, it can be used when a contraction of volatility (IV) is expected. An example is the following: shortly before a company's earnings report (where there is a high IV), a butterfly opens and waits until there is a contraction of the IV (after the report), accompanied by little or no price movement. The long butterfly spread can be used with puts when a sideways or slightly bearish move is expected. If we expect a lateral or slightly bullish movement, we should do the butterfly with contracts on the call side.

**Comparison with other strategies**

The long butterfly spread thrives on the erosion of time value, yet it possesses a capped potential risk in contrast to a short straddle or short strangle. However, the potential earnings from a long butterfly spread are low compared to a short straddle or short strangle, not to mention the commissions are higher as well. If volatility is constant, the long butterfly spread butterfly will not increase in value or show a large gain until it is very close to expiration and the stock price is close to the core strike price. Conversely, short straddles and short strangles show gains soon after the position is opened, as long as the stock price does not break even.

Another difference is that a long butterfly spread is usually recommended to be closed with a low profit percentage. Therefore, to get the same dollar amount that a single short straddle and short strangle can give us, it will be necessary to open several long butterfly positions, which implies a higher cost of commissions.

In summary, the Long Butterfly Spread should be distinct from the Short Butterfly Spread strategy used in different conditions. It should also be separate from the Broken wing butterfly strategy, which is also different.

More than an entry strategy, the butterfly or long butterfly spread manages another previous strategy: the iron condor. This means that when entering the market, you choose IC[Iron Condor] as your initial strategy, and if the price goes up or down to one of your short strikes, then the butterfly is used to get more credit, cut losses, and even exit with profits. The long butterfly spread can help us under certain market conditions, so it is essential to know it and know how to execute it at the right time. It is recommended to do it more with call contracts. It is a neutral strategy with low risk and significant profits if opened in environments of high volatility and little movement in the asset price. If you have a small account, this strategy may favor you due to the low capital required to open the position. You can diversify with other strategies and with other assets.

EXPLORING SHORT BUTTERFLY SPREADS FOR TARGETED SPREADS FOR TARGETED MARKET SCENARIOS.

**What is Short Butterfly Spread?**

The Short Butterfly strategy is a strategy that maintains options neutrality, allowing for potential gains from heightened volatility and significant movements in the underlying asset's price. This strategy, like many other options strategies, will limit your losses and profits and will consider, unlike other simpler strategies, the purchase or sale of 3 different options in which both calls and puts can be used:

- Sell 1 Call that is ITM (In the Money).
- Buy 2 ATM calls (At the Money).
- Sell 1 call OTM (Out of the Money).

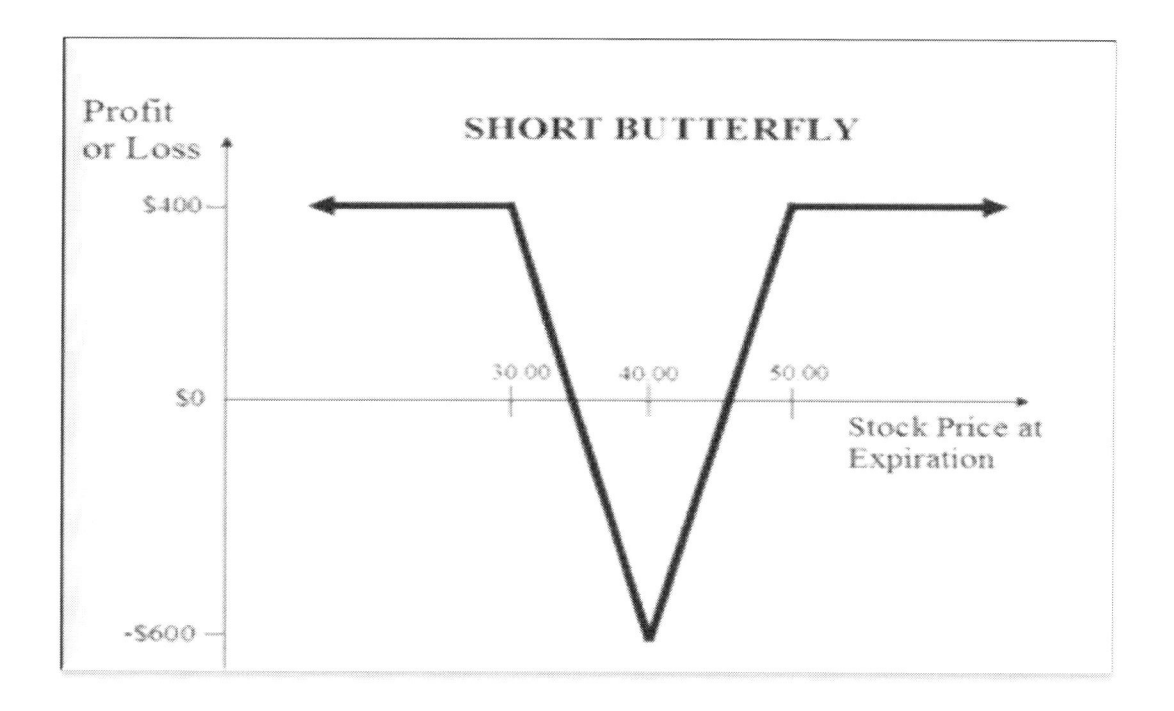

**GRAPH ILLUSTRATING A SHORT BUTTERFLY SPREAD**

In simple language, the Short Butterfly strategy will be used when we believe the underlying price will increase or decrease over time.

We can use its antonym defined by the prefix "Long" if the price will remain stable over time. Therefore, both forms will be built similarly but changing the type of contracts that we acquire or sell. However, both will have the same purpose: limiting both profits and losses and reducing risk due to the negative effect that the passage of time has, for example, on our contracts, if the movements we expected do not occur. So, we will explain the Short Butterfly described above and give some examples.

**How does the Short Butterfly strategy work?**

We will carry out the operation of, using call options, selling one ITM, buying two ATMs, and selling the last OTM, paying a certain amount to enter the position, resulting in:
- Take a profit when the underlying price crosses the major strike's limit.
- Obtaining profits if the underlying price is below the minor strike's price.
- The worst that could happen is that the underlying price would stay equal to the price of the higher strike on the expiration date, in which case we would lose the profits of the two calls due to the losses on the sale of the call made.

Therefore, one of the positive things about this strategy is undoubtedly reducing the maximum loss, which will only occur when the underlying asset remains sideways.
- The maximum profit will be defined by the difference of strikes (sold-bought). It will be calculated by adding the premium of the lower strike call put to the premium of the higher strike call put and subtracting the premium of the two calls bought.
- The maximum loss will be calculated by subtracting from the strike of the call bought the lowest strike of the call sold and subtracting from this the maximum profit to be received.
- The lower threshold will be calculated by adding the maximum profit to the lowest strike of the call sale.
- The upper threshold will be calculated by subtracting the maximum profit from the upper call sale.

## REAL-LIFE EXAMPLES SHOWCASING BUTTERFLY SPREADS' EFFECTIVENESS

**Case Study 1**

Our first tale transports us to the world of tech stocks and the anticipation of quarterly earnings. A savvy trader, Alex, predicts that a renowned tech giant's stock, currently trading at $250, will experience minimal movement post-earnings due to market expectations. Instead of risking directional trades, Alex turns to the butterfly spread.

With a central strike price of $250, Alex purchases a $240 call option, sells two $250 call options, and finally buys a $260 call option. The strategy pays off beautifully as the stock, despite the earnings report, barely budges. The short calls' value erodes due to the limited price movement, while the long calls retain their worth. Alex walks away with a well-earned profit, proving the precision of the butterfly spread in capturing subtle shifts.

**Case Study 2**

Next, we join Sarah, a trader who closely monitors economic events, especially the Federal Reserve's announcements. Aware of the potential market turbulence that could follow, Sarah crafts a butterfly spread around a key stock index ETF trading at $300.

She purchases a $290 put option, sells two $300 put options, and acquires a $310 put option. As the market reacts to the Fed's pronouncements, the ETF displays minimal movement, precisely what Sarah anticipated. The short puts' value erodes due to the calm, while the long puts appreciate slightly. Sarah's strategic maneuver navigates her portfolio through the storm, showcasing the butterfly spread's resilience against volatile gales.

**Case Study 3**

Meet Chris, an astute trader with an eye for stocks known for oscillating within specific ranges. Observing a pharmaceutical company trading around $150, Chris crafts a butterfly spread with a $150 central strike price.

He buys a $140 call option, sells two $150 call options, and acquires a $160 call option. The stock remains true to its range-bound behavior, barely straying from $150. Chris's well-timed strategy results in the short calls losing value due to the stock's confined movement while the long calls preserve their worth. His patience and precision reap the rewards, proving the butterfly spread's potency in range-bound scenarios.

These real-life stories testify to the butterfly spread's elegance in options trading. Like an artist who carefully blends colors on a canvas to create a masterpiece, traders employ butterfly spreads to craft strategic triumphs within precise parameters. Through careful strike price selection and impeccable timing, these traders harness the strategy's potential for profit in scenarios where many others would falter.

As traders continue their journey through the dynamic landscape of options, the butterfly spread is a remarkable tool that navigates the intricate balance between risk and reward. Each case study illuminates a distinct facet of its effectiveness, inspiring readers to embrace the artistry of options trading and employ butterfly spreads to their advantage. If this book has helped you in any way so far feel free to leave a short review for this book.

## CHAPTER 2
## CALENDAR SPREADS: TIME AS YOUR TRADING ALLY

In the fast-paced realm of options trading, where market trends shift like winds on the open sea, the calendar spread is a masterful strategy that harnesses the ebb and flow of time. Imagine orchestrating a trade where the passage of time becomes your ally, a reliable force that works in your favor. Welcome to the realm of calendar spreads, a dynamic trading approach that can offer traders an elegant way to navigate the complex currents of the financial markets.

**Understanding a Calendar Spread**

At its core, a calendar spread is a multi-dimensional strategy that involves simultaneously buying and selling options contracts with the same strike price but different expiration dates. The magic happens when the trader capitalizes on the difference in time decay (theta) between these two options. While both options are affected by theta, the near-term option loses its value faster than the longer-term one, presenting an opportunity for astute traders.

Think of it as a symphony of time. Like a fleeting melody, the near-term option fades away faster, while the longer-term option, akin to a resonant chord, sustains its value. Traders proficient in this strategy learn to play these temporal variations to compose a harmonious tune of profit.

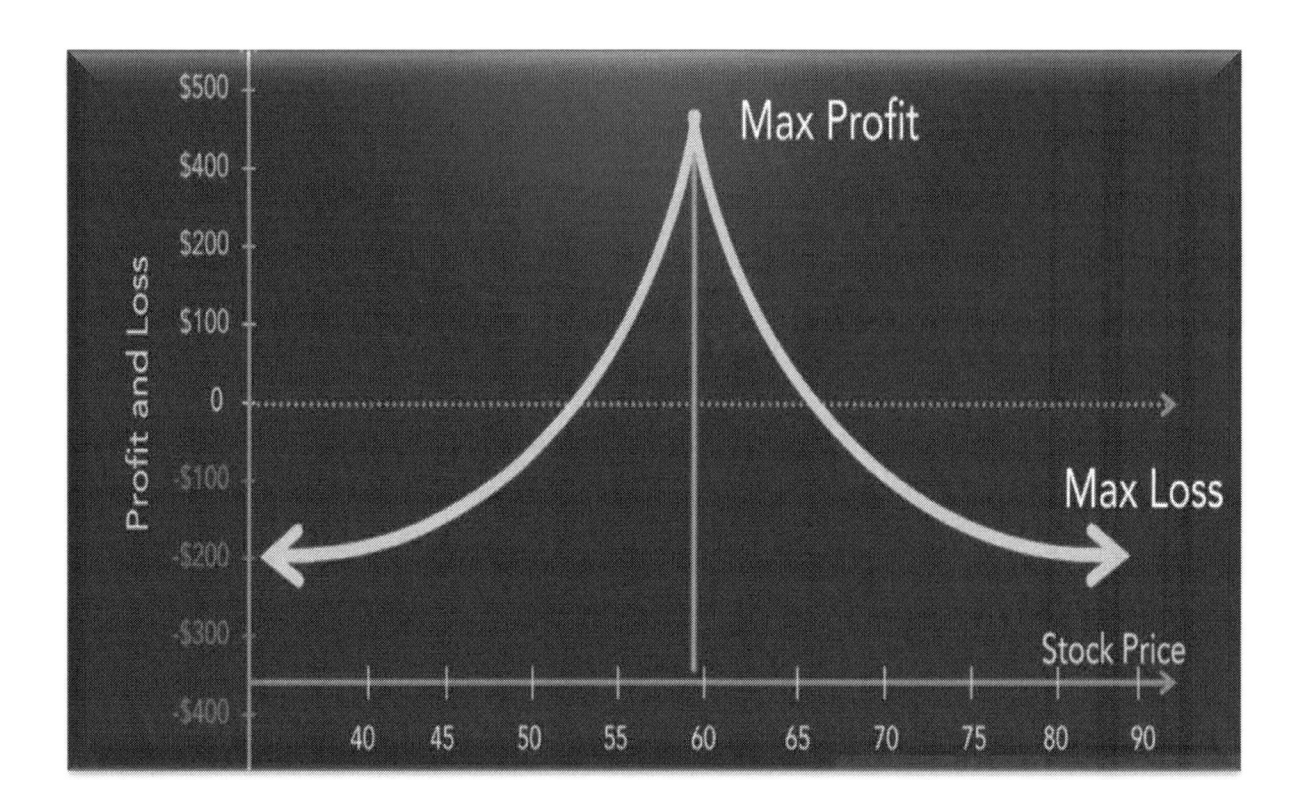

**GRAPH ILLUSTRATING A CALENDAR SPREAD**

**Risk, Reward, and the Art of Balance**

One of the most captivating aspects of the calendar spread is its inherent balance between risk and reward. It's akin to tightrope walking with a safety net below – a delicate dance that requires precision and understanding. The maximum potential loss in a calendar spread is the initial debit paid to establish the position. This capped risk sets it apart from riskier strategies that can result in unlimited losses.

On the flip side, the potential for profit arises from the differing time decay rates of the options. If the trader's muted short-term price movement prediction comes to fruition, the spread could potentially yield substantial gains. It's the art of exploiting the nuances of time and volatility to craft a well-balanced, dynamic trade.

**Real-Life Mastery: The Symphony of Experience**

As traders delve into the world of calendar spreads, they navigate not just market fluctuations but also their understanding of market behavior, volatility shifts, and real-time scenarios. Real-life experience is the compass that guides them toward mastery. Learning how various market conditions impact the effectiveness of a calendar spread is akin to fine-tuning the notes of a symphony for maximum resonance.

Calendar spreads are not just about trading; they are about honing the craft of capturing value from the progression of time itself. This strategy beckons traders to dive deep into the intricacies of market dynamics, seize opportunities where others might overlook them, and experience the thrill of crafting a trade that resonates with the rhythms of the financial world.


LEVERAGING LONG CALENDAR SPREADS FOR TIME-BASED TRADES.

In the bustling world of options trading, where opportunities and risks surge like waves, the long calendar spread emerges as a captivating strategy that harnesses the power of time to sculpt potential profits. Imagine embarking on a trade where time becomes your partner, an ally that can amplify your gains and temper your risks. Welcome to the world of long calendar spreads, a strategic approach allowing traders to navigate time currents to their advantage.

At its essence, a long calendar spread involves purchasing a longer-term option while simultaneously selling a shorter-term option with the same strike price. The crux of this strategy rests on the concept of time decay, where the shorter-term option loses its value faster than the longer-term one. The trader capitalizes on this temporal discrepancy by seeking to benefit from the erosion of the short-term option's value while retaining the longer-term option for potential price movement.

**Picture this:** You anticipate that a particular stock will experience limited price movement soon, but you expect more substantial fluctuations in the coming months. To execute a long calendar spread strategy, an option trader would initiate a position by acquiring a call option with a later expiration date and simultaneously selling a call option with a nearer expiration date, both at the same strike price.

Long calendar spreads are a delicate balance between risk and reward, akin to traversing a tightrope while juggling. The beauty of this strategy lies in its limited risk potential. The potential downside is capped at the net debit incurred when initiating the spread, equal to the disparity between the premiums paid and received for the respective options.

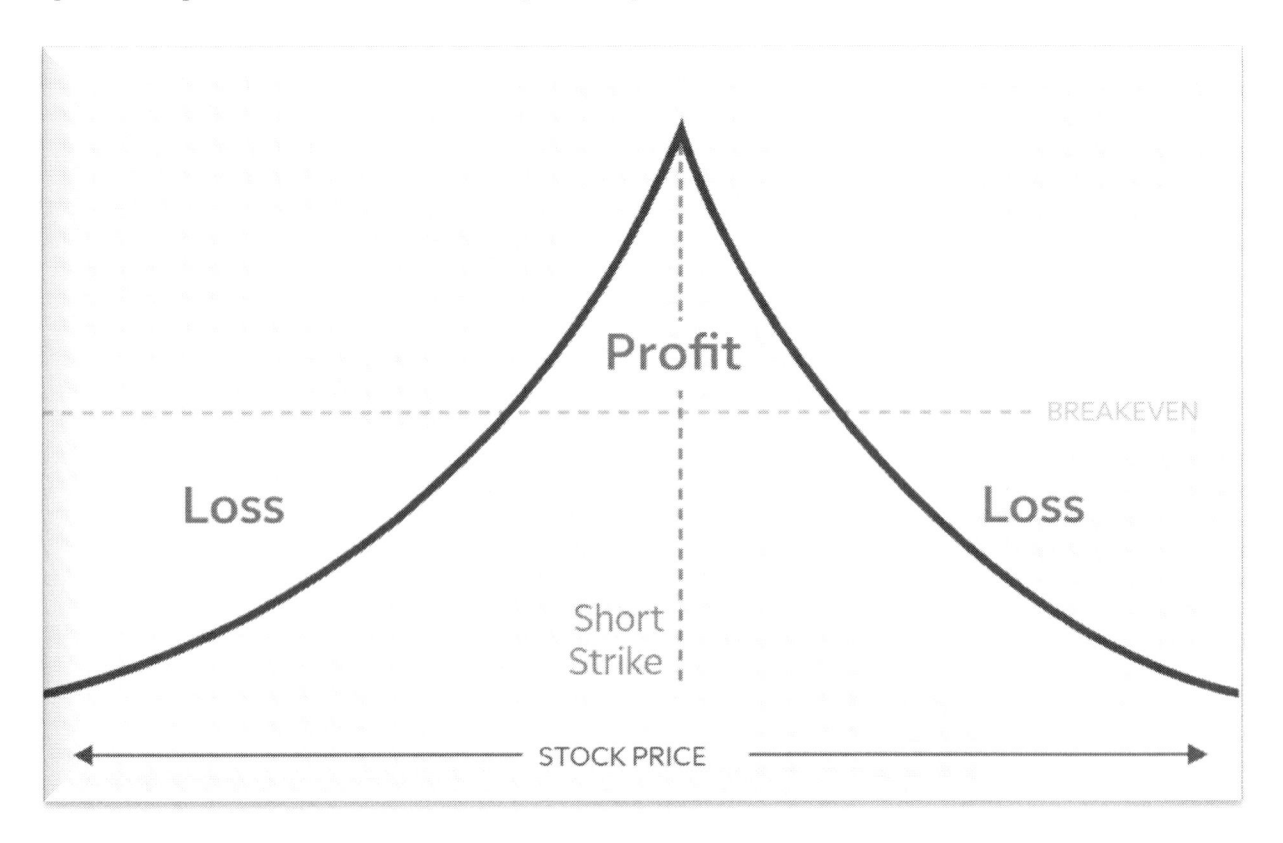

**GRAPH ILLUSTRATING A LONG CALENDAR SPREAD**

On the other side of the coin is the potential for reward, which is multifaceted. If the stock's price remains relatively stable and the shorter-term option experiences rapid time decay, you could profit from the difference in its value. Additionally, if the stock's price eventually moves in the desired direction, the longer-term option you hold could be appreciated. It's a symphony of possibilities orchestrated by the passage of time and the ever-changing tides of the market.

**Mastery Through Experience: Navigating the Rapids**

Long calendar spreads are not just trades; they are journeys. Each trade becomes an expedition into the intricate landscape of time and market dynamics. Every experience, whether a triumph or a lesson, contributes to your navigation skills. Just as a skilled sailor learns to read the wind and waves, you, as a trader, learn to decipher the currents of time and volatility.

With each executed long calendar spread, you gain insights that shape your approach to subsequent trades. You become adept at setting up spreads that capitalize on the right timing, managing positions through market fluctuations, and ultimately reaping the rewards of your strategic decisions.

## UTILIZING SHORT CALENDAR SPREADS FOR VOLATILE MARKET CONDITIONS

A short calendar spread, or a time spread or horizontal spread, involves selling a shorter-term option while simultaneously buying a longer-term option with the same strike price. This strategy thrives in heightened volatility, where short-term options experience faster time decay than their longer-term counterparts.

Imagine a scenario where a company is about to announce its quarterly earnings, a classic catalyst for market turbulence. Anticipating increased volatility, you decide to employ a short calendar spread. You sell a call option with a nearer expiration date and simultaneously purchase a call option with a later expiration date, both at the same strike price.

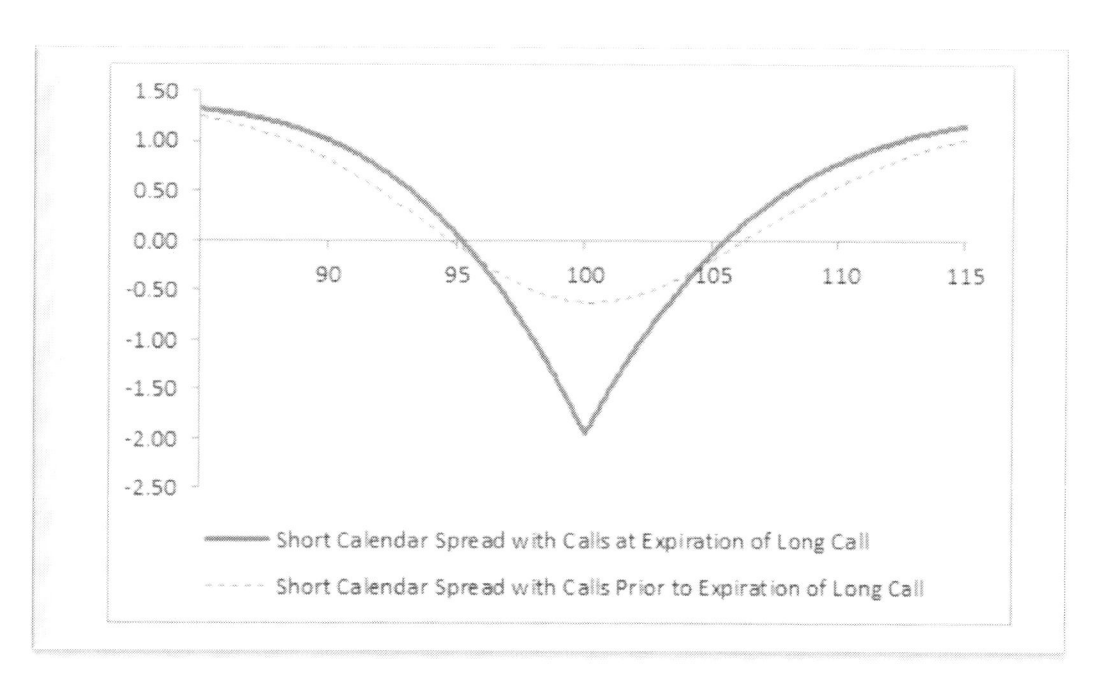

**GRAPH ILLUSTRATING A LONG CALENDAR SPREAD**

### Capitalizing on Time Decay and Volatility

The magic of short calendar spreads lies in capitalizing on two key factors: time decay and volatility. As the short-term option loses value more rapidly due to time decay, you stand to profit from the differential between the premiums received and paid. Additionally, in a volatile market, fluctuating prices can amplify the potential gains of the strategy.

Think of it as maneuvering through a turbulent sea. The choppy waves represent market volatility, and your strategic sail-trimming allows you to ride those waves for potential profit. However, just as a sailor needs to watch the changing wind, a trader employing short calendar spreads must monitor the market closely, adjusting their position if conditions change.

As with any trading strategy, short calendar spreads come with their risk profile. The maximum potential loss is the initial cost of establishing the spread, which occurs if the market makes a solid and sustained move in the direction opposite to your position. However, the rewards can be substantial, especially during pronounced volatility.

Consider a pharmaceutical company awaiting regulatory approval for a new drug. The uncertainty surrounding this event can lead to increased price swings. You could benefit from these price fluctuations by strategically utilizing a short calendar spread.

In this way, short calendar spreads become more than a trading strategy; they become a way to embrace market turbulence with confidence and finesse. So, set your sails, chart your course, and navigate the high seas of volatility with short calendar spreads as your trusted ally.

APPLYING CALENDAR SPREADS EFFECTIVELY IN DIFFERENT MARKET SCENARIOS

A calendar spread, also called a time spread, entails the simultaneous purchase and sale of options of an identical type (calls or puts) at a very strike price, albeit with varying expiration dates. Its adaptability makes it a valuable asset in the toolkit of any trader looking to navigate diverse market conditions.

**Scenario 1: Sideways Markets**

Imagine a market that seems meandering along, needing a clear trend. In such situations, a calendar spread can be a powerful choice. By selecting strike prices near the current stock price, traders can benefit from the passage of time as both the near-term and longer-term options experience decay, potentially resulting in profits even without a significant price movement.

**Scenario 2: Volatile Markets**

When market volatility rises, traders may hesitate to commit to directional trades. This is where the calendar spread truly shines. By selling the near-term option and buying the longer-term one, traders can leverage increased time decay in the near-term option while maintaining exposure to potential price movements through the longer-term option. This strategy capitalizes on the market's inherent unpredictability.

**Scenario 3: Bull or Bear Bias**

Market sentiment isn't always evenly split between bullish and bearish. Traders often lean towards a particular direction. Here's where the calendar spread proves its worth. If you have a bullish outlook, establish a calendar spread with calls by selling a near-term option and buying a longer-term one. Conversely, the same can be done using put options for a bearish stance. This strategy allows you to tailor your trade to your market sentiment.

The practical application of calendar spreads across diverse market scenarios is a journey of adaptation. Just as a traveler immerses themselves in different cultures, a trader must immerse themselves in the nuances of the market. The ability to recognize when to employ this strategy, whether in sideways markets, volatile times, earnings seasons, or with a specific directional bias, is akin to the art of discerning the right path in unfamiliar terrain.

# CHAPTER 3
## TRADING VOLATILITY WITH STRADDLES AND STRANGLES

Volatility is one of the statistics commonly used to measure investment risk and constitutes an asset in which you can invest. One of the methods used for this, the most used without a doubt, is to do it through options and, more specifically, with two strategies, although in reality, it is the same one that has two versions: Straddle (Cone) and Strangle (Cradle). It is very simple; it consists of the simultaneous purchase or sale of a Call and a Put. If they use options with the same exercise price and expiration, it is called a Straddle or Cone, and if it is done at different exercise prices, it is called a Strangle or Cradle.

- Straddles and strangles are standard options that involve buying (selling) a call and a pot of the same support and expiration.
- Long loads and crashes benefit from large and volatile price fluctuations, either up or down.
- A short straddle or strangle is profitable when the base price faces low volatility and does not move much after expiration.

In a Straddle Buy, being bought with options, the passage of time and the decrease in volatility affect you negatively, while you benefit from increases in implied volatility. We must distinguish the two types of volatility that affect these strategies: - Implicit volatility, which is the volatility with which the option is valued, that is, the one that is expected, on the day it is appreciated, that the underlying asset will perform. Throughout the time remaining to maturity, or what is the same, the estimate of future volatility. - Volatility that the underlying asset performs, that is, how much or little the underlying asset moves until the expiration date.

**Embracing the Volatility Storm**

Volatility – a term that ignites both excitement and trepidation among traders. It's the force that sends prices on a rollercoaster ride, creating profit potential but also carrying risks. Enter the straddle strategy, a dynamic duo of call and put options purchased at the same strike price and expiration date. This two-pronged approach captures gains from significant price movements, regardless of direction.

Imagine a pharmaceutical company about to unveil a groundbreaking drug. Traders around the world anticipate a seismic price shift. Sarah, a seasoned trader, decides to deploy a straddle. She purchases a call option to profit from a potential surge and a put option to gain from a plunge. When the company's announcement triggers a surge, Sarah reaps the rewards of her strategic move. Her journey mirrors the essence of the straddle strategy – harnessing the power of volatility to secure profit, no matter the outcome.

Remember, trading volatility isn't a solitary endeavor; it's an invitation to embrace the thrill of uncertainty. As traders set sail into the world of straddles and strangles, let them be guided by the wisdom of experienced captains who understand that success requires both knowledge and intuition. Whether it's a storm or a whisper in the market, may they find their course and discover the hidden treasures within the waves of volatility.

## MASTERING LONG STRADDLE STRATEGY FOR CAPTURING

In options trading, capturing volatility is a skill that can elevate your strategies to new heights. At the heart of this skill lies the long straddle strategy – a powerful tool that allows traders to ride the storm, harnessing price fluctuations to their advantage. So, let's unfurl the sails of knowledge and delve into the art of mastering the long straddle strategy as we navigate the captivating world of volatility.

**What is the Straddle Strategy?**

The straddle strategy is recognized as a market-neutral approach. This implies that they allow you to generate profits irrespective of the direction in which the price of the underlying asset moves. To execute this strategy, you simultaneously purchase a put option and a call option on the identical underlying asset, featuring an equivalent expiration date and strike price. This must be close to the underlying price ("at the money").

**When Is It More Appropriate to Use A Straddle?**

As you have just seen, for executing a straddle to be profitable, it is necessary that there is or will be a moment of significant volatility in the market and that you choose an asset that is prone to move widely. This can happen when:

- A company presents its quarterly or annual results
- News related to interest rates, unemployment, or monetary policy adjustments is published
- The value of an asset approaches a relevant support or resistance

Example: Putting a Straddle into Practice

The stock price of a software company is approaching resistance at $85.00. Historically, it is a point where there have been several rejections, and the price fell sharply after touching it. However, the current economic situation has been causing solid increases in this value and its entire sector. Some indications point to a possible support smash.

Not being clear about what will happen in this context, you choose to buy a put and a call option, both for ten days from now, with USD 85.00 as the strike price. You pay a total of $5.6 (per share) for the premiums of both.

If the price breaks the resistance and goes higher, you will take a profit by executing the call option. If the opposite happens, your profits will come from the put option. In both cases, the price needs to move more than $5.6 one way or the other to cover the premium expense.

**The Long Straddle**

One such option strategy is the long straddle. A long-term investor buys a call option and puts the option at the same value and strike price. A subsequent move-up allows you to exercise the call option and buy the security at the strike price, now at a deep discount. The investor can sell the security at its highest market value for an instant profit.

If the security falls in price, the investor exercises the put option. This allows you to sell the security at a higher price than the amount currently trading. The investor makes good profits from a significant movement in the security's price, either up or down. Whichever option doesn't execute expires; the investor loses nothing more than the small premium he paid.

**Long straddle**

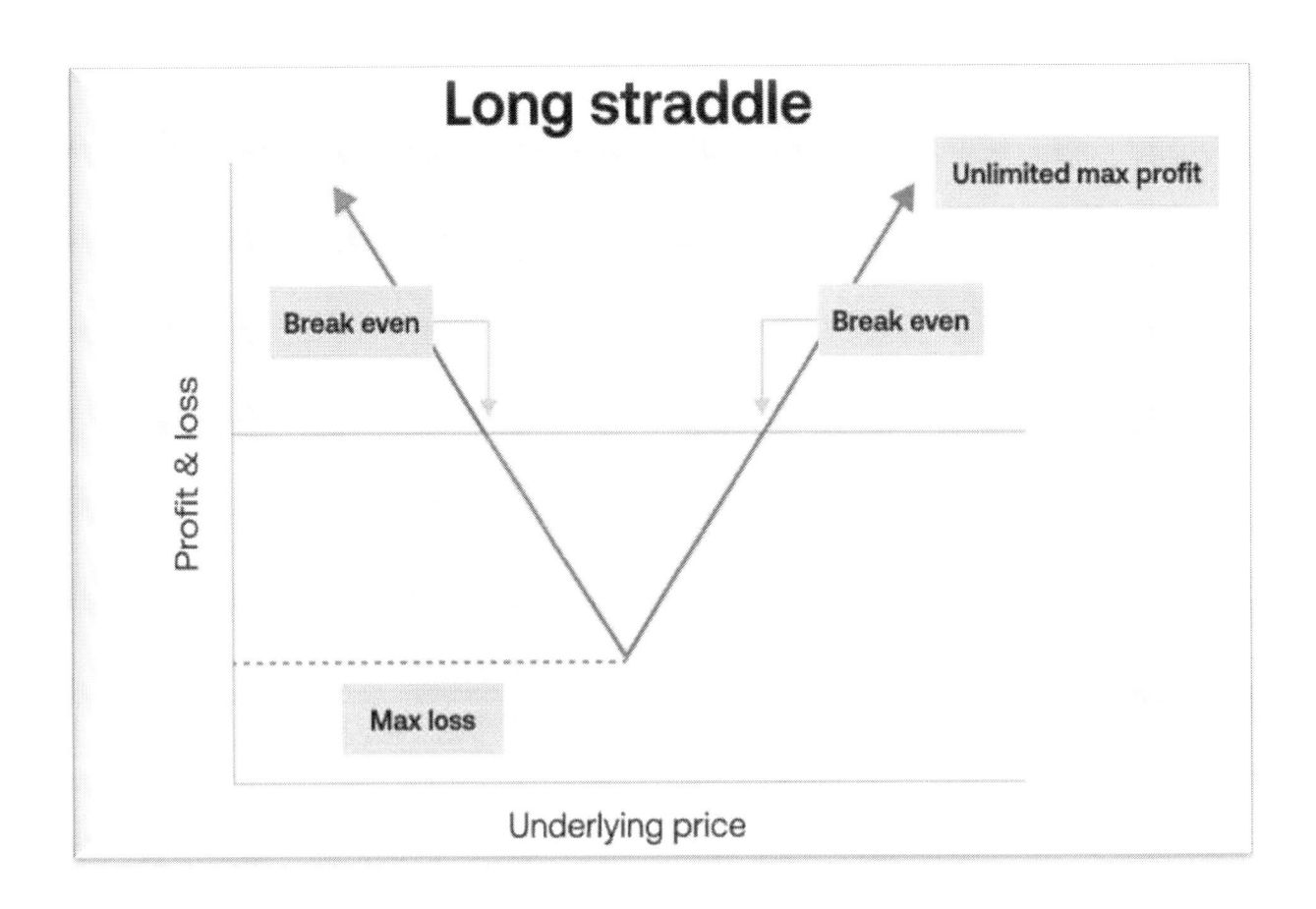

*(Profit & loss vs Underlying price: Break even points on either side of Max loss, Unlimited max profit on both ends)*

**GRAPH ILLUSTRATING A SHORT STRADDLE**

**The Essence of the Long Straddle**

Picture this: a calm sea suddenly whipped into a frenzy by the winds of uncertainty. Such is the essence of market volatility – an unpredictable force that can make or break trades. Enter the long straddle strategy, a time-tested technique that arms traders with the means to profit regardless of whether prices surge skyward or plummet to the depths.

Imagine you're Trader Ava, and you sense that Company XYZ is about to unleash a game-changing announcement. The question is: Will it send the stock soaring or spiraling? Here's where the long straddle strategy comes into play. Ava purchases both a call option and a put option at the same strike price, allowing her to profit from significant price movements in either direction. As the announcement hits, volatility surges, inflating the premiums of both options. Ava reaps the benefits, having secured the potential for gain no matter the outcome. This real-life tale exemplifies the long straddle's power to transform market uncertainty into profit potential.

Ultimately, the long straddle strategy isn't just about capturing price movements; it's about capturing the essence of trading – the thrill, the uncertainty, and the profit potential. As traders embark on their journeys with the long straddle strategy, may they find success and the wisdom to ride the whirlwind with grace and mastery.

## UNDERSTANDING SHORT STRADDLE AND STRANGLE FOR RANGE-BOUND MARKET STRATEGIES

As we set sail on our journey of advanced strategies and volatility, the winds of opportunity often blow in unexpected directions. In the heart of the trading world, where markets can meander without a clear sense of direction, the short straddle and short strangle strategies emerge as steadfast companions. These strategies are the compass and sextant for traders seeking to harness the power of range-bound markets, where price fluctuations create waves that can be skillfully navigated. So, let's embark on an expedition to decode the art of leveraging short straddles and strangles in the quest for profit as we uncover the hidden treasures that await within the realm of range-bound markets.

**What is a Strangle?**

The strangle is very similar to the straddle, which also seeks to obtain profitability in highly volatile market contexts where you do not know if the price will go up or down. The price must also make a wide move for it to be profitable. As is done with the straddle, in the strangle, simultaneous positions are opened in put and call options on the same underlying asset for the same expiration date. However, in the strangle, the strike prices of both are different.

**The Short Straddle Approach**

Imagine the stock market as a tranquil harbor, where price movements gently ebb and flow within a well-defined range. This is the ideal backdrop for the short straddle strategy, where traders aim to capitalize on limited price oscillations. In this narrative, let's dive into a real-life scenario to illuminate the strategy's essence.

Meet Trader Alex, who recognizes that Stock XYZ has entered a period of stability. Alex employs the short straddle strategy, executing a simultaneous sale of a call option and a put option with an identical strike price. As the stock's price remains tethered within a narrow corridor, the call option and put option premiums decay, allowing Alex to pocket the maximum profit. This strategy is akin to casting a net in calm waters, capturing the theta decay as the days pass. The real-life takeaway is that short straddles can transform range-bound markets into profitable playgrounds, reminding us that opportunities abound even in tranquility.

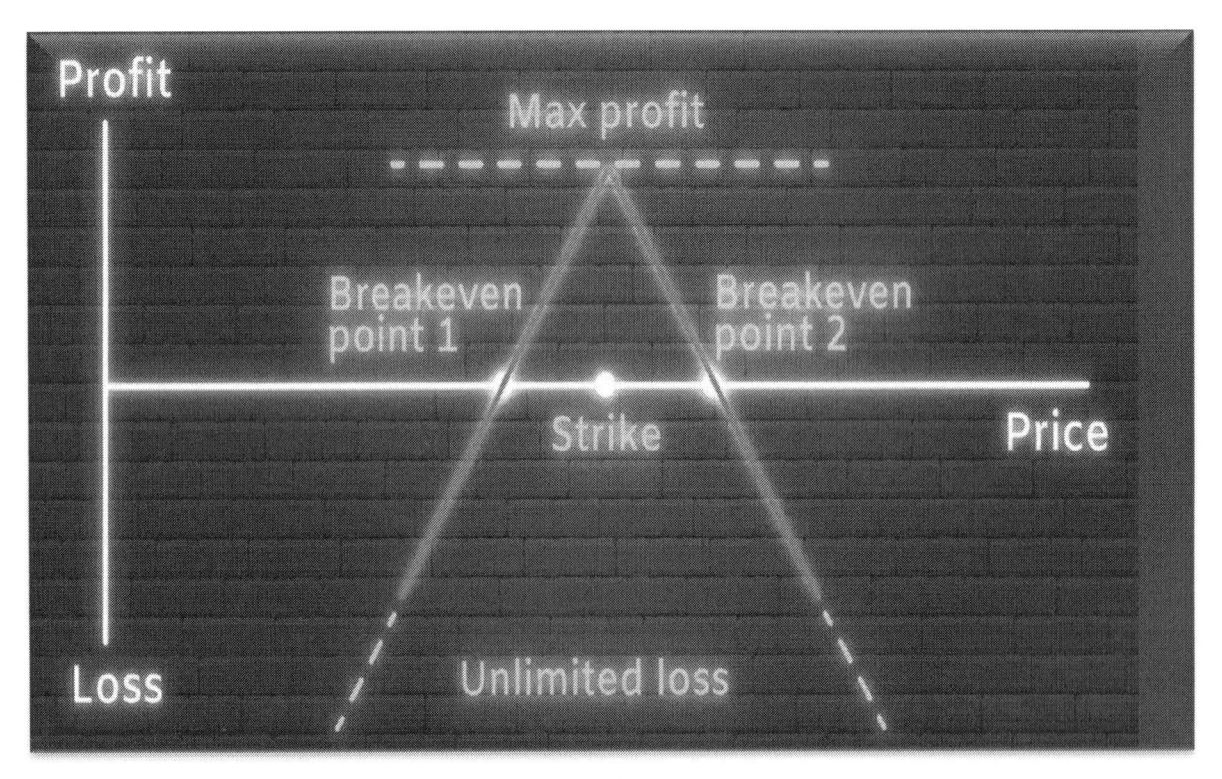

**GRAPH ILLUSTRATING A SHORT STRADDLE**

**The Short Strangle Approach**

Now, shift your gaze to a market that's anything but docile, where price fluctuations paint a dynamic canvas. This is the realm where the short-strangle strategy unfurls its sails. A short strangle involves selling an out-of-the-money call option and an out-of-the-money put option simultaneously. Traders leverage this strategy when they foresee a period of high volatility but expect prices to remain confined within a specific range.

Imagine the energy sector, where Company Energy Wise is on the brink of unveiling a groundbreaking announcement. Traders sense an impending storm, and the short strangle strategy becomes their beacon. As Energy Wise's stock price surges and dips, the call-and-put options' premiums inflate due to heightened volatility. Our traders capitalize on this price dance, capturing premium on both ends of the spectrum. This real-life tale underscores that even in turbulent waters, the short strangle strategy offers a path to profit, affirming that the range-bound market isn't just a challenge but an opportunity.

**The Spectrum of Experience: Navigating the Range**

As we conclude our journey through the realm of short straddles and strangles, the depth of their versatility and potential becomes clear. These strategies aren't confined to algorithms; they're brought to life by the stories of traders who venture into the ever-shifting seas of the financial markets. It's a reminder that in trading, as in life, adaptability is vital. As traders weave these strategies into their repertoire, they can weather the unpredictability of the markets, finding profit even in the absence of clear trends.

The short straddle and short strangle strategies are more than just lines on a chart; they're the tools that empower traders to read the currents of range-bound markets and transform the ebb and flow of price fluctuations into a symphony of profit. So, as readers explore this chapter, let them immerse themselves in the experiences of those who've ventured into the range, capturing the essence of these strategies that transform market challenges into opportunities for growth.

The straddle and strangle are advanced strategies used when trading options. They allow you to profit when you think the market may move sharply, but you can't tell which way. For example, when high-impact news is published, or companies present their income statements.

In both cases, put and call options are purchased simultaneously for the same asset and expiration date. In the case of the straddle, they are at the same strike price, and in the strangle, they have different prices.


## REAL-LIFE USE CASES OF VOLATILITY TRADING WITH STRADDLES AND STRANGLES

In the stormy sea of financial markets, where waves of uncertainty can either capsize portfolios or propel them to newfound heights, strategies that harness volatility become the compass by which traders steer their ships. Among these strategies, the trusty straddles and strangles stand as beacons, guiding traders through tumultuous waters to the shores of profit. Let's embark on a voyage through real-life tales of volatility trading, where straddles and strangles emerge as heroes, shaping destinies and redefining success.

**Daring to Embrace the Unpredictable: The Earnings Announcement**

Picture yourself on the precipice of a corporate earnings announcement – a moment that can send ripples through financial markets. As a trader, you're at a crossroads, faced with the daunting task of predicting market reactions to this pivotal event. This is where the straddle strategy takes center stage, and real-life stories come alive.

In the realm of technology giants, Company XYZ is preparing to unveil its quarterly earnings report. Traders sense the looming storm and turn to the straddle strategy. By strategically acquiring both a call option and a put option at an identical strike price and expiration date, one can capitalize on favorable market movements, be it a substantial surge or a significant decline in the underlying stock. When the earnings report hits, and the stock's price swing is as wild as the wind, the straddle strategy reveals its power. Traders celebrate their ability to capture profits from the volatility, showcasing the strategy's uncanny ability to navigate uncertainty.

**Embracing Opportunity Amidst Turbulence: The Market Shaker**
Let's switch our lens to a broader landscape – a geopolitical event that sends shockwaves across global markets. This is where the strangle strategy makes its grand entrance. In the face of market-shaking news, predicting the precise direction of price movement becomes a Herculean task. The strangle strategy, characterized by purchasing a higher strike price call option and a lower strike price put option, is ideally suited for capitalizing on moderate price fluctuations.

Imagine Company ABC, a biotech player on the cusp of unveiling groundbreaking news. Aware of potential price ripples, traders employ the strangle strategy to capture profit from moderate price movements. When the information arrives, and the stock registers a controlled surge, the call option dances to its rhythm. Yet, even when a minor hiccup casts a brief shadow, the put option stands firm, showcasing the strategy's adaptability and ability to thrive amidst market whispers.

As we journey through the real-life narratives of straddles and strangles, their effectiveness comes to life. These strategies aren't mere lines of code on a trading platform; they're the tools traders wield to revolutionize risk and seize opportunity. But remember, the art of volatility trading is full of challenges. Mastering these strategies demands skill, experience, and a keen understanding of market dynamics.

As you chart your course through the pages of volatility trading, straddles, and strangles become your loyal companions – the wind in your sails, the stars in your night sky. They're the strategies that empower you to embrace uncertainty, leverage it to your advantage, and confidently navigate the tides of financial markets.

# GLOSSARY

**Butterfly spread:** Butterfly spread refers to an options strategy that combines bull and bear spreads with a fixed risk and capped profit. These spreads are intended as a market-neutral strategy and pay off the most if the underlying asset does not move prior to option expiration.

**ATM:** At the money (ATM) is a situation where an option's strike price is identical to the current market price of the underlying security. An ATM option has a delta of ±0.50, positive if it is a call, negative for a put.

**ITM:** A call option is in the money (ITM) if the market price is above the strike price. A put option is in the money if the market price is below the strike price. An option can also be out of the money (OTM) or at the money (ATM). In-the-money options contracts have higher premiums than other options that are not ITM.

**OTM**: Out of the money" (OTM) is an expression used to describe an option contract that only contains extrinsic value. These options will have a delta of less than 0.50. An OTM call option will have a strike price that is higher than the market price of the underlying asset.

**Calendar spread:** A calendar spread is an options or futures strategy established by simultaneously entering a long and short position on the same underlying asset but with different delivery dates. In a typical calendar spread, one would buy a longer-term contract and go short a nearer-term option with the same strike price.

**Strangle:** A strangle is an options strategy in which the investor holds a position in both a call and a put option with different strike prices, but with the same expiration date and underlying asset.

**Straddle:** A straddle involves buying (or selling) both a call and a put with the same strike price and expiration on the same underlying asset.

# REFERENCES

"Butterfly Spread: What It Is, with Types Explained & Example." *Investopedia*, 10 June 2022, www.investopedia.com/terms/b/butterflyspread.asp#:~:text=The%20term%20butterfly%20spread%20refers.

Kaeppel, Jay. "Advanced Option Trading: The Modified Butterfly Spread." *Investopedia*, 17 Jan. 2022, www.investopedia.com/articles/optioninvestor/10/modified-butterfly-spread.asp.

Kohler, Jeff. "Using Calendar Trading and Spread Option Strategies." *Investopedia*, 21 Aug. 2021, www.investopedia.com/articles/optioninvestor/08/calendar-spread-options-strategy.asp#:~:text=calendar%20put%20spread.-.

Rebellion, Market. "Straddles & Strangles: Option Strategies Designed to Thrive in Volatility." *TheStreet*, 14 June 2022, www.thestreet.com/investing/options/straddles-strangles-option-strategies-designed-to-thrive-in-volatility.

"Simple Strategy 2: Straddle and Strangle." *IG*, www.ig.com/en/ig-academy/how-cfd-options-work/simple-strategy-2-straddle-and-strangle.

"Straddles and Strangles: What's the Difference?" *Investopedia*, 18 June 2021, www.investopedia.com/ask/answers/05/052805.asp.

Tape, Ticker. "Calendar Spreads: Learn the Roll Decision, Strategy and Risks - Ticker Tape." *The Ticker Tape*, 14 Feb. 2023, tickertape.tdameritrade.com/trading/options-calendar-spread-trading-16172.

"What Is Butterfly Spread Option? Definition of Butterfly Spread Option, Butterfly Spread Option Meaning." *The Economic Times*, 14 Aug. 2023, economictimes.indiatimes.com/definition/butterfly-spread-option.

# BOOK 6

## "OPTIONS PROBABILITY: MASTERING RISK MANAGEMENT AND TRADE ADJUSTMENT"

# TABLE OF CONTENTS

CHAPTER 1 ........................................................................................................................ 3
THE ART OF RISK MANAGEMENT: SAFEGUARDING YOUR TRADING QUEST ........................ 3
    UNDERSTANDING AND IMPLEMENTING RISK MANAGEMENT PRINCIPLES IN OPTIONS TRADING........ 7
    SETTING STOP-LOSS LEVELS, MANAGING POSITION SIZES, AND DIVERSIFYING ................... 9
    UTILIZING PROTECTIVE STRATEGIES TO MITIGATE POTENTIAL LOSSES .......................... 10
CHAPTER 2 ...................................................................................................................... 14
TRADE ADJUSTMENTS TECHNIQUES: NAVIGATING MARKET SHIFTING WINDS ................ 14
    MAKING ADJUSTMENTS TO OPTIONS POSITIONS BASED ON MARKET CHANGES ............ 16
    ENHANCING WINNING TRADES AND MITIGATING LOSSES WITH STRATEGIC MOVES ....... 17
    REAL-LIFE EXAMPLES OF TRADE ADJUSTMENTS IN VARIOUS MARKET CONDITIONS ........ 18
GLOSSARY ....................................................................................................................... 21
REFERENCES .................................................................................................................... 22

## CHAPTER 1
## THE ART OF RISK MANAGEMENT: SAFEGUARDING YOUR TRADING QUEST

Risk management is one of the most important, if not the most important, issues regarding trading. On the one hand, traders want to minimize potential losses, but on the other hand, traders also want to get as much potential gain as possible from each trade. One of the factors contributing to financial losses among traders is not solely attributed to their lack of experience or market knowledge but rather stems from inadequate risk management practices. Effective risk management is a fundamental requirement for achieving success in the field of trading.

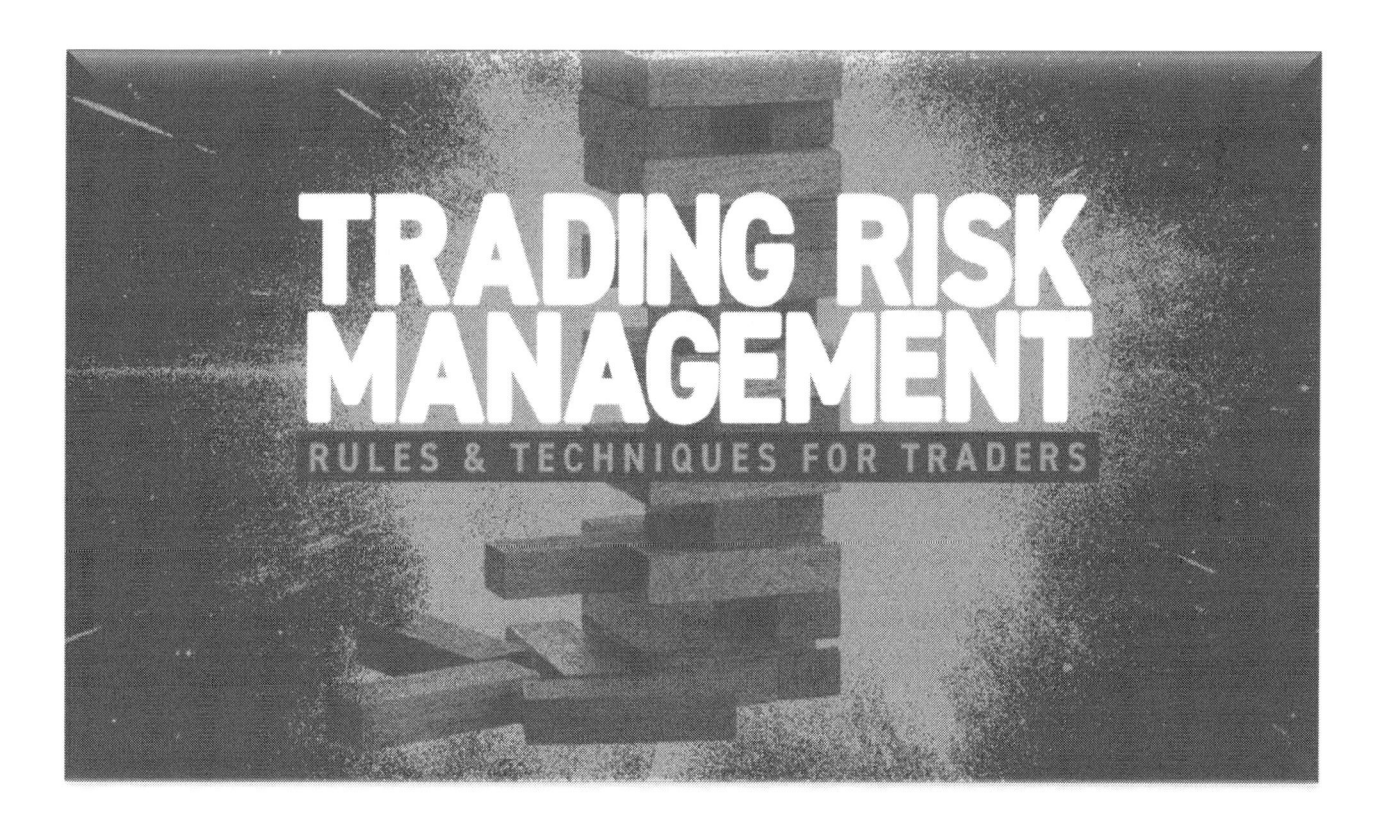

When it comes to trading any instrument, the fundamentals of risk management are highly similar and remain the same regardless of whether you are interested in options trading, futures trading, commodity trading, or stock trading.

These risks can include:
- **Market Risk:** The most prevalent type of risk in trading is known as market risk, which refers to the possibility that the market will behave in a manner that contradicts your

expectations. For instance, if you believe that the value of the US Dollar will increase in comparison to the Euro and, as a result, opt to buy the currency pair EURUSD only to see it go down, you will incur a financial loss.

- **Leverage Risk:** Leverage puts traders at risk because it allows them to open transactions with considerably larger sums of money than they have available in their trading accounts. This could lead to a loss that is greater than the amount of money that was initially deposited into the account in some circumstances.

- **Interest Rate Risk:** An economy's interest rate may affect the value of that economy's currency, meaning traders may be exposed to the risk of unexpected changes in interest rates.

- **Liquidity Risk:** Some forms of currency and financial instruments have a higher degree of liquidity than others. When a currency pair has high liquidity, this indicates a healthy balance of supply and demand for it, and as a result, trades may be carried out in a concise amount of time. There may be a delay between opening or closing trade on your trading platform and the actual execution when dealing with currencies with lower demand. Because of this, the deal may not be conducted at the anticipated price, resulting in a reduced profit or possibly even a loss for you.

**Risk of ruin:** The risk of running out of capital to execute trades. Imagine you have a long-term strategy of how you think the value of a security will change, but it's moving in the opposite direction. It would help if you withstood this movement until the security moves in your desired direction. If you lack sufficient capital, your trade could be promptly closed, and you could lose everything you invested, even if the security later moves in the desired direction.

You should now be entirely aware of the risks of trading options and any other instrument! For this reason, as you will no doubt appreciate, the issue of risk management in option trading is significant.

**Five tips for risk management in trading**

Here are the ten top risk management tips that will help you reduce your risk whether you are a new trader or a pro:

- Educate yourself about option risk and trading
- Use a stop-loss
- Use a Take Profit to lock in your profits
- Avoid assuming more risk than you can afford to lose.
- Limit your leverage

**1) Educate yourself about option risk and trading**

What is the first rule of trading? If you are new to trading, you must educate yourself as much as possible. No matter how experienced you are with options trading, there is always a new lesson to learn! Read on and find out about all things options trading.

**2) Use a Stop Loss**

You may have wondered, "Do traders lose money?" Sure. You lose money regularly. However, the objective is to ensure that the net gains exceed the net losses by the end of the trading session. A stop-loss mechanism is one effective risk management strategy to mitigate significant financial losses. A stop loss is a tool that enables investors to safeguard their investments against unforeseen fluctuations in market conditions. It empowers them to establish a predetermined price level at which their position will be automatically liquidated. However, if you enter a position in the market hoping that the asset will appreciate and it falls when it reaches your Stop Loss price, the trade will be closed to prevent further losses.

However, it is crucial to acknowledge that stop losses do not provide a guarantee. There are occasions when the market exhibits erratic behavior and experiences price gaps. The execution of the stop loss order will not occur at the predetermined level in this particular scenario. Instead, it will be activated when the price reaches that level again. This occurrence is commonly referred to as slippage. Establishing a stop loss level that ensures a maximum loss of 2% of your trading balance for each trade is advisable.

Once you set your stop loss, you should keep the loss margin the same. Installing a safety net is possible if you use it properly. If you find yourself losing with a stop loss, analyze your stops and see how many were useful. It might be time to adjust your levels for better trading results.

**3) Use a Take Profit to lock in your profits**

A Take Profit is comparable to a Stop Loss, but, as the name suggests, its primary goal is not to reduce losses but to increase earnings as much as possible. A Stop Loss aims to execute the automatic closure of trades to mitigate potential losses. Conversely, a Take Profit is intended to close trades once they attain a specific profit level automatically. Establishing well-defined expectations for each trade can effectively set a profit target and determine an appropriate take profit level. Additionally, this approach enables the trader to assess and determine the suitable level of risk associated with the trade. Most traders aim for a reward-to-risk ratio of at least 2:1, with the expected reward being twice the risk they are willing to take on a trade.

In short, think about what levels you are aiming up and what level of loss down you can reasonably sustain. This will assist you in upholding your discipline during trading. Additionally, it will foster a mindset that considers the concepts of risk and reward.

**4) Avoid assuming more risk than you can afford to lose.**

One fundamental principle of risk management is to ensure that you only expose yourself to risk within your capacity to absorb potential losses. Despite its fundamental importance, the mistake of breaking this rule is prevalent, especially among those new to trading. The financial markets exhibit a high degree of unpredictability. Thus, traders who exceed their financial capacity expose themselves to significant vulnerability. If a small string of losses would be enough to wipe out most of your trading capital, this indicates that each trade is taking too much risk.

Covering lost capital is challenging since you must reclaim a significant proportion of the money in your trading account to compensate for what you have lost. Imagine you have a trading account of EUR 5,000 and lose EUR 1,000. The percentage loss is 20%. However, to recoup this loss, you need to make a 25% profit from the remaining capital in your account (EUR 4,000).

Conducting a thorough risk assessment before engaging in trading activities is essential. When the odds of winning are less than the profit to be made, exit the trade. You may want to use a trading calculator to help with your risk management. It is advisable to adhere to a prudent guideline of not exposing more than 2% of your account balance per trade. Moreover, it is common practice for numerous traders to modify their position sizes to align with the volatility of the specific currency pair they are engaging in trading activities with. A more volatile currency requires a smaller position than a less volatile pair.

Eventually, you may suffer a heavy loss or burn up a significant part of your trading capital. There is a temptation to try to get your investment back on the next trade after a big loss. However, increasing risk when your account balance is already low is not advisable, as this is considered the least opportune time for such a decision.

Instead, consider reducing your trade size on a losing streak or pausing until you can identify a high-probability trade. Always stay emotional and balanced with your position sizes.

## 5) Limit your leverage

Leverage allows you to magnify your profits made with your trading account, but it can also magnify your losses and increase risk potential. For example, an account with a leverage of 1:30 means that you can place trades worth up to EUR 30,000 on an account with EUR 1,000. If the market moves in your favor, you will take full advantage of that EUR 30,000 trade even though you only invested EUR 1,000. However, the opposite is true when the market moves against you.

Your risk is, therefore, higher with higher leverage. For individuals new to the field, adopting a prudent risk management strategy that involves minimizing exposure by refraining from utilizing high leverage levels is advisable. Only consider using leverage if you clearly understand the potential losses. By implementing this strategy, you can mitigate significant losses in your portfolio and minimize the risk of being on the unfavorable side of the market.

Admirals offer different levels of leverage based on trader status. Traders fall into two categories: retail traders and professional traders. Admirals offers 1:30 leverage for retail investors and 1:500 leverage for experienced traders.

Risk management is easy to understand. The tricky part is having enough self-discipline to stick to these risk management rules when the market moves against a position.

With this in mind, you can manage your risk by ensuring that a particular investment vehicle is a part of your portfolio, not everything.

As with all aspects of trading, what works best in risk management depends on your preferences and profile as a trader. Some traders are willing and able to take more risk than others. If you are a beginner, the best tip for reducing your risk, no matter who you are, is to start conservatively.

## UNDERSTANDING AND IMPLEMENTING RISK MANAGEMENT PRINCIPLES IN OPTIONS TRADING

In the exciting realm of options trading, where possibilities and potential gains abound, there's an essential skill that every trader must master: risk management. Imagine embarking on a journey across treacherous waters without a reliable compass or a skilled navigator - it's a recipe for disaster. Similarly, navigating without proper risk management can lead to turbulent outcomes in options trading. This chapter is your guiding compass, your skilled navigator, through the art of risk management - a vital element to safeguarding your trading quest.

**Understanding the Heartbeat of Risk Management.**

Risk management isn't just a phrase; it's the heartbeat that sustains your trading journey. Fundamentally, risk management entails safeguarding your capital, maintaining your profits, and securing your long-term participation in the market. It's akin to putting on a life jacket before setting sail. But understanding risk management goes beyond the metaphor - it's about comprehending the principles that underpin it.

Consider this: Every trade involves an element of uncertainty. Like a ship battling unpredictable tides, markets can shift unexpectedly. Risk management is your anchor, providing stability amidst uncertainty. It begins with acknowledging that losses are a natural part of trading. Just as no sailor can control the weather, no trader can predict every market movement. However, you can control how much you're willing to risk on each trade.

**RISK MANAGEMENT STRATEGIES**

- **Mitigate Risks**: Long term returns over short terms Gains.
- **Strategy**: Minimize Losses with effective know-how
- **Risk/Reward Ratio**: Know how much you stand to Gain or Loose in a trade.
- **Risk Management**: Control your exposure to price movement
- **Trade Size**: Calculate the Risk Percentage and market conditions
- **Stop LOSS**: Trade without being worried about Losses.
- **OnePercent Rule**: Stay in the game Longer

**Implementation of Risk Management**

Implementing risk management principles is where theory becomes practice, and the real magic happens. Just as a seasoned captain charts a course before setting sail, a trader plans before executing a trade. This planning involves placing stop-loss orders - predefined points at which you'll exit a trade to limit losses. Think of it as your emergency lifeboat, preventing you from sinking further in rough market waters.

Moreover, diversification is another crucial aspect of risk management. Imagine having a well-equipped vessel with multiple sails, each capable of steering you in a different direction. Similarly, diversifying your portfolio means putting only some of your capital into a single trade. It spreads risk across various positions, ensuring one unfavorable trade doesn't sink your entire ship.

**Applying Risk Management**

Real-life stories provide powerful anchors to the concepts we're discussing. Consider the tale of a trader who neglected risk management, believing they could predict market movements flawlessly. A series of wrong predictions left their account in shambles, akin to a shipwreck on uncharted shores. But in contrast, a trader who embraced risk management weathered storms by respecting stop-loss levels and diversifying their trades.

Risk management isn't just about saving you from disasters but creating a sustainable trading practice. As navigators study charts, currents, and stars, traders must analyze markets, trends, and economic indicators. Applying risk management ensures that you're not just sailing for today but for the long haul.

As you set sail on the unpredictable waters of options trading, remember that risk management is your trusted compass, your unwavering anchor. The principles you'll grasp in this chapter are more than rules; they're the wisdom of experienced sailors who've weathered countless storms. The stories of those who've faltered and flourished serve as guiding lights, reminding us that risk management is not an option but an imperative.

The art of risk management is your compass, your tool, and your guiding star, leading you toward your chosen destination in the exhilarating world of options trading.

## SETTING STOP-LOSS LEVELS, MANAGING POSITION SIZES, AND DIVERSIFYING

In the dynamic world of options trading, where market movements can be as unpredictable as the tides, risk management becomes your compass, guiding you to safer waters. This voyage requires a combination of well-calibrated tools and a strategic mindset. Just as seasoned sailor relies on their navigational tools and charts, a successful trader relies on robust risk management strategies to navigate the unpredictable seas of the market. In this chapter, we'll delve into the practical and actionable techniques that form the bedrock of risk management: setting stop-loss levels, managing position sizes, and diversifying.

**Setting Stop-Loss Levels: Safeguarding Against Stormy Markets**

Setting stop-loss levels is like securing your trading capital against adverse market movements. It's your safety net, ensuring that if the market takes an unexpected turn, you exit the trade before substantial losses occur.

However, the art of setting stop-loss levels requires finesse. Placing them too close may lead to premature exits, while putting them too wide may expose you to excessive risk. Consider the recent stormy weather analogy - if you anchor too close to the shore, you're susceptible to crashing waves; if you anchor too far, you risk drifting into uncharted waters. Finding the right balance is vital.

**Managing Position Sizes: Sailing Steadily Amidst Market Volatility**

Imagine you're a sailor on a small boat. Loading it with too much cargo makes it unstable and prone to capsizing. Similarly, managing position sizes in trading is about maintaining stability in your portfolio. Refrain from overloading a single trade with too much capital, as it can lead to disproportionate losses.

Just as a skilled captain knows the weight their vessel can handle; a trader must determine how much capital they're willing to allocate to each trade. This prevents excessive losses and ensures that a string of losing trades is manageable for your entire trading ship. Balancing risk and reward is the essence of successful position sizing.

**Diversification: Navigating the Trading Waters with Multiple Sails**

Imagine embarking on a voyage with a fleet of ships instead of just one. If one ship faces turbulent waters, the others can still chart a course to success. Diversifying your trading portfolio operates on the same principle. Rather than putting all your capital into a single trade, allocate it across different trades and asset classes.

Just as a diversified fleet can weather various sea conditions, a diversified trading portfolio can endure market volatility. If one trade doesn't go as planned, others may flourish, mitigating potential losses. Diversification is the compass that guides you through market storms, ensuring your overall success even when some trades hit rough waters.

As you traverse the trading waters, remember that successful risk management is about more than survival – it's about thriving. By setting stop-loss levels, managing position sizes, and diversifying, you're not just shielding yourself from potential losses – you're positioning yourself for sustainable success. Just as a skilled sailor adapts to changing winds and currents, a successful trader adapts their risk management strategies to evolving market conditions. Your trading journey is an expedition; these risk management techniques are your navigational tools. As you proceed, remember that the seas may be unpredictable, but with these strategies, you can master them and steer towards prosperous horizons.

## UTILIZING PROTECTIVE STRATEGIES TO MITIGATE POTENTIAL LOSSES

Engaging in options trading is a dynamic and potentially profitable undertaking; however, it is essential to acknowledge the inherent risks associated with this activity. One of the key principles seasoned traders understand is the importance of mitigating potential losses through protective strategies. These strategies serve as a safety net, helping traders navigate the unpredictable nature of the financial markets while safeguarding their investments. In this chapter, we'll delve into protective strategies and explore how they can be effectively employed to manage risk and protect your capital.

**The Foundation of Protective Strategies: Risk Management**

Before diving into specific protective strategies, it's crucial to emphasize the foundational principle of risk management. Successful traders understand that while gains are enticing, the preservation of capital is equally, if not more, important. Protective strategies are designed with this principle to limit the downside risk of a trade or portfolio.

### Hedging with Options: A Multi-Faceted Approach

One of the primary ways to utilize protective strategies is through hedging. Hedging involves taking on positions that counterbalance potential losses in other positions. This could mean holding options contracts that act inversely to the market movement of your primary position. The two most common types of protective strategies in this context are:

- **Protective Puts:** A protective put involves purchasing put options on a security you already own. If the price of the security drops, the put option can offset the loss by gaining in value. It's akin to having an insurance policy against a significant downturn in the market.

- **Collars:** A collar strategy combines protective puts with covered call writing. It involves buying a protective put to limit downside risk and selling a covered call to generate income. The protective put acts as insurance, while the covered call helps fund the cost of the put.

### Diversification and Allocation: Spreading Risk

Another crucial element of protective strategies is diversification. Diversification entails the allocation of investments across various assets or sectors. Doing so reduces the impact of a poor-performing asset on your overall portfolio. Diversification is an essential strategy for risk mitigation that can effectively minimize the influence of market volatility.

### Market Volatility and Protective Strategies

Protective strategies become particularly valuable during periods of heightened market volatility. Volatile markets can lead to rapid and unpredictable price swings, causing significant losses for unprotected positions. During such times, employing protective strategies like buying protective puts or implementing collars can help mitigate potential losses and provide peace of mind.

### Taking Action: Implementing Protective Strategies

Implementing protective strategies requires a proactive approach and careful consideration. Here are some practical steps to effectively utilize these strategies:

1. **Assess Your Portfolio:** Regularly assess your portfolio to identify positions at risk due to market conditions or potential events. This proactive assessment will help determine which assets might benefit from protective strategies.

2. **Understand Your Options:** Before implementing any protective strategy, thoroughly understand your options. Different strategies have varying costs, benefits, and potential outcomes. Educate yourself on how protective puts, collars, and other strategies work.

3. **Risk-Reward Balance:** Consider the trade-off between the cost of implementing a protective strategy and the potential benefits. While these strategies can limit losses, they may also impact potential gains. Finding the right balance is vital.

4. **Market Timing:** Be mindful of market conditions when implementing protective strategies. While waiting until the last minute is tempting, it's often more effective to establish protection before volatility spikes or significant events occur.

5. **Stay Informed:** It is advisable to stay informed about market news, economic indicators, and other factors potentially impacting asset prices. Staying informed allows you to make timely decisions regarding your protective strategies.

6. **Regular Review:** Continuously monitor the performance of your protective strategies. As market conditions change, your protective needs may also evolve. Regularly reassess your positions to ensure they align with your risk management goals.

**The Psychology of Protective Strategies**

Understanding the psychology behind protective strategies is just as important as knowing the mechanics. Emotions often play a significant role in trading decisions. Protective strategies provide a level of comfort and confidence that can help traders navigate the emotional highs and lows of the market.

Consider a scenario where a trader has a substantial position in a particular stock. Anxiety and fear can cloud judgment if the stock's price starts to plummet. However, protective puts can alleviate some emotional burden, allowing the trader to make rational decisions based on strategy rather than panic.

**Real-Life Applications and Lessons Learned**

To truly grasp the power of protective strategies, looking at real-life examples is essential. Consider the market crash of 2008. Traders with protective puts in place could limit their losses significantly, providing a cushion during a tumultuous time. Similarly, the recent market turmoil caused by the COVID-19 pandemic highlighted the effectiveness of protective strategies in managing downside risk.

In the options trading world, protecting your capital is as crucial as making profits. Utilizing protective strategies offers a way to navigate the volatile nature of the market while reducing the potential for substantial losses. Whether through protective puts, collars, diversification, or other risk management techniques, these strategies give traders the confidence to weather market storms and continue their journey with resilience.

Incorporating protective strategies into your options trading arsenal is about more than managing risk – it's about empowering your trading journey. The objective is to equip oneself with the necessary tools and strategies to effectively navigate the intricacies of the market with a sense of assurance. By implementing proactive measures to safeguard your investments, you position yourself strategically to navigate market volatility and seize potential opportunities that may arise.

As you venture into options trading, remember that risk management isn't just a strategy – it's a mindset. By embracing protective strategies and understanding their real-world applications, you're equipping yourself with the knowledge and skills to safeguard your trading quest and elevate your overall trading experience.

## CHAPTER 2
## TRADE ADJUSTMENTS TECHNIQUES: NAVIGATING MARKET SHIFTING WINDS

In the world of options trading, the market's shifting winds demand the flexibility to adjust your trades. Mastering trade adjustment techniques is crucial for options traders navigating the ever-changing tides of the market. This chapter delves into the world of trade adjustments—a skill that separates the savvy trader from the rest.

**The Need for Trade Adjustments**

Markets are like the ever-changing sea, influenced by many factors, from economic news to geopolitical events. Even the most meticulously planned trades can be affected by unexpected shifts. This is where trade adjustments come into play—techniques that enable traders to respond to changing market dynamics without abandoning their trades entirely.

Trading, like sailing, demands flexibility. The market is known for its capricious nature, often shifting direction without notice. Trade adjustment techniques are the tools for responding to these shifts, ensuring that even in turbulent times, you can remain in control and make the most of your trades.

**Rolling and Unrolling Trades: Akin to Adjusting Sails**

One of the fundamental trade adjustment techniques is rolling—a strategy that involves changing the parameters of your existing trade to adapt to new circumstances. Just as a sailor adjusts the sails to harness the winds in a different direction, traders can roll options positions by closing an existing position and opening a new one with modified parameters.

For instance, imagine you hold a bullish call option, but the stock's price starts moving against your prediction. Instead of letting the trade sink, you can roll the call option to a later expiration date or a different strike price. This adjustment allows you to extend your trading timeline or adjust your outlook to match the changing market conditions.

**Strategic Position Management: Navigating Market-Shifting Winds**

Traders adjust their positions strategically to manage risk and enhance potential rewards. This could involve using additional option contracts to create spreads, straddles, or multi-leg strategies. These techniques allow traders to adjust the risk-reward profile of their positions, offering more flexibility in the face of changing market conditions.

**Balancing Acts: Ensuring Adequate Coverage**

Just as a sailor navigates waters with a balanced weight distribution to prevent capsizing, a trader employs trade adjustments to balance risk exposure. For example, if you hold a bullish position and notice a bearish turn in the market, consider opening a bearish position to offset potential losses.

**Rolling Strategies in Action**

Imagine your trade isn't sailing smoothly—it's headed for choppy waters. Instead of panicking, a trader proficient in adjustment techniques applies the art of rolling. Rolling involves closing an existing position and opening a new one with different parameters. It's like changing your sail's angle to harness the wind's energy. For instance, you might roll a losing call option trade to a higher strike price and further expiration date, giving your trade more room to recover.

**Protecting and Pivoting: Effective Hedging Techniques**

Sailing through turbulent waters requires knowing when to batten down the hatches. Similarly, you can employ hedge techniques to protect your positions from sudden market shifts in trading. These techniques include using options to create positions that counteract the risk in your existing trades. Think of it as deploying a sea anchor to stabilize your boat during a storm.

**Turning Adjustments into Advantage**

Adaptability isn't just about avoiding losses; it's also about seizing opportunities. Skilled sailors know how to adjust their sails to catch wind gusts, propelling them forward. Likewise, in trading, savvy adjustments can transform a losing trade into a winning one or enhance your profit potential.

**Navigating the Learning Curve**

As with any skill, mastering trade adjustment techniques takes practice. Just as a sailor becomes more adept at reading the wind and waves over time, traders refine their instincts for recognizing when adjustments are needed. And just as seasoned sailors share tales of their most challenging voyages, successful traders learn from their adjustments, gaining insights that guide their future decisions.

In conclusion, trade adjustment techniques are the rudder that steers your trading ship. Just as a skilled sailor anticipates shifts in the wind, a proficient trader expects market movements and adapts accordingly. In options trading, trade adjustments are not signs of failure but symbols of adaptability. Just as a sailor learns to read the winds and adjust their sails, a skilled trader learns to read the market and change their positions. With the proper techniques and a keen understanding of market dynamics, you can navigate the shifting winds of trading, adjusting your trades with precision and steering your journey toward success. These techniques empower you to manage risk and capitalize on changing conditions. Remember, mastering trade adjustments is rewarding, leading to more confident, strategic, and ultimately booming trading.

## MAKING ADJUSTMENTS TO OPTIONS POSITIONS BASED ON MARKET CHANGES

Welcome to the heart of the trading storm—where market shifts and tides of change can toss your options positions like a ship on restless waters. As markets ebb and flow, traders must recognize trends, volatility, and underlying asset price shifts. In this chapter, we're diving headfirst into adjusting your options positions based on the capricious winds of market changes. This isn't about just surviving; it's about thriving amid market turbulence.

Markets serve as a manifestation of collective sentiment, which has the potential to undergo rapid fluctuations. As a trader, your positions are intrinsically linked to market conditions. They rise and fall with the tides of market shifts. Embracing this dynamic nature is the first step towards mastering the art of adjustments. Think of market changes as the wind at your back or a storm brewing on the horizon. Recognizing opportunities in these shifts is like a sailor spotting land after days at sea. When volatility spikes or prices swing unexpectedly, it's not just chaos—it's your chance to recalibrate your sails. Options trading isn't a calm sea; it's a stormy ocean with waves of volatility and currents of uncertainty. Before you, a canvas of potential gains and losses unfurls, shaped by the capricious whims of the market. Your ability to adapt and adjust is your compass, guiding you toward success even in the most tumultuous waters.

**Recognizing the Call for Adjustment:**

Adjustments aren't a one-size-fits-all solution; they're your toolkit of possibilities. Just like a carpenter selects the right tool for the job, you have a variety of adjustment strategies. Whether rolling options, spreading your position, or adding protection, these tools are lifeboats for your trades when the waters get rough. As a sailor scans the horizon for storm clouds, traders must vigilantly monitor their positions for signs of trouble. Economic data releases, geopolitical events, or unexpected news might trigger market changes. These shifts can lead to sudden price swings or changes in volatility, potentially putting your trades at risk. Recognizing these signals early empowers you to take pre-emptive action.

Much like a sailor's toolkit contains tools for every repair scenario, traders have a range of adjustment strategies at their disposal. Rolling your options, spreading your position, or adding hedges are just a few techniques that can be employed. These tools can be customized to address the specific market changes you encounter, enabling you to refine your position without beginning anew. That's what making adjustments is all about. It's not just about reacting; it's about staying ahead of the storm. Your ability to adapt is your rudder, steering your trades through the market's ever-changing landscape.

Adjustments are more than just reactive maneuvers; they're a harmonious blend of flexibility and strategic foresight. It's about staying true to your trading goals while adapting to market dynamics. Just as a sailor uses the wind to their advantage, you can use market changes to enhance your position's potential.

In the heart of every trader, the psychological aspect of adjustments looms large. It's easy to become emotionally attached to a trade, hoping for it to turn around. However, the art of making adjustments demand an objective approach. Being willing to cut losses, shift strategies, or exit trades based on market changes is a hallmark of a seasoned trader. Trading isn't just about numbers but your emotions and psychology. Just as a captain needs a steady hand during a storm, you need a clear mind when adjusting trades. Overcoming attachment to a trade's outcome and being willing to change course is essential for thriving in ever-shifting markets.

In this dynamic dance with the market, every adjustment is a lesson. It's about learning from the market's whispers and shouts, refining your strategy, and enhancing your ability to read its signals. Each adjustment is a chapter in your trading story—a narrative of resilience and growth.

In the vast expanse of the trading landscape, making adjustments based on market changes is your compass. It's a testament to your ability to read the market's language and respond with finesse. Like a mariner guided by the stars, you're driven by experience and insights. Through skillful adjustments, you can confidently navigate market shifts, harnessing the ever-changing currents to steer your options toward success.

## ENHANCING WINNING TRADES AND MITIGATING LOSSES WITH STRATEGIC MOVES

In the world of trading, success is often painted by your ability to maneuver with finesse, enhancing profitable trades while nimbly navigating the shoals of potential losses. This chapter unveils the intricate tapestry of strategic moves that elevate your trading from mundane to masterful. Buckle up as we delve deeper into enhancing wins and strategically cushioning losses.

Trading isn't a mere transaction; it's an art form. Just like a painter adds layers to a canvas, a trader layers strategic moves upon their positions. Each decision becomes a brushstroke that accentuates gains while providing a cushion against potential downturns. The key is to recognize when to intensify your stance or adjust your sail, always keeping your journey forward in mind. Trading is as much about psychology as it is about numbers. The strategic trader navigates the intricate terrain of emotions with the precision of a cartographer. They acknowledge their biases, remain disciplined in executing their strategies, and maintain a clear head when adjusting their positions.

Strategic moves aren't a one-size-fits-all solution but a toolkit brimming with possibilities. From scaling into positions with careful precision to locking in profits at strategic milestones, you're the architect of your success. Employing options to hedge your positions or employing trailing stops to safeguard your gains are like the varied colors on your palette—each chosen thoughtfully for the masterpiece you're crafting. The beauty of strategic moves lies in their versatility. You're not locked into a single note; you have an entire keyboard of possibilities. Scaling into positions, locking in profits with trailing stops, or hedging with options are your instruments of choice. They offer the flexibility to amplify your gains and erect a shield against potential losses. Losses don't daunt the strategic trader; they sculpt them into stepping-stones. Defensive maneuvers, like deploying options to mitigate losses or using stop orders to curtail declines, are the tools that shape adversity into resilience. Rather than letting losses define their journey, strategic traders wield them as growth tools. In the arena of trading, psychology is as crucial as strategy. The strategic trader is a virtuoso of the mind, recognizing biases, maintaining discipline in executing plans, and adapting with grace when adjustments are needed. The ability to stay composed amidst turbulence is the hallmark of a true strategist.

Each strategic move is a gem, a brilliant facet in the mosaic of your trading expedition. Every win maximized, every loss mitigated, teaches invaluable lessons. It's not just about celebrating victory; it's about understanding how each strategic move contributes to the symphony of your growth.

Losses are part and parcel of trading, but how you deal with them sets you apart. Strategic moves aren't solely about chasing profits; they're about acknowledging losses and harnessing them to refine your strategy. Just as a blacksmith tempers steel to strengthen it, a trader tempers their approach to grow in adversity.

As we delve into the realm of strategic prowess, remember that you're not just executing trades; you're orchestrating a symphony of calculated moves. Each decision amplifies your resonance in the market, letting you harmonize wins and soften losses. Trading isn't merely a quest for profits; it's a journey of self-discovery and skillful navigation. As you read on, let the strategies shared become your companions in this exciting expedition toward trading excellence.

In the trading realm, strategic moves aren't just actions; they're the conductor's baton guiding the symphony. As you tread the fine line between triumph and resilience, remember that each strategic move is a note, a brushstroke, a dance move. With each execution, you're weaving a narrative that defies mere numbers—a saga of artistry, mastery, and the ultimate voyage toward trading excellence.

REAL-LIFE EXAMPLES OF TRADE ADJUSTMENTS IN VARIOUS MARKET CONDITIONS

In the trading world, no two days are alike, and no market condition remains static—the ever-changing landscape challenges traders to be adaptable, resilient, and innovative. Enter the realm of trade adjustments—a strategic toolkit that allows traders to recalibrate their positions in response to market shifts. Embarking on the path of trade adjustments requires a deep understanding of strategies and the ability to apply them effectively in real-world scenarios. In this chapter, we will immerse ourselves in real-life examples illuminating how trade adjustments can be wielded with finesse across a spectrum of market scenarios.

**1. The Volatility Vortex: Navigating Through High Volatility**

Market turbulence can be both exhilarating and unnerving. In times of heightened volatility, the straddle and strangle strategies shine. The straddle strategy comprises buying both a call option and a put option at the same price to profit from price fluctuations in the underlying asset. On the other hand, a strangle strategy follows a similar approach but involves purchasing call-and-pull options with different strike prices. These trades capitalize on the anticipated price swings that come with increased volatility. For instance, uncertainty can trigger significant price fluctuations during an earnings announcement. Traders can deploy a straddle to profit from these substantial moves, regardless of the direction they take.

**2. Navigating Bear Markets**

Bear markets instill fear and uncertainty, but they also present opportunities. When stocks take a nosedive, put options become invaluable tools. By employing the protective put strategy, traders can safeguard their portfolios against steep declines. Imagine a trader anticipating a market downturn and holding a significant stock position. They effectively secure the right to sell at a predetermined price by purchasing put options. If the stock value does plummet, the put options act as a safety net, preventing excessive losses.

**3. The Bullish Charge: Capitalizing on Bull Markets**

Bull markets come with optimism and an upward momentum. But even in these favorable times, adjustments play a role. Covered call writing is a popular strategy where a trader holds a long stock position and sells a call option against it. This allows them to generate extra income from the premium while potentially limiting upside gains if the stock surges beyond the strike price. During bullish trends, traders can enhance their returns by regularly selling covered calls and capturing premiums while benefiting from the stock's appreciation.

**4. The Momentum Surge: Riding the Trend Wave**

Trends are a trader's best friend, and riding the momentum can lead to substantial gains. But trends can change direction abruptly, potentially catching traders off-guard. This is where the diagonal spread strategy steps in. By purchasing a longer-term option and selling a shorter-term option of the same type, traders create a safety buffer. For instance, if the stock trend suddenly reverses, the short option will expire faster, minimizing potential losses. Meanwhile, the long option can be appreciated, offering protection.

**5. The Challenging Consolidation: Capturing Breakout Potential**

A stock consolidating within a narrow range might foreshadow an imminent breakout. The long strangle strategy comes into play in such scenarios. Traders anticipate a significant move by purchasing both an OTM call and put option. If the stock price breaks out, the winning leg can more than compensate for the loss on the other leg. This strategy thrives because the breakout will outweigh the premium paid for both options.

**6. The Protective Pursuit: Safeguarding Profits**

Imagine a trader who bought a stock that has appreciated significantly. They can employ the collar strategy to protect their gains while allowing room for further upside. This involves simultaneously purchasing a protective put option and selling a covered call. The protective put protects against downside risk, while the covered call generates premium income. It's a nuanced balancing act that offers protection without capping potential profits too tightly.

### 7. The Swing of the Pendulum: Butterfly Spread's Symphony

A butterfly spread strategy came to the fore in a market oscillating between bullish and bearish sentiments. A trader, observing a stock repeatedly moving between two price points, initiated a butterfly spread. They benefited from the stock's oscillations by combining long and short option positions at three different strike prices. The profit from the short leg offset potential losses from the long legs, showcasing the finesse of range-bound strategies.

### 8. The Unforeseen Surge: The Collar's Protective Embrace

An unexpected surge in a stock's price can catch even seasoned traders off guard. One trader, holding a substantial position in a stock, implemented the collar strategy for protection. By purchasing a put option to shield against downside risk while simultaneously selling a covered call to generate income, the trader found a balance between safeguarding gains and allowing for potential upside.

### 9. Riding the Momentum: Adjusting with Vertical Spreads

In a market propelled by momentum, a trader executing vertical spreads demonstrated their adaptability. As the stock gained momentum, the trader initially opened a vertical spread to capture potential gains. However, when a shift in market sentiment threatened the position, they swiftly adjusted by closing the initial spread and opening a new one with more suitable strike prices.

These real-life stories embody the essence of trade adjustments—flexibility, creativity, and quick thinking. They underscore that no strategy is a fixed blueprint but a canvas for traders to craft their responses to market shifts. These stories are a testament to the dynamic nature of options trading. Through them, readers learn techniques and witness the traders' thought processes, adaptability, and determination in action.

As we walk through these real-life examples, remember that every market scenario demands different tools. The art of trade adjustments involves discerning which strategy aligns with the ever-changing market winds. It's about navigating the storms, seizing opportunities, and minimizing risks. In your journey as a trader, consider these examples as guideposts, enabling you to adapt, adjust, and conquer the intricate dance of market dynamics.

# GLOSSARY

**Risk management:** Risk management is anticipating prospective dangers, evaluating them, and adopting preventative measures to reduce or eliminate them.

**Investment:** Investment is placing money into an asset that has the potential to increase in value, generate income, or do both. For instance, purchasing equity stock in a publicly traded firm can increase your chances of getting monthly dividend payments and capital gains through share price growth.

**Stop loss:** A stop-loss is a forewarned order to sell an asset when it hits a specific price level. It is employed to cap gain or loss in a transaction. The idea can be applied to both short-term and long-term trading.

**Profit:** Profit is total revenue minus total expenses. It reveals how much your company made after expenses. Profit is a crystal-clear indicator of how your firm operates and performs in the market because the main objective of every business is to make money.

**Portfolio:** A portfolio is a collection of financial investments such as closed-end and exchange-traded funds (ETFs), options, equities, bonds, commodities, cash, and cash equivalents.

**Trading psychology:** Trading psychology is the study and comprehension of the psychological and emotional factors affecting traders' behavior, decision-making, and performance in the financial markets.

**Capital:** A trader's capital is the money available to purchase and sell securities.

**Market value:** The price at which buyers and sellers agree to trade something is known as the market value. The phrase refers to a stock, futures, or option's market price.

# REFERENCES

Corporate Finance Institute. "Risk Management." *Corporate Finance Institute*, 27 Oct. 2022, corporatefinanceinstitute.com/resources/risk-management/risk-management/.

Kuepper, Justin. "Risk Management Techniques for Active Traders." *Investopedia*, 12 June 2023, www.investopedia.com/articles/trading/09/risk-management.asp.

Nicholls, Harry. "The 5 Most Effective Risk Management Techniques That the Pros Use." *Medium*, 25 Oct. 2018, harrynicholls.medium.com/the-5-most-effective-risk-management-techniques-that-the-pros-use-a3bf7191f682.

Renno, Yves. "Understanding Trading Positions and Managing Risk." *Crypto-Friendly Currency Accounts*, 27 June 2023, wirexapp.com/blog/post/understanding-trading-positions-and-managing-risk-0766.

Stempler, Mariano. "The Art of Risk Management and the Safeguarding Success." *Www.linkedin.com*, 18 May 2023, www.linkedin.com/pulse/art-risk-management-safeguarding-success-mariano.

# BOOK 7

## "OPTIONS MINDSET: HARNESSING PSYCHOLOGY AND BUILDING YOUR TRADING PLAN."

# TABLE OF CONTENTS

**CHAPTER 1** ............................................................................................................................ 3

**MASTERING TRADING PSYCHOLOGY: YOUR PATH TO TRADING SUCCESS** ........................... 3

    RECOGNIZING COMMON PSYCHOLOGICAL CHALLENGES FACED BY TRADERS .................. 4

    DEVELOPING THE TRADING MINDSET: THE IMPORTANCE OF THE TRADING MINDSET ...... 6

    DEVELOPING EMOTIONAL DISCIPLINE AND RESILIENCE TO HANDLE TRADING PRESSURES ................. 8

    ADOPTING A POSITIVE AND GROWTH-ORIENTED MINDSET FOR TRADING SUCCESS ........ 13

**CHAPTER 2** .......................................................................................................................... 15

**CRAFTING YOUR OPINIONS TRADING PLAN: YOUR BLUEPRINT FOR TRADING ADVENTURE** ................. 15

    SETTING CLEAR TRADING GOALS, DEFINING RISK TOLERANCE, AND ESTABLISHING TIME FRAMES. 16

    CREATING A COMPREHENSIVE TRADING PLAN THAT ALIGNS WITH YOUR OBJECTIVES ..... 17

    INCORPORATING A TRADING JOURNAL FOR PERFORMANCE TRACKING AND CONTINUOUS IMPROVEMENT ............................................................................................................... 19

**CONCLUSION** ..................................................................................................................... 22

**GLOSSARY** .......................................................................................................................... 23

**REFERENCES** ...................................................................................................................... 25

# CHAPTER 1
## MASTERING TRADING PSYCHOLOGY: YOUR PATH TO TRADING SUCCESS

Trader psychology is one of the essential traits to be a successful trader since it is decisive for your performance in the medium and long term. However, it is often one of the most overlooked aspects of trading. Your ability to trade successfully may be significantly improved by investing the time to learn about trading psychology. With your new perspective, it can assist you in making wiser decisions and in finding solutions to issues.

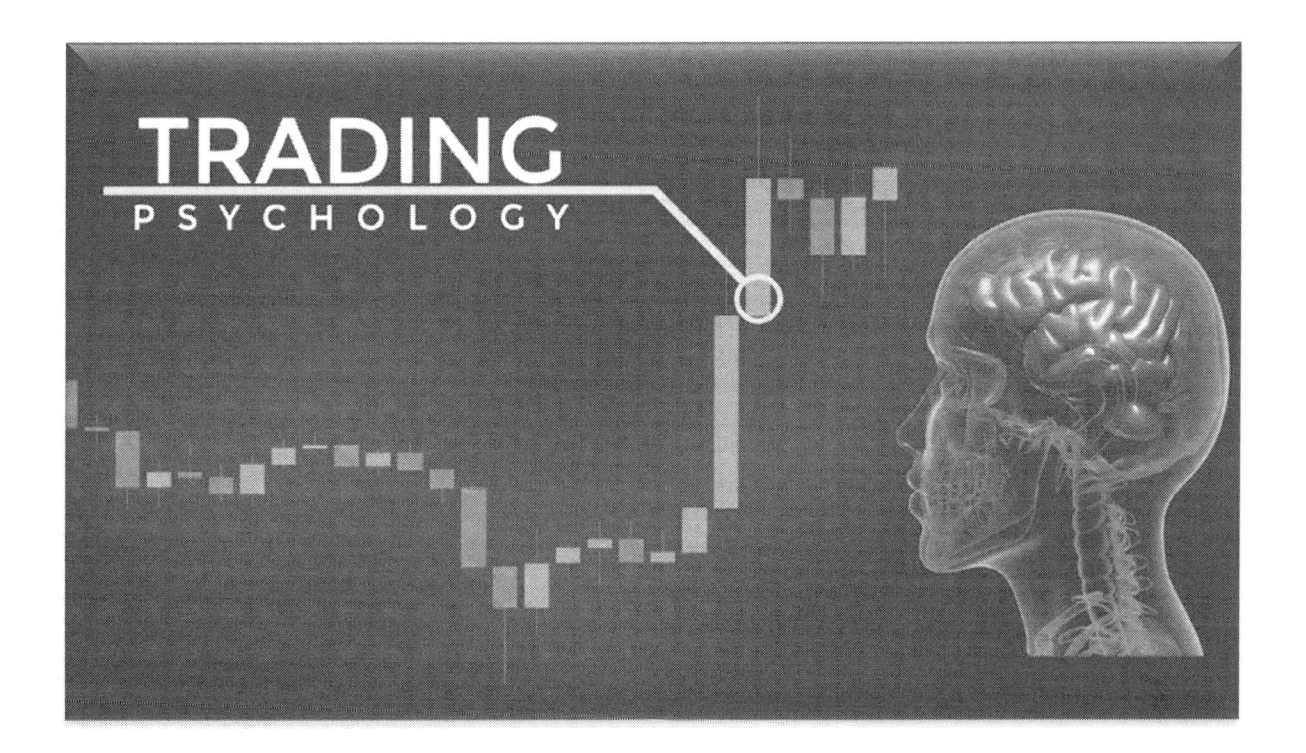

The first step to understanding trade psychology is emotional control. Understanding and controlling both good and negative emotions are crucial life skills. It would be best to arm yourself with the right tools and strategies. Impatience, negativity, and cognitive biases may all be addressed by an effective business strategy. You can develop the skill of accepting losses, which is essential to any profession in trading.

Additionally, you'll discover how uncertainty impacts your capacity for trading and your ability to make decisions. Understanding the interplay between emotions, thoughts, and perception will help you lessen underlying personality flaws that may hinder success.

Healthy emotional restraint is a crucial factor in the success of the best traders. Positive thinking helps increase your self-assurance and remaining composed and level-headed will help you stay steady in choppy markets.

The most significant emotion in trading is greed. This is usually experienced at the end of a bull market. Traders' greed may drive people to take up dangerous positions. It might also be a barrier to your success if you let it control you.

The myth of sunk costs is another psychological phenomenon. People tend to embrace the status quo in corporate strategy rather than changing and improving because of a cognitive bias. It could lead to losses that snowball or inspire despair. It may also result in the use of improper trading methods and tactics. Knowledge of psychological attitudes and one's complexes, control of emotions, and working with conscious attitudes allows investors to avoid this situation. Furthermore, a trader who understands how the market "crowd" will behave can predict the value dynamics of financial instruments.

Long-term outcomes will increase if you have a positive outlook on trading. This book covers the value of a solid trading strategy, how to handle unsuccessful transactions, and how to keep your momentum going. It is an excellent resource for learning about the psychology and science of option trading.

You'll discover how to cultivate self-control and conquer impatience. It's critical to keep in mind that trading is a mental game. Consistency should be emphasized across a succession of operations. It would be challenging for you to follow a trading plan if you lack discipline.

RECOGNIZING COMMON PSYCHOLOGICAL CHALLENGES FACED BY TRADERS

The emotional and mental condition that influences whether a trader will succeed, or fail is described by trading psychology. It is a complex concept, representing various behavioral traits and aspects of your character. The psychology of trading is the engine that drives the decisions you make. It reflects your trading profile and motivations. For example, how fear and greed influence your behavior and your decisions.

Trading psychology encompasses emotional discipline, mindset, discipline, recognizing and overcoming cognitive biases, etc.

Think of trading psychology as the ability to maintain a clear and stable state of mind at all times, regardless of market conditions and external factors. Or what is the same, the power of a trader to maintain rationality and coolness even when things do not go the way he wants or when he may be tempted to act against his trading plan?

"Successful trading is about knowing your psychology, not predicting the markets." –Mark Douglas.

Although often overlooked, trading psychology can be just as important as understanding the mechanics of financial markets, fundamentals of technical and fundamental analysis, trading experience, etc. In high-stress situations, such as volatile market periods, it is frequently the determinant of whether or not a deal is profitable for the investor.

A trader who lacks a resilient psychology is prone to making bad decisions, even going against his trading plan.

For example, traders with a poor psychological profile need better discipline. As a result, they may become victims of excessive greed and pursue high-risk trades (for example, trading with high leverage during volatile periods). In this situation, a slight market movement against the trader's position is enough for his entire portfolio to disappear instantly. On the other hand, it can also cause trades to be lost due to excessive fear.

Maintaining a stable trading psychology ensures that your rationality and judgment are not clouded, and you do not violate your trading strategy.

Trading psychology is essential for long-term success. Although even the most adventurous or undisciplined traders could succeed in the short term, it would be mostly by luck. In the long run, the results will even out, and outliers will quickly become losses without the proper psychological profile.

The psyche comprises two distinct components: the personal aspect, which encompasses emotions and volition, and the cognitive aspect. The behaviors of individuals are influenced by the processes and states associated with them. In daily life, individuals experience a state of conditional equilibrium that varies based on the level of influence on their activities. This equilibrium point is unique to each person—a disruption of equilibrium results in a deviation from the typical behavior patterns.

**Psychological Challenges Faced by Traders:**

1. **Fear and greed:** These are two influential emotions that have the potential to influence trading decisions significantly. Fear of losing money can lead to hesitation, missed opportunities, and exiting trades prematurely. On the other hand, greed can push traders to take excessive risks for potential high returns.

2. **Overtrading:** The desire to be constantly active in the market can lead to overtrading. This can result in impulsive decisions, increased transaction costs, and emotional exhaustion.

3. **Confirmation Bias:** Traders often seek information confirming their beliefs while ignoring contradictory evidence. This bias has the potential to result in suboptimal decision-making and overlooked opportunities.

4. **Loss Aversion:** Traders tend to feel the pain of losses more intensely than the joy of gains. This behavior may result in retaining unprofitable positions for an extended period with the expectation that the market will eventually reverse.

5. **Impatience:** Impatience can lead to entering trades prematurely or closing them too soon. Traders may need help to wait for optimal setups and instead act on impulse.

6. **Lack of Discipline:** Following a trading plan and adhering to rules is essential, but a lack of discipline can prevent traders from deviating from their strategy, leading to inconsistent results.

7. **Anxiety and Stress:** The volatile nature of the markets can create high anxiety and stress levels. This can impair one's ability to make sound judgments and may result in irrational decision-making.

8. **Overconfidence:** Success in a few trades can lead to overconfidence, causing traders to take larger risks without proper analysis.

DEVELOPING THE TRADING MINDSET: THE IMPORTANCE OF THE TRADING MINDSET

Think of mindset as a set of traits determining your success in trading (or any other aspect of your life). Having the right attitude can decide how you perceive certain situations and how they affect you. People with a winning mentality, who never give up, will remain calm and collected even when it seems like their whole world is falling apart.

Having the right mindset is an integral part of trading psychology. It is a set of personality traits and various abilities, such as emotions of acceptance, discipline, motivation, self-determination, the will to excel, adaptability, and flexibility.

**Mentality mistakes to avoid**

Indeed, you have heard the expression: "You are your own worst enemy." This is precisely the case when it comes to the trading mindset. Often, traders are only subject to their self-imposed limitations. These limitations are often the result of your mindset.

Listed below are some widespread mindset mistakes to avoid if you want to become a better trader:

- **Greed** – Weak-minded traders are prone to chasing bigger profits even when extremely risky.
- **Fear** – As opposed to greed, fear is when traders are too scared to enter the market, even when the chances of losing are slim.
- **Recklessness** – Sometimes traders get carried away with the moment and make a wrong decision that goes against their trading plan (for example, when trading out of revenge to try to make up for a loss)
- **Overconfidence** -Know-it-all traders always find that no one knows better than the market the hard way. Having a big ego also prevents traders from improving their skills.
- **Obstinacy** – Traders who continue to cling to an approach that has proven not to work well are guaranteed failure in the short and long term.
- **Lack of dedication** - Trading the markets is not a sprint but a marathon, and those who are not willing to undertake the long journey are the first to fail.
- **Indecision** – If you spend too much time perfecting your strategy or trading a demo account, you will procrastinate rather than make progress.

**Addressing Psychological Challenges:**

1. **Awareness:** Recognize and acknowledge your emotions while trading. Developing an understanding of your emotional triggers can facilitate the process of making more logical and reasoned decisions.
2. **Education:** Learn about trading psychology and techniques to manage emotions. This could include mindfulness exercises, deep breathing, or breaks during stressful periods.
3. **Trading Strategy:** Create a well-rounded trading plan encompassing precise entry and exit parameters, effective risk management techniques, and strategic approaches for diverse market scenarios. Stick to your plan to avoid impulsive decisions.
4. **Risk Management:** It is imperative to establish well-defined risk-reward ratios and refrain from jeopardizing an amount that exceeds your financial capacity to bear losses on a single trade. This helps reduce the emotional impact of losses.

5. **Journaling:** Keep a trading journal to document your thoughts and emotions during trades. Reviewing past trades can help identify patterns in your decision-making process.
6. **Mindset:** Cultivate a growth mindset, prioritizing ongoing learning and advancement over immediate outcomes.
7. **Support System:** Connect with other traders and mentors or join trading communities to share experiences and gain insights.
8. **Healthy Lifestyle:** Prioritizing a healthy lifestyle entail ensuring sufficient sleep, engaging in regular physical activity, and consuming a well-balanced diet.
9. **Physical well-being:** can positively impact mental clarity and decision-making.

Incorporating these strategies can significantly improve your ability to navigate the psychological challenges of trading. Remember, trading is as much about mastering your emotions as it is about analyzing the markets.

**How do you work on your psychology when trading?**

Working on your trading psychology is an ongoing process that requires self-awareness, discipline, and a willingness to learn and grow. Here are some tips to help you work on your feelings and emotions:

1. **Identify your emotions** – Identify the emotions impacting your trading decisions. Common emotions that can affect traders include fear, greed, and hope. Once you have identified the emotions, develop strategies to manage them.

2. **Develop a trading plan** – A trading plan can help you stay disciplined and avoid rash decisions. Your trading plan should include rules for entering and exiting trades, risk management strategies, and guidelines for managing your emotions.

3. **Seek support** - Engaging in trading can often result in a sense of solitude. It is highly recommended that you research the possibility of becoming a member of a trading community or obtaining the aid of a mentor or coach who can offer priceless support and direction.

DEVELOPING EMOTIONAL DISCIPLINE AND RESILIENCE TO HANDLE TRADING PRESSURES

Emotional Discipline refers to the ability to control and manage one's emotions in situations that require focus, decision-making, and resilience. It involves maintaining a level-headed approach even when faced with emotional challenges, stress, or pressure.

There are many different emotions, including joy, fear, wrath, and complacency. Emotionally unstable people are more likely to act impulsively and are not always capable of controlling their conduct. On the other hand, the absence of emotion in a person's conduct causes it to resemble that of a mechanism, which is another thing that is not very desirable.

The cognitive realm, which comprises thinking, memory, attention, perception, and comprehension, in addition to other processes and states, also affects people's activities. This component of the mind is accountable for the behavior directed, the decisions made, and the actions resulting from those decisions.

The fast speed of perception, the capacity to concentrate for extended periods, and the ability to evaluate information are all helpful skills for a trader in options trading. On the other hand, excessive functioning of the cognitive domain quickly leads to overall mental tiredness, which in turn hurts the outcomes of the investor's job. This also applies to prejudices, both in the rational and emotional spheres. A state of conditional balance of mind refers to an optimal condition that enables consistent and profitable trading.

The optimal mental state of the trader should be tailored to their psychological characteristics, mainly if they are prominent. For example, an individual who experiences heightened emotional responses should be able to regulate their emotions before engaging in bidding activities. Any given character trait possesses the potential to enhance business outcomes.

Adhering to the regulations governing psychological state control, maintaining disciplined adherence to the selected trading strategy, cultivating practical, rational attitudes, and exercising emotional control are the primary techniques for mental management.

**Mandatory rules:**

The first thing a trader has to do is guard against the emergence of mental conditions that will hinder the efficiency of his actions. In spite of the fact that adhering to these guidelines is one of the most effective ways to exert influence on one's mental state, the vast majority still need to do so. Therefore, to improve the performance of options, the following steps are taken:

- Ensuring a minimum of seven hours of sleep per day is recommended. Adequate sleep has been found to regulate an individual's emotional state and enhance cognitive functioning. For instance, a trader who has obtained sufficient rest will exhibit greater attentiveness during work than a trader who has commenced trading following a night spent at a club.
- Get regular physical activity.
- It is advised to refrain from using antidepressants and other substances with active effects before and during work. It is imperative to establish a direct correlation between trading and driving. It is crucial to exercise complete control over one's actions before operating a trading terminal or getting behind the wheel.
- Take a break from trading for 5 to 10 minutes every hour. Go for a walk and warm up. Try not to think about trading during your break.
- It is advisable to refrain from commencing work if one is experiencing intense emotions. Emotional states such as euphoria, stress, fear, violence, and joy can hinder an individual's capacity to evaluate market conditions objectively.

**Formation of effective rational attitudes:**

Throughout psychology and psychotherapy, the idea of a "rational attitude" is utilized to identify consistent thought patterns that significantly impact individual behavior. "No one can be trusted" and "I have no luck with money" are examples of misbehavior. "I have the right to be wrong," Fear and challenges are valuable guides because they motivate people to take action.

1. Identify some basic concepts that will give positive results. "Bad trades and losses teach me to understand the market better" – this is an example of correct thinking for the exact options strategy. Follow these steps to start positively impacting trading results: Create a helpful mindset from your perspective and document it. Take some time to digest the recorded statement. What you've written, do you think?

2. Repeating the rational layout on paper 20–30 more times is recommended. Then, it would help if you repeated it aloud. You will, therefore, assist the mentality in accepting it.

3. Always keep a notebook or piece of paper near the workplace on which all the rules are written. They should be read again and again.

4. Effective rational settings help the options trader when using real options signals and everyday life.

**Control of emotions:**

1. The ability to control emotions is one of the most essential qualities we all need.

2. Use the "fear attack" technique used in rational-emotive therapy to cope with fear. Its essence lies in that you must first perform the actions that the person is afraid of. For example, if, for some reason, you are afraid to use the main options signals, then do so regardless of possible losses.

You may also envision what might happen if your fear is confirmed. For example, consider the scenario if you are worried about losing your whole investment owing to poor trading judgments. Consider it; you may discover something positive in this circumstance.

Furthermore, seek out and implement new psychological approaches to manage emotions regularly and successfully. Knowing its strengths and weaknesses, a trader can better understand how options trading signals work than others and change their strategy or trading style in time.

**The importance of discipline in trading**

In the book "The Disciplined Trader," Mark Douglas says, "In the market environment, you have to set the rules of the game and then have the discipline to stick to them, even if the market moves in ways that tempt you." constantly making you believe that this time you don't need to follow your rules."

Discipline is the ability to follow a plan or strategy and never go against it, even when it seems you should. Discipline comes from within and is a quality built over time to respond appropriately to feelings such as trust, fear, greed, etc. Think of discipline as your shield against irrational and emotional decisions. Some experts believe that trading discipline is even more critical than profit-making. Although this may sound controversial, Mark Douglas explains it well in his book. He says that, as a trader, it is more important always to follow his rules than to make money because whatever money he makes, he will inevitably lose it if he doesn't follow his rules.

**Strategies to develop trading discipline**

Developing trading discipline is a complicated process, but we can boil it down to three main elements:

**1. Set your rules**

Establishing rules is essential, whether it is a trading strategy, the habit of keeping a trading journal, or back-testing a risk management strategy. They will be the foundation that will determine your long-term success.

**2. Follow your rules**

Think of your trading rules as if they were the law: They are there for a reason, and you should not break them.

**3. Take responsibility for your actions**

Use the carrot and stick method. Reward yourself when you execute your strategy flawlessly and punish yourself when you go against it. The exact rewards and punishments are up to you, but the main thing is that they are enough to motivate him to follow your rules and prevent him from breaking them.

**The impact of discipline on long-term trading success**

Discipline is critical to long-term trading success, and studies show it.

According to "DALBAR", over the past 30 years, the average investor has consistently underperformed the S&P 500 by as much as 3.5%. The study attributes this mainly to emotion-driven decision-making and poor trading discipline. According to other studies, the discipline of trading evolved. The more mature a trader is, the more disciplined he tends to be.

People with solid trading discipline are best positioned to ensure long-term success. By following a well-defined trading plan, sticking to their risk management strategy, and avoiding making emotional decisions, traders can improve their performance and earn consistent profits over time.

**The significance of risk management in the field of trading psychology**

Risk management is an aspect of the trading field that significantly influences the psychological aspects involved. It will not only help you minimize losses and maximize profits, thus helping to increase your confidence, but it will also protect you against a possible spiral of negative emotions.

This is especially important for beginning and not-so-disciplined traders. The reason is that a series of losing trades can quickly throw you off track and distort rational decision-making. Appropriate risk management can serve as a shield or safety net against these situations since you will know the scope of the consequences if your strategy does not go as planned. This will protect you against negative surprises and all potential impacts from them.

In addition, risk management plays a critical role in managing stress levels. Think of risk management as your silent watchdog that will help you, even if your emotions run wild. Knowing it's there will ensure peace of mind even when trading becomes very stressful (as it often does). This practice will assist you in cultivating a constructive mindset and mitigate the potential pitfalls of emotional trading.

**Strategies to improve emotional discipline in trading**

Let's start by saying that recognizing positive and negative emotions on the spot can be very difficult. They are often only apparent in hindsight, and what may seem negative when it happens may be positive in retrospect. Nevertheless, several strategies can be implemented to enhance one's ability to interpret situations and cultivate a higher level of emotional intelligence. They are:

- **Practice self-awareness:** Learn to understand when doing something deliberately or unconsciously. Analyze how it makes you feel based on how you're doing it, especially when you have yet to find yourself.

- **Learn to accept all emotions**: Whether positive or negative, there is no escaping emotions. Learn to watch from the sidelines, and don't let emotions get the better of you or try to suppress them. Be sure to identify your feelings to make the process more accessible in the future.

- **Accept that you will not always be in control**: And what is good? We're all control freaks to some degree, but there's a limit beyond which this becomes a real problem. If you cannot accept that you will not always be in control of trading, you will start to build up pressure and anxiety to a point where everything will explode.

- **Consider everything as a lesson:** Be sure to accept every situation, good or bad, as a step toward your growth. This will help you control your emotions; negative situations will affect you less.

- **Look back and create a feedback loop:** Return to your memory chest to see how you've reacted to certain situations. Many times, similar or even the same scenarios could be repeated in the future and comparing the way you have responded in both cases will help you recognize your emotional growth.

- **Don't compare yourself to others:** Judging the emotions that a particular situation has triggered in oneself based on the response it has provoked in others is a recipe for disaster. Not everyone has the same emotional intelligence, is at the same stage of their life/career or has similar personality traits. Therefore, it is entirely normal to react differently.

Alexander Elder, one of the most famous traders in the world, says that beginners focus on analysis. Still, professionals operate in a three-dimensional space: the psychology of trading, your feelings, and the mass psychology of the markets.

The importance of trading psychology cannot be stressed enough. Personality traits, such as discipline, mentality, and emotional discipline, are just as important, if not more, than the strategy itself. It should be noted that even the best trading system will only succeed if you learn to follow it.

ADOPTING A POSITIVE AND GROWTH-ORIENTED MINDSET FOR TRADING SUCCESS.

A positive and growth-oriented mindset is crucial for achieving long-term success in trading. It's not just about making profits; it's about developing resilience, managing emotions, and continuously learning and adapting. In this chapter, we'll explore the importance of adopting such a mindset and provide insights into how traders can cultivate it for their benefit.

**The Mindset Factor in Trading**

Trading can be an emotional roller coaster. The market's unpredictable nature can lead to both highs of excitement and lows of frustration. Traders often face challenges such as fear of losses, overconfidence, impatience, and the temptation to chase after quick gains. These emotional reactions can lead to impulsive decisions that result in losses. This is where the mindset factor comes into play.

A positive mindset involves maintaining an optimistic outlook, regardless of short-term results. It's about understanding that losses are a natural part of trading and viewing them as learning opportunities rather than failures. A growth-oriented mindset, on the other hand, emphasizes continuous learning and improvement. Traders with this mindset are open to new strategies, techniques, and market insights. They recognize that there's always something to learn from both successes and failures.

**Cultivating a Positive and Growth-Oriented Mindset**

1. **Self-Awareness:** Recognize your emotions and their impact on your trading decisions. Be mindful of when fear, greed, or impatience influence your actions. Having this awareness can assist you in making more logical decisions.

2. **Embrace Learning:** Instead of dwelling on losses, focus on learning from them. Conduct a thorough analysis of your errors, ascertain the factors that contributed to their occurrence, and devise strategies to prevent the recurrence of similar situations. Each mistake is a stepping-stone toward improvement.

3. **Set Realistic Goals:** Set achievable trading goals that align with your risk tolerance and experience. Unrealistic expectations can lead to frustration and poor decision-making.

4. **Practice Patience:** Successful trading requires patience. Only some trades will yield immediate results. Forbearance allows you to wait for the right opportunities and avoid impulsive actions.

5. **Maintain a Trading Journal:** Keep a detailed journal of your trades, including the reasoning behind each decision. This helps you track your progress, identify patterns, and learn from your experiences.

6. **Focus on Process, Not Just Results**: Instead of fixating solely on profits and losses, focus on executing your trading plan effectively. Trusting your process can help alleviate emotional reactions.

7. **Adaptability:** The markets are constantly changing. It is essential to demonstrate a willingness to adjust strategies and approaches in response to prevailing market conditions. Flexibility is vital to long-term success.

8. **Practice Mindfulness:** Incorporate mindfulness techniques to stay present and manage emotions. Practices such as deep breathing and visualization can assist individuals in maintaining composure during periods of market volatility.

**Real-Life Examples of Mindset in Action**

To illustrate the significance of mindset in trading, let's consider two traders, Alex and Sarah:

**Alex**: Alex is a trader with a positive and growth-oriented mindset. He views losses as opportunities to learn and refine his strategies. After a series of losses, Alex takes a step back to analyze his approach, identifies areas for improvement, and adjusts his risk management. Over time, his disciplined approach and commitment to learning led to consistent profitability.

**Sarah**: On the other hand, Sarah is prone to negative emotions after losses. She becomes frustrated and makes impulsive decisions to recover losses quickly. Unfortunately, this approach leads to even more significant losses. Sarah's unwillingness to learn from her mistakes prevents her from achieving long-term success.

Trading success goes beyond charts and analysis; it requires a positive and growth-oriented mindset. Adopting such a mindset helps traders manage emotions, learn from experiences, and make informed decisions. By cultivating self-awareness, embracing learning, and staying adaptable, traders can enhance their ability to navigate the challenges of the market with resilience and ultimately achieve their goals. Remember, trading is a journey, and a strong mindset is your compass for success.

## CHAPTER 2
## CRAFTING YOUR OPINIONS TRADING PLAN: YOUR BLUEPRINT FOR TRADING ADVENTURE

Welcome, fellow trader, to a realm where the wind shifts swiftly and tides can turn in the blink of an eye. In the exciting world of options trading, success doesn't just happen by chance—it's meticulously crafted, like a masterful piece of art. And at the heart of your triumphant journey lies your trading plan—an indispensable blueprint that maps your course and guides your decisions on option trading.

**Understanding the Essence of Your Trading Plan**

1. **Setting Your Sails with Clear Goals:** Every legendary journey begins with a purpose. Determine your trading goals—are you seeking steady income, exhilarating growth, or a balance? Clarify your intentions; they will be your lighthouse when the seas get rough.

2. **Navigating the Choppy Seas of Risk Management**: Just as a wise mariner plots their route to avoid treacherous waters, you must define your risk tolerance. Establish boundaries for your risk exposure, ensuring that you sail forth with confidence even during storms.

3. **Plotting the Right Trading Course:** Different ports call for different strategies. Choose your trading strategies wisely, just as you'd select a sturdy vessel for specific voyages. Will you navigate the covered call shores or venture into the iron condor currents? The choice is yours.

4. **Casting Anchor with Entry and Exit Rules:** Anchors keep a ship steady amidst the waves. Similarly, your trading plan must outline precise entry and exit rules. Whether you rely on technical signals, market sentiment, or a combination, your rules ensure you stay on track.

**Beyond the Horizon: Navigating with Foresight**

Every great seafarer anticipates the unexpected. As a trader, your journey will be no different. Consider these scenarios:

- Weathering Storms with Position Sizing: Just as you wouldn't overload a boat, manage your risk by allocating the right portion of your capital to each trade. It's the secret to staying afloat when market waves get wild.
- Adjusting Sails for Changing Winds: Markets are erratic, much like the wind. Embrace trade adjustments as a seasoned sailor would adjust sails. Be ready to shift your strategies and adapt to changing market conditions.
- Reviewing the Voyage: A seasoned mariner reviews their course after a voyage. Similarly, regularly assess your trades. It is essential to acknowledge and commemorate your successes, derive valuable lessons from your setbacks, and implement necessary adjustments by referring to your trading journal.

**Trading Plan in Action: Setting Sail on a Trading Adventure**

Allow me to introduce two traders, each with their distinct voyage:

- **Ella the Explorer:** Ella crafts a trading plan geared toward consistent income. She focuses on covered calls and cash-secured puts, utilizing them on quality stocks she'd be comfortable owning long-term. By sticking to her plan and managing risk, Ella generates a steady income that supports her financial goals.

- **Liam the Voyager:** Liam is a more daring trader, seeking rapid growth through volatile trades. His plan involves straddles and strangles, allowing him to profit from sharp market movements. Yet, his plan includes strict stop-loss and exit strategies to protect his capital. Liam's journey requires constant vigilance and a deep understanding of his chosen strategies.

**The Power of Adaptation and Discipline**

A trading plan isn't set in stone; it's a dynamic tool that evolves as you gain experience and the market changes. While having a plan is essential, adapting and staying disciplined is equally crucial. Emotional control, sticking to your rules, and continuous learning are the pillars that support your trading journey. Crafting your trading plan isn't just about putting words on paper—it's about embodying a disciplined approach to the market. Just like explorers adapt to changing conditions, traders must evolve with market shifts. Your anchors will be emotional resilience, adherence to your plan, and an eagerness to learn.

Remember, crafting a trading plan is a personal process. It reflects your financial goals, risk appetite, and trading style. It's not just a guideline; it's your blueprint for success in options trading. Therefore, take the time to craft your plan thoughtfully, and let it be your guide as you navigate the exciting and rewarding realm of options trading.

## SETTING CLEAR TRADING GOALS, DEFINING RISK TOLERANCE, AND ESTABLISHING TIME FRAMES

Setting clear trading goals, defining risk tolerance, and establishing time frames are not isolated factors; they interact and influence each other. Your goals determine your risk appetite, affecting the most suitable time frames. A dynamic synergy creates a harmonious trading strategy, ensuring that your actions align with your aspirations.

While clear goals, risk tolerance, and time frames provide a structured framework, adaptability is the rudder that steers your ship through changing waters. Markets are dynamic, and unexpected events can disrupt even the most meticulously planned voyages. Being open to adjusting your goals, risk tolerance, or time frames as circumstances evolve is essential to maintaining a successful trading journey.

Clear trading goals, risk tolerance, and time frames also have a profound psychological impact. Knowing your goals provides motivation and a sense of purpose while understanding your risk tolerance helps manage emotions during market fluctuations. Defined time frames prevent impulsive decisions driven by short-term market noise. When these factors are harmonized, traders are better equipped to stay disciplined, patient, and focused.

**Setting Clear Trading Goals**

Trading without clear goals is akin to sailing without a destination. Setting specific and achievable trading goals is the compass that guides your decisions and actions. Do you seek consistent income, long-term wealth accumulation, or speculative gains? Defining your goals not only provides direction but also influences your trading strategy. It's the difference between wandering and progressing purposefully towards your financial aspirations.

**Defining Risk Tolerance**

Every journey has its challenges and risks, and trading is no different. Defining your risk tolerance is like determining how much rough sea you're willing to endure. Understanding how much loss you can comfortably absorb is crucial before emotions cloud your judgment. You remain level-headed and rational by establishing precise risk tolerance levels, even when faced with market turbulence.

**Establishing Time Frames**

Time is the essence of trading. Just as a sailor must consider weather conditions when planning their voyage, traders must establish time frames that suit their objectives. Are you a short-term trader seeking quick gains, a medium-term trader aiming for trend captures, or a long-term investor looking for sustainable growth? Your chosen time frames define the rhythm of your trading activities, aligning your strategy with your goals.

In trading, success doesn't come by chance; it results from deliberate planning and strategic execution. Setting clear trading goals, defining risk tolerance, and establishing time frames are the compass, the safety net, and the navigation tools that guide traders on their journey. With these elements in place, traders can confidently navigate the seas of uncertainty, making informed decisions and steering towards profitable shores. As you embark on your trading adventure, remember that your goals, risk tolerance, and time frames are not just tools – they're your strategic allies on the path to trading mastery.

CREATING A COMPREHENSIVE TRADING PLAN THAT ALIGNS WITH YOUR OBJECTIVES

Engaging in financial market trading can offer excitement and the potential for profitability. However, having a carefully crafted trading plan in place is crucial to mitigate risks and avoid feeling overwhelmed. A comprehensive trading plan is your roadmap in the complex trading world, helping you navigate the challenges and make informed decisions. It's like building a sturdy ship before embarking on a voyage – you need a solid foundation to weather the unpredictable seas of the market.

**Setting Clear Trading Goals:**

Defining your trading goals is the first step in creating a comprehensive trading plan. What do you aim to achieve through trading? Are you looking for consistent income, long-term growth, or capital preservation? Establishing clear and attainable objectives aids in maintaining focus and mitigating the risk of becoming overwhelmed amidst the market's complexities. It is advisable to ensure that your goals are specific, measurable, achievable, relevant, and time-bound, commonly called SMART. For instance, when aiming to attain a specific percentage of returns within a designated period, ensuring that the objective is realistic and aligned with your risk tolerance is crucial.

**Defining Risk Tolerance:**

Understanding your risk tolerance is crucial in crafting a trading plan. Risk tolerance measures your comfort level in assuming risk in pursuit of potential returns. This varies from person to person based on financial situation, psychological makeup, and investment objectives. Assessing your risk tolerance helps you determine the types of assets to trade, position sizes, and risk management strategies. Maintaining a sincere self-assessment regarding one's capacity to manage risk without incurring excessive stress is imperative.

**Establishing Time Frames:**

Time frames are the periods within which you expect your trades to unfold. They can range from short-term (intraday) to medium-term (swing trading) to long-term (position trading). Your time frames should align with your trading goals and risk tolerance. For instance, day trading might be suitable if you're comfortable with higher risks and want to capitalize on short-term price movements. On the other hand, if you prefer more stable and longer-term trades, position trading could be a better fit.

**Creating a Trading Strategy:**

Once you have your goals, risk tolerance, and time frames, it's time to develop a trading strategy. Your strategy should outline how you'll enter and exit trades, the types of assets you'll trade, technical and fundamental analysis methods, and risk management techniques. Having a well-defined strategy provides you with a systematic approach to trading and prevents you from making impulsive decisions based on emotions.

**Risk Management:**

Incorporating risk management into your trading plan is vital for preserving your capital. Determine the maximum amount of capital you're willing to risk on each trade and use tools like stop-loss orders to limit potential losses. Risk management also involves diversification – spreading your investments across different assets to minimize the impact of a single failure.

**Continuous Evaluation and Adjustment:**

A comprehensive trading plan is not static; it should be dynamic and adaptable. Regularly evaluate your trading performance against your goals and make adjustments as needed. If specific strategies are consistently underperforming, consider refining or replacing them. Likewise, if market conditions change, your plan should be flexible enough to accommodate new insights.

In summary, developing a comprehensive trading plan is essential to success as a trader. It provides structure, discipline, and a clear path toward your financial objectives. By setting clear goals, defining your risk tolerance, establishing suitable time frames, crafting a solid trading strategy, implementing robust risk management, and continuously evaluating your plan, you increase your chances of navigating the markets effectively and achieving sustainable trading success. Remember, a well-crafted trading plan is your compass in the volatile trading world, helping you steer toward your destination with confidence and purpose.

## INCORPORATING A TRADING JOURNAL FOR PERFORMANCE TRACKING AND CONTINUOUS IMPROVEMENT

Trading in the financial markets is a dynamic and challenging endeavor. The ever-changing market conditions, the influx of information, and the emotional rollercoaster of gains and losses can make it challenging to keep track of your trading decisions and assess your performance objectively. This is where a trading journal comes into play – a powerful tool that can provide invaluable insights, enhance your decision-making process and drive continuous improvement in your trading journey.

**The Power of a Trading Journal:**

A trading journal is much more than a simple record-keeping tool; it's a treasure trove of information about your trading activities, thought processes, emotions, and outcomes. It's a comprehensive documentation of your trades, strategies, and the reasoning behind your decisions. By meticulously logging your transactions and analyzing them, you create a data repository that can reveal patterns, strengths, weaknesses, and areas for improvement.

**Benefits of Keeping a Trading Journal**

1. **Objective Self-Assessment:** A trading journal lets you evaluate your trading decisions and outcomes objectively. It helps you identify both successful and unsuccessful trades, enabling you to refine your strategies and cut out practices that are detrimental to your performance.

2. **Identifying Patterns:** With a trading journal, you can recognize patterns in your trading behavior. Are there certain times of the day when you perform better? Do you tend to overtrade during certain market conditions? Identifying patterns can lead to targeted improvements.

3. **Emotional Awareness:** Trading emotions can be both your ally and your enemy. A trading journal helps you become more aware of how emotions like fear, greed, and overconfidence influence your decisions. By acknowledging these emotions, you can work towards controlling them.

4. **Improving Decision-Making:** Reviewing your trading journal can reveal whether your decisions were based on sound analysis or impulsive reactions. This insight helps you make more informed decisions and avoid repeating past mistakes.

5. **Refining Strategies:** Over time, your trading journal can highlight which strategies consistently yield positive results and which need adjustment. This iterative process of refining your strategy is essential for sustained success.

6. **Learning from Losses:** Losses are an inevitable part of trading. Instead of dwelling on them, a trading journal helps you learn from them. Examining unsuccessful trades can offer valuable insights into the factors that contributed to their failure and guide on preventing similar errors from occurring in subsequent endeavors.

**Components of an Effective Trading Journal:**

1. **Trade Details:** Include the date, time, asset traded, entry and exit prices, position size, and type of trade (buy/sell, long/short).

2. **Trading Strategy:** Describe the rationale behind each trade. What technical or fundamental analysis led to your decision? Was the trade based on a pattern or indicator?

3. **Emotional State:** Note your emotions before, during, and after the trade. Were you feeling confident, anxious, or hesitant? This helps you recognize patterns in emotional responses.

4. **Outcome and Analysis:** Record the trade's profit, loss, or breakeven results. Perform a post-trade analysis, evaluating whether the trade adhered to your strategy and what you could have done differently.

5. Notes and Observations: Jot down any observations or lessons learned from the trade. Did you notice a new pattern? Did you deviate from your plan? These insights contribute to your growth as a trader.

**Consistency is Key:**

To fully reap the benefits of a trading journal, consistency is essential. Make journaling a routine part of your trading process. Reflecting on each trade and analyzing your decision-making is an investment in your trading skills. Over time, your trading journal becomes a repository of wisdom, offering a glimpse into your evolution as a trader and guiding your path toward becoming a more prosperous and disciplined participant in the markets.

Incorporating a trading journal into your trading routine can be a game-changer. It's not just about documenting trades; it's about understanding your strengths, weaknesses, and emotional triggers. By leveraging the insights from your journal, you can refine your strategies, make better decisions, and ultimately pave the way for consistent growth and success in the world of trading.

## **CONCLUSION**

We've come a long way together in this crash course on options trading. From understanding the basics to exploring the potential rewards and risks, this book aims to give you a clear starting point.

Trading options provide flexibility and opportunity, making it a potentially useful instrument in your investment strategy. But, as with all investments, it's essential to approach it with caution and knowledge. The strategies and insights you've gained here will help but always remember the importance of making informed decisions.

As you progress, use this book as a reference, continue learning, and always be mindful of the risks involved. The world of options trading awaits, and with the foundation you've built, you're well on your way.

If this book has helped you with Options Trading and you enjoyed it, go ahead and leave a review for this book. Thank you for diving into this beginner's guide. Wishing you all the best in your trading adventures!

# GLOSSARY

**Trading psychology:** Trading psychology refers to the study and understanding of the psychological and emotional aspects that influence traders' decision-making, behavior, and performance in the financial markets.

**Greed:** Greed can be described as an intense desire for something and often manifests as the intense desire for wealth. This can easily get out of hand when the market moves against traders but is equally likely to negatively influence trading decisions on winning trades.

**Myth:** A myth is a well-known story which was made up in the past to explain natural events or to justify religious beliefs or social customs.

**Rationality:** Rationality the quality of being based on clear thought and reason, or of making decisions based on clear thought and reason.

**Volatile:** Volatility refers to the fluctuations in the market price of the underlying asset. It is a metric for the speed and amount of movement for underlying asset prices. Cognizance of volatility allows investors to better comprehend why option prices behave in certain ways.

**Determinant:** Determinant is an element that identifies or determines the nature of something or that fixes or conditions an outcome.

**Volition:** an act of making a choice or decision, also the power of choosing or determining.

**Cognitive:** Cognitive means relating to the mental process involved in knowing, learning, and understanding things.

**Equilibrium:** Equilibrium is a state of balance between opposing forces or actions. Equilibrium is the state in which market supply and demand balance each other, and as a result prices become stable.

**Psychotherapy:** Psychotherapy refers to a variety of treatments that aim to help a person identify and change troubling emotions, thoughts, and behaviors.

**Voyager:** Voyager is used for trading, investing, swaps, and asset management. Users can also earn rewards on stable coin loans, based on interest fees, and can earn compound interest on holdings in over 30 supported cryptos, including Bitcoin (BTC) and Ethereum (ETH).

**Explorer:** An explorer is a person who investigates unknown regions, areas of knowledge, or experiences with the purpose of discovery.

**Excitement:** Excitement is a feeling or situation full of activity, joy, exhilaration, or upheaval.

# REFERENCES

Aziz, Andrew. *MASTERING TRADING PSYCHOLOGY in Collaboration with MIKE BAEHR*. Blackman, Matt, and CMT. "10 Steps to Building a Winning Trading Plan." *Investopedia*, 5 July 2021, www.investopedia.com/articles/trading/04/042104.asp.

"How to Create a Successful Trading Plan." *IG*, www.ig.com/en/trading-strategies/how-to-create-a-successful-trading-plan-181210.

"How to Master Trading Psychology." *Tradervue*, 20 May 2022, www.tradervue.com/site/2022/05/20/trading-psychology/.

Rich, Stanley R., and David E. Gumpert. "How to Write a Winning Business Plan." *Harvard Business Review*, hbr.org/1985/05/how-to-write-a-winning-business-plan.

Made in United States
Troutdale, OR
11/09/2023